The History of Religions

The History of Religions

Retrospect and Prospect

A collection of original essays by
Mircea Eliade, Paul Ricoeur, Michel Meslin,
Ugo Bianchi, Ninian Smart, Charles H. Long,
Kurt Rudolph, and Joseph M. Kitagawa

Edited by Joseph M. Kitagawa

with an Afterword by
Gregory D. Alles and the Editor

MACMILLAN PUBLISHING COMPANY
A Division of Macmillan, Inc.
NEW YORK
COLLIER MACMILLAN PUBLISHERS
LONDON

Macmillan Publishing Company
A Division of Macmillan, Inc.
866 Third Avenue, New York, N. Y. 10022

Collier Macmillan Canada, Inc.

Library of Congress Catalog Card Number: 84–17191

Printed in the United States of America

printing number
1 2 3 4 5 6 7 8 9 10

Library of Congress Cataloging in Publication Data
Main entry under title:

The History of religions.

Includes presentations at a Divinity School, University of Chicago conference on the history of religions held in May, 1983.
Includes bibliographies and index.
1. Religions—History—Addresses, essays, lectures.
I. Kitagawa, Joseph M. II. University of Chicago. Divinity School.
BL87.H57 1985 200'.9 84–17191
ISBN 0-02-916490-7

In gratitude
to the past and present faculty
of The History of Religions
The University of Chicago

George Stephen Goodspeed (†1905)
George Burman Foster (†1918)
Albert Eustace Haydon (†1975)
Joachim Wach (†1955)
Mircea Eliade
Charles H. Long
Jonathan Z. Smith
Gösta Ahlström
Wendy D. O'Flaherty
Frank E. Reynolds

and to

THE HISTORY OF RELIGIONS ALUMNI

Contents

About the Contributors

Gregory D. Alles is teaching classics and the history of religions at Valparaiso University, Valparaiso, Indiana.

Ugo Bianchi is professor of the history of religions, Faculty of Letters and Philosophy, at the University of Rome and a vice-president of the International Association for the History of Religions. In addition to works in his native Italian, he has published in English volumes entitled *The Greek Mysteries* and *The History of Religions.*

Mircea Eliade is the Sewell L. Avery Distinguished Service Professor, Emeritus, of the History of Religions at the Divinity School, the University of Chicago. He has also taught at the University of Bucharest and the Ecole des Hautes Etudes (the Sorbonne) in Paris. His writings include such well-known works as *The Myth of the Eternal Return (Cosmos and History), The Sacred and the Profane, Patterns in Comparative Religion, Yoga—Immortality and Freedom, Shamanism: Archaic Techniques of Ecstasy,* and *A History of Religious Ideas* (3 volumes), as well as many novels and short stories.

Joseph M. Kitagawa is professor of the history of religions and former dean of the Divinity School, the University of Chicago. He is a vice-president of the International Association for the History of Religions and has served as chairman of the Committee on the History of Religions of the American Council of Learned Societies. He has written *Religion in Japanese History* and *Religions of the East* and has edited several volumes, including Joachim Wach's *The Comparative Study of Religion.*

Charles H. Long is William Rand Kenan Professor of the History of Religions at the University of North Carolina, Chapel Hill, and professor of the history of religions at Duke University. A past president of the American Academy of Religion, he has also taught at the University of Chicago. He is the author of *Alpha: The Myths of Creation* and other works.

Michel Meslin is professor of the history of religions and vice-president of the University of Paris-Sorbonne and director of the department of sciences of religions in the Institute of History there. He has also served as president of the French Society for the History of Religions (Société Ernest Renan). His publications include *La Fête des kalendes de janvier dans l'empire romain: Etudes d'un rituel* *de nouvel an, Le Christianisme dans l'empire romain,* and *Pour une science des religions.*

Paul Ricoeur is John Nuveen Professor, Emeritus, of Philosophical Theology at the Divinity School, the University of Chicago, and Professor Emeritus at the University of Paris-Sorbonne. He has also taught at the University of Strasbourg. His publications include *The Symbolism of Evil, Freud and Philosophy, Interpretation Theory: Discourse and the Surplus of Meaning, The Conflict of Interpretations,* and *Hermeneutics and the Human Sciences.*

Kurt Rudolph held until recently the professorial chair in the history of religions at Karl Marx University, Leipzig. In addition to *Die Religionsgeschichte an der Leipziger Universität und die Entwicklung der Religionswissenschaft, Gnosis, Mandaeism,* and *Die Mandäer* (2 volumes), he has written widely on the study of the history of religions and its historical foundations, Gnosticism, especially the modern Gnostic community of the Mandaeans, and the Qur'an and early Islam.

Ninian Smart is professor of religious studies at the University of California, Santa Barbara, and at the University of Lancaster, England. His publications are well-known in the English-speaking world and include *Philosophers and Religious Truth, World Religions: A Dialogue, The Phenomenon of Religion, The Science of Religion and the Sociology of Knowledge,* and *Worldviews.*

Introduction

The title of this book, *The History of Religions: Retrospect and Prospect,* is not meant to imply that its contents present a neatly packaged account of the historical background, contemporary state, and future outlook of the discipline of the history of religions (*Religionswissenschaft*). Nor is this volume designed to show "how to study" or "how to teach" the history of religions. Rather, it contains a series of reflections by leading scholars and practitioners of the discipline regarding the significance of its scholarly tradition and its problems. As one would expect, the different contributors reflect various perspectives. Thus, the volume does not advocate any party line. It hopes instead to evoke further discussion and reflection on the part of its readers.

The history of religions has never tried—and is not likely to try—to develop a rigidly defined methodological orthodoxy. But like many other disciplines, it is keenly conscious of its historical "given," that is, of the formation of its original character in the cultural milieu of the European Enlightenment. To take an analogy from art, by the eighteenth century there had already been hung a richly brocaded "scholarly" tapestry, woven with threads from the Hellenistic, Jewish, Christian, and Islamic traditions, embroidered with threads from the Renaissance, and embellished with a growing knowledge of non-Western religions and cultures. To be sure, the nineteenth- and early twentieth-century pioneers of the history of religions were conscious of this historic tapestry, but they attempted to weave their own patterns. These new "weavers" had been trained in various fields of ethnology, philology, biblical studies, history, art, philosophy, and theology as well as in the newly emerging human sciences, but all of them were self-conscious about developing an alternative approach to the study of religion, an approach different from the philosophy of religion and from theology. True to their Enlightenment heritage, those early historians of religions relied on reason. They used historical and comparative methods, and they were motivated by their concern with the origin, pattern of development, and universal character of religious phenomena.

For a number of reasons, this early history of religions did not win its independence easily. On the one hand, religiously committed Europeans did not readily accept an alternative method in the study of religion which compared Jewish and Christian traditions with other religions of the world on the same plane. Furthermore, the teaching of *Religionswissenschaft* was often done in the theological faculties of universities, faculties not inclined to trust the new discipline and its rationalistic and/or evolutionary thrust. On the other hand, those who *were* "scientifically oriented" suspected hidden religious or theological agendas behind what claimed to be an objective approach. Nevertheless, in the course of time, the historical study of religions (*Religionsgeschichte*) and the comparative study of religions on certain levels were accepted in various European quarters, and later, serious attempts were made to formulate a coherent approach to *Religionswissenschaft* as a whole.

In comparison with Europe, nineteenth-century North America was more hospitable to the historical study of religions ("history of religions" in a primarily historical sense) and the comparative study of religions, but not to the more fully developed discipline of the history of religions (*Religionswissenschaft*), which was yet to be introduced. Humanistically oriented historical study was exemplified by the establishment of the prestigious "American Lectures on the History of Religions" in 1891, while comparative study, which was more religiously motivated, was dramatically symbolized by the World's Parliament of Religions held in Chicago in 1893. The popularity of historical and comparative studies of religions was enhanced by liberalism during the first quarter of the century, but it eroded quickly in the 1930s. Historical, comparative, and humanistic studies of religions in North America barely survived. Where they survived, they did so mainly in private graduate universities and particularly in the divinity schools of such universities.

The cultural climate in North America since the end of World War II has become more conducive to the growth of the history of religions (*Religionswissenschaft*) and its related disciplines—comparative mythology, sociology of religion, psychology of religion, cultural area studies, and scholarly studies of particular religious traditions such as Hinduism, Buddhism, Islam, Chinese and Japanese religions, and "primitive" religions. In comparison with the cultural provincialism of prewar days, many North Americans have become more and more interested in Asian, African, and South American cultures and religions, which now find their places in the curricula of many colleges and universities. By far the most significant new factor in recent decades has been the sudden proliferation of departments of religion or of religious studies as integral parts of liberal arts faculties in many public and private colleges and universities. This is a new context for the history of religions, and the discipline now faces new challenges and new tasks.

Among the many and varied problems that confront the discipline of the history of religions in our time, especially in North America, are three crucial issues: (1) the mode of cooperation with other disciplines represented in the liberal arts faculty and particularly in the department of religious studies; (2) the self-identity of the history of religions as a discipline; and (3) an effective communication of these two issues to colleagues, students, and society at large.

1. It is easier to advocate the necessity of cooperation between the history of religions and other disciplines than to articulate a legitimate and acceptable mode for this cooperation, especially because of the wide variety of institutional arrangements found in North American colleges and universities. In principle, undergraduate education has two aims: first, to liberalize the minds of students so that they learn the meaning and value of being human for living in contemporary society and this world; second, to prepare students for graduate studies in specific areas or for professional training in professional schools. In the undergraduate context, the task of the historian of religions is similar to that of the sociologist of religion, the psychologist of religion, and those who teach the scriptures, histories, thoughts, and ethics of particular religious traditions, or, for that matter, those who teach various literatures, philosophies, and civilizational studies. By necessity, historians of religions, like all their colleagues, must "vulgarize" their scholarship—in the French sense of the term—and present oversimplified generalizations to undergraduate students. But even then historians of religions must be clear about their task; that is, they must present the multidimensional reality of religion by presenting exemplary features of religion taken from some of the specific religious traditions or from certain phases of the long history of the religious experience of humankind. The cooperative enterprise of liberal education greatly needs the contribution of historians of religions if undergraduate education is to be more cross-cultural and better grounded in a historical perspective of the entire world.

For those students who pursue some aspect of the study of religion in graduate study or who seek professional training in a religious field, historians of religions must make a more technical contribution. As members of cooperating educational teams, they are experts on a methodological alternative which approaches, say, Judaism, Buddhism, or Christianity, or such topics as myths, symbols, and cults, not as objects of study in themselves but as integral parts of the whole history of the religious experience and expressions of humankind. Usually a historian of religions is well-versed in one or two of the related disciplinary approaches, such as cultural anthropology, psychology, sociology, or philosophy, in special topics, and in one or two historical religious traditions. But the most significant contribution that historians of religions can make to cooperative inquiry and teaching on the graduate level derives from the perspective and the approach of their discipline in reference to the diverse religious phenomena.

Unlike undergraduate education, graduate education aims at developing competence in research and scholarship and only secondarily at training undergraduate teachers. In graduate education, the historian of religions is constantly involved in at least three different but related areas of cooperation: (1) cooperation with fellow historians of religions near and far, often as participants in learned societies and as contributors to and referees for journals, but at times as collaborators in joint research projects; (2) cooperation with colleagues on a particular faculty who are engaged in research in various other aspects of religion(s); and (3) cooperation with a group of graduate students who are initially apprentices but who gradually become junior partners on one's research team. Ironically, graduate programs in some institutions are erroneously conceived as a slightly higher level of undergraduate education or as primarily a training program for undergraduate teachers. They offer too many introductory and "tool" courses on specific areas or topics and not enough research opportunities in which senior partners (faculty) and junior partners (graduate students) together engage in hammering out learned generalizations and general interpretive schemes relevant to dealing with diverse religious phenomena. In principle, most graduate courses or seminars should be concerned with exemplary data and problems, from which graduate students learn the art and spirit of research for the enhancement of their own scholarship. The aim of graduate education is to prepare students for *competent* research and scholarship in the hope that some of them may achieve *great* scholarship in the future. Unfortunately, there is no assurance that competent researchers make effective undergraduate teachers. Still, no one can remain an effective teacher without the continuing research that sustains his or her own scholarship.

2. The self-identity of the history of religions is a serious issue today. In the popular mind, the discipline is often confused with other related and legitimate approaches to the study of religion(s) such as (a) independent studies of "primitive" or "archaic" religions, Hinduism, Islam, Buddhism, and Chinese and Japanese religions; (b) comparative studies of various religious forms and traditions; (c) comparative studies of the doctrinal systems and truth claims of various religious traditions, with or without an attempt to promote meaningful "dialogue" among adherents of various traditions; and (d) sociological, anthropological, psychological, cultural, and other "scientific" approaches to various features of religions, with or without an attempt to make gener-

al statements about the nature of religion. In addition, there exists also (e) a serious effort on the part of Roman Catholic and Protestant theologians to make theological sense of the reality of religious pluralism, a phenomenon that has great affinity to item (c). In our time, popular confusion of these different but related enterprises has penetrated academic circles; and some administrators and colleagues—and, sadly, even some scholars who teach the history of religions—have been affected by such a confused image of the discipline.

In a sense, this popular confusion is understandable. A historian of religions is often engaged in research on phenomena of certain specific religious traditions or in comparative research, just as a scholar of linguistics is sometimes engaged in research on a particular language or in the comparative study of a certain number of languages. Moreover, any historian of religions will try to keep up with the research of scholars in these related areas. Often research by such scholars will inspire and illumine the historian of religions' own perspectives and approaches. But if the history of religions is to make its distinct contribution to the cooperative inquiry into religion(s), its scholars must bring to bear on the cooperative endeavor the perspectives and approaches of their discipline, which is an important alternative to other disciplines.

3. How to communicate effectively the nature of a discipline and the meaningful mode of cooperation between it and other disciplines is not a problem unique to the history of religions. In fact, all disciplines face the same problem. Admittedly, certain disciplines—some of the physical and biological sciences, for example—have been far more successful than the history of religions in identifying different audiences and developing appropriate forms and levels of discourse addressed to each audience. By contrast, the history of religions has displayed admirable intellectual honesty in its preoccupation with a self-critical soul-searching of its disciplinary integrity. But thus far it has done little to identify different audiences or to develop kinds of discourse appropriate to them.

The history of religions has certain basic structures and approaches; but in dealing with very diverse religious phenomena, it allows a great variety of scholarly temperaments and methodological options. Any discipline so broad can advance only by constant self-criticism and mutual criticism among peers and by discussion with scholars in other disciplines. At the same time, as a discipline represented in institutions of higher learning, the history of religions has a responsibility to articulate both its own nature and task and its relation to other disciplines and to communicate them to colleagues in different fields, to graduate students in religious studies, and to undergraduate students. It must also seek to be understood by the scholars and leaders of various religious communities—Jewish, Christian, Buddhist, Hindu, and what have you—as well as by society at large. To some extent, all these kinds of discourse involve oversimplification and generalization, but they must be part of a continuum. They should not distort the basic character of the discipline.

In the past, European scholars took several steps to reach an audience outside the narrow confines of their discipline. In addition to scholarly treatises, they wrote less technical essays conveying their insights and perspectives to a wider audience. A good example is Joachim Wach's *Meister und Jünger*. In North America, Mircea Eliade has been particularly successful in addressing a variety of audiences in his lucid and engaging style at levels appropriate to each. Moreover, past scholars devoted much time and serious attention to the composition of *Lehrbücher*, surveys of the field for educational purposes. For example, A. Bertholet and E. Lehmann carefully reedited the fourth edition of Pierre Daniel Chantepie de la Saussaye's *Lehrbuch*. Roughly contemporaneously, Nathan Søderblom was reediting Cornelis P. Tiele's *Compendium*. Also significant were several major encyclopedias, to which the best scholars of the day contributed, not only encyclopedias limited to religion, such as James Hastings' well-known *Encyclopedia of Religion and Ethics* and *Die Religion in Geschichte und Gegenwart*, but also first-class general encyclopedias such as the *Encyclopaedia Britannica*. Fortunately, there are today signs of renewed interest in these enterprises.

The history of religions is a relatively young discipline. It must continue to define its nature and task. At the same time, its grand vision of trying to understand the profound religious dimension in human experience and history must be presented to challenge the imagination and the intellect of both scholarly and lay audiences. The discipline's health and survival require articulate and effective communication of what it is and what it can be.

The present volume follows the pattern of two earlier publications, *The History of Religions: Essays in Methodology* (1959) and *The History of Religions: Essays on the Problem of Understanding* (1967). The tradition of the history of religions at the University of Chicago dates back to the university's inception in 1892. At that time, George Stephen Goodspeed was called to the chair of comparative religions and ancient history. He was succeeded by George Burman Foster, who served from 1905 to 1918, and by Albert Eustace Haydon, who served between 1919 and 1945. In 1945, Joachim Wach was called to the chair of the history of religions and served until his death in 1955. After Mircea Eliade's arrival in 1956, there arose a new interest in gradually developing the entire enterprise of the history of religions. In an attempt to sort out the issues, the first volume mentioned above was published. It contained essays from a number of scholars of varying perspectives: Wilfred Cantwell Smith, Raffaele Pettazzoni, Jean Daniélou, Louis Massignon, Ernst Benz, Friedrich Heiler, and its editors, Mircea Eliade and Joseph M. Kitagawa. A few years later, Eliade was instrumental in founding the journal, *History of Religions*. In 1965, the first conference on the history of religions was held in Chicago. The presentations, most of which were by Wach's former students, were published in the second volume mentioned above, together with papers by Wach, Eliade, Paul Tillich, Kitagawa, and Charles H. Long.

In 1983, a second conference on the history of religions was held at Chicago. It was designed to include reflections by European, British, and American scholars with invited responses from North American colleagues. In addition, two special lectures were given by Eliade and Paul Ricoeur. On May 8, 1983, following the opening of the conference by Franklin I. Gamwell, dean of the Divinity School, Professor Jonathan Z. Smith introduced Professor Eliade, and on the next day, Professor Bernard McGinn introduced Professor Ricoeur.

The working sessions were chaired successively by Professors Wendy O'Flaherty, Frank E. Reynolds, and Joseph M. Kitagawa. Professors Lawrence Sullivan (University of Missouri-Columbia), Diana Eck (Harvard University), and Kees W. Bolle (University of California, Los Angeles) responded to the presentation by Professor Michel Meslin (the Sorbonne); Professors William Scott Green (University of Rochester), Alf Hiltebeitel (George Washington University), and David Carrasco (University of Colorado) responded to the presentation by Professor Ugo Bianchi (Rome); Professors Bruce Lincoln (University of Minnesota), Joanne Punzo Waghorne (University of Massachusetts-Boston), and Richard Martin (Arizona State University) responded to the presentation by Professor Ninian Smart (Lancaster, England, and the University of California, Santa Barbara); and Professors Willard G. Oxtoby (University of Toronto), Judith Berling (Indiana University), and Benjamin Ray (University of Virginia) responded to the presentation by Professor Charles H. Long (University of North Carolina and Duke University).

Comments and discussions by other participants followed the prepared responses. Dr. Henry Pernet, a Chicago alumnus from Switzerland, offered his services as interpreter for Professor Meslin. Professor Kurt Rudolph (University of Leipzig) was invited to the conference but could not attend. He graciously contributed an article to this volume. The editor's paper, originally prepared for discussion at a retreat of the University of Chicago's Divinity School faculty, is also included here.

The 1983 conference attracted many colleagues from various institutions in North America, nearly half of whom were Chicago alumni. They recalled with gratitude the noble tradition of the history of religions at Chicago, faithfully nurtured by past and current faculty members and by the alumni, to all of whom the present volume is dedicated.

J. M. K.

Summer, 1984
Swift Hall
University of Chicago

Acknowledgments

The editor is grateful to graduate students Gail Hinich, David Haberman, and Rob Campany, who assisted Gregory Alles in recording the conference sessions. In writing the Afterword, Mr. Alles and the editor gratefully acknowledge their faithful service as recorders and their input. David White, also a graduate student at Chicago, translated Professor Meslin's paper from the French for the benefit of the conference participants. His translation appears here, revised by Mr. Alles, who also translated Professor Rudolph's contribution from the German original. In addition, thanks are due to Peter Chemery, Don Pittman, and Jane Swanberg for their valuable comments on an early draft of the Afterword.

This volume would not have appeared were it not for the encouragement of Dean Franklin I. Gamwell and of Charles E. Smith, vice-president and publisher of Macmillan Publishing Company. The editor is greatly indebted to Gregory Alles (now on the faculty of Valparaiso University) and Martha Morrow-Vojacek for their able assistance in the preparation of the volume; again to Mr. Alles for his efforts in proofreading the manuscript and in preparing the index in the midst of his busy teaching schedule; and to Margaret Sandford Norbeck for her tireless efforts on behalf of the conference.

The History of Religions

Homo Faber and *Homo Religiosus*

MIRCEA ELIADE

It has been remarked that the last few decades have been paradoxically characterized by the coexistence of a tragic, neurotic pessimism and a robust, almost candid optimism. A great number of scientists, sociologists, and economists draw increasing attention to the imminent catastrophes that menace our world, not only our Western type of culture and sociopolitical institutions but mankind in general and even life on our planet. Other authors, less numerous but equally energetic, exalt the great scientific discoveries and the fantastic technological conquests accomplished or begun in recent decades. I shall recall here only a few of the arguments and opinions expressed by representatives of both trends of thought. Although these thinkers approach their subjects from opposing positions, they illustrate different aspects of the same cultural process. They share the conviction that we are witnessing the end of our world and are thus on the threshold of some decisive event—either a total extinction or the beginning of a new creation.

. . . Solvet saeclum in favilla . . .

I begin with a few examples from contemporary arts, selected particularly from poetic and musical compositions and films enthusiastically admired by the younger generation. Rock music, discovered and glorified by American and European youth in the 1960s, began under the sign of political, social, and moral revolution. It is significant that at its apex rock music proclaimed the imminent death of the world.[1] In 1962, Bob Dylan became the spokesman for a youth protest movement with his famous "Blowin' in the Wind" and "A Hard Rain's Gonna

Fall." In 1964, the British group The Rolling Stones inaugurated their career by playing the most desperately sad blues. Later these young men took to drugs and eventually seemed to espouse satanism. Their singing was a means to end the world as well as a way to their own destruction. The quartet The Doors, formed in 1967 at Los Angeles under the leadership of Jim Morrison, brought out a number of very popular records, inspired by such taboo themes as patricide. Jim Morrison died of alcoholism in Paris in 1971. Magma, a group of French jazz musicians, was organized in 1970. Their leader, Christian Vander, wanted to depict the impending destruction of the world. One famous cut, "Mekanik Destructiw Kommandöh," describes the end of our planet.

"The creatures of rage," wrote a French critic, "the choirs, the music of iron and ice, the apocalyptic uproar—these creatures of rage come to smash the Earth to powder and sweep away the multitudes. And the unlimited putrid chaos of our world is delivered up to the angels of darkness, who come to punish the insane pride of the earthlings."[2] A similar apocalyptic vision inspired the Blue Oyster Cult, founded in New York in 1971. "We are constructing our music in order that it will be the last programme on the computer at the end of the world. . . ."

In the last twenty years, a number of films have portrayed the end of the world or the more or less total annihilation of mankind as a result of nuclear war.[3] No less striking is the pessimistic tone of the most recent science-fiction novels. In their essay, "De la science-fiction à la science-affliction," Igor and Grichka Bogdanoff observe that, whereas the science-fiction produced from 1945 until the 1960s was dominated by the specter of atomic war, during the last fifteen years the mortal danger has been ecological: excessive pollution, the population explosion, the destruction of nature, the scarcity of resources, and so on.[4] In his novel, *Stand on Zanzibar* (New York, 1968), J. Brunner dramatizes the end of the world, brought on by a demographic explosion impossible to control. In *The Sheep Look Up* (1972), the rains contain powerful doses of acids, air is respirable only at certain hours of the day, water is only rarely drinkable, and so on. Such a world is a caricature of our own. The end of the world is not in the future, it has already begun: "under our eyes, our world is wasting and grows rotten."[5]

Of course, these terrors—illustrated in the most popular rock music and in so many films about the future and works of science-fiction—are not without foundation. Leaving aside the apocalyptic consequences of a thermonuclear war, the present ecological situation and the population explosion do constitute extremely serious problems. The planetary pollution, which brought thousands of animal species to the verge of extinction and even "killed" a sea,[6] increases continually. In a recent issue of *The Ecologist: Journal of the Post Industrial Age* (vol. 10, January–February 1980), a desperate appeal is made to world authorities, "A Plan to Save the Tropical Forests." One reads such terrifying sentences as: "The tropical rain forests are the world's richest gene banks, and as they start to disappear so do our options for the future. It is just like walking out along a plank and starting to cut away at the wood behind with a saw." "If a culture sins against the forests," writes Ehrenfried Pfeiffer, "its biological decline is inevitable. . . . Sixty million years of evolution is being converted into worthless paper packaging. . . ."

I will not quote the famous and radically pessimistic report of the *Club of Rome,* many of whose predictions are controversial. But Carl Amery, in his book, *The End of the Providence* (1972; French translation, Paris, 1976), argues that industrial and demographic explosions condemn our species and the entire biosphere to extinction. According to Amery, the end is only a generation or two ahead of us. A similarly pessimistic vision of the future is eloquently presented by Robert L. Heilbroner in *An Inquiry into the Human Prospect* (New York, 1974):

> Our movement into the future will be a descent into the black cave of bare and unrelieved survival, a survival characterized by overcrowding, material wants, rigidly determined systems of life and authoritarian government. . . . Doubling the population of the earth's poorer regions every quarter of a century, it threatens, unless checked by mass starvation, to place here forty billion persons (as opposed to the present three-and-a-half) in 100 years. Such a growth in population seems to require an almost infinite agricultural and industrial expansion if the most tragic levels of starvation are to be averted.[7]

But then, writes Heilbroner, the consequence will be

> the depletion of the earth's resources, which seems certain surprisingly soon to demand a slow-down and then a halt to industrial expansion. In league with that, there is as well the danger of overreaching the thermal limit for the atmosphere, which long before the extinction limit is reached in a century-and-a-half (three or four generations) will also require a slow-down and a halt to industrial growth. . . . The only alternative to such industrial contraction is in the end death.[8]

The "Anti-Sinistrose"

The French writer Louis Pauwels, founder and director of the monthly *Question de,* coined the expression "sinistrose" to designate all forms of despair, pessimism, and nihilistic prophecies regarding the future of our world. A special issue of his magazine, a 320-page volume entitled *La Fin du Monde?,* was devoted to the analysis and refutation of some recent expressions of "sinistrose." Here I will use freely the documentation collected in his volume.

A tout seigneur, tout honneur. When presenting an optimistic interpretation of the future, one must begin by evoking the famous scientist-theologian Pierre Teilhard de Chardin.[9] Between 1920 and 1955, Teilhard wrote many books and essays (published posthumously) on cosmic evolution and cosmic redemption. By cosmic redemption, he meant redemption through Christ, that is to say, the transmutation of cosmic matter through the sacrament of the Mass, evidently achieved by the voyages of men in the galaxies during the next several hundred thousand years.

Such an optimistic view of the future—minus Teilhard's theological hope—is shared by a number of economists and scientists. In an interview a few years ago, Herman Kahn affirmed that a population of six billion with a per capita income of $18,000 is not beyond our possibilities. In his book, *The Next 200 Years* (New York, 1976), Kahn proclaims that the world is moving not toward a period of austerity but into universal prosperity. Thus the great problem of the future will be mankind's adaptation to a life of abundance and leisure. This sort of optimism is rejected by one of the contributors to *La Fin du Monde?*[10]

A more adequate analysis of the available data concerning the population explosion and other catastrophic predictions is Pauwels's article, "L'anti-sinistrose" (*La Fin du Monde?*, pp. 227–244). According to Pauwels's sources, the demographic growth of the Third World will be stabilized by the year 2000 (p. 236); the scarcity of food-stuffs is a myth (pp. 236–238). Among the anticatastrophic authors, Pauwels quotes Adrian Berry who, in his book, *The Next Ten Thousand Years* (New York, 1974), makes the case that even in the event of nuclear war progress will be only temporarily restrained, not stopped; in fact, there is no limit to what science and technology may accomplish. Berry announces that man will remodel the entire solar system; he speaks of autonomous floating cities and of "domesticated planets."

In an article published in *Analog* and partially translated in *La Fin du Monde?* (pp. 245–254), Arthur Clarke summarized his views on the next 120 years. Very soon, space technology will enable man to set up special installations on Mercury in order to obtain solar energy more easily and more abundantly. Clarke predicted visits to planets by 1980 and their colonization by 2000. Some twenty years later, we will begin interstellar explorations, and by 2030, we will contact extraterrestrial beings. For 2100, Clarke foresees an encounter with extraterrestrial beings, a world-brain, and human immortality.[11]

Tragically pessimistic or utterly optimistic, both trends of thought proclaim the imminent end of our world. Both predictions—that of an Apocalypse and that of a Golden Age—are founded exclusively upon the spectacular development of science and technology. If, following the pessimistic interpretation, our world is to be destroyed, it will not be destroyed for religious reasons (for example, God punishing us for our sins) but simply as a result of our technological progress. Likewise, the Golden Age and the conquest of immortality predicted by optimists for the next few hundred years will not be gifts of God but the inevitable consequence of man's scientific genius and technological abilities. Nevertheless, both predictions have a religious structure, in the sense that they partake of religious symbolism. Of course, the representatives of these two opposite trends are not aware of the religious implications of their despair or of their hopes. What is significant is that all of them relate the inevitability and the imminence of *our* world's end to the fantastic realizations of human workmanship.

Making Things More Rapidly Than Nature

For a historian of religion, this apotheosis of *homo faber* is particularly interesting. It reminds him of a whole world of archaic symbols, myths, and rituals. Science and technology began their uninterrupted progress with the discovery of metallurgy. That is, their progress began when man understood that he could collaborate with nature, and finally come to dominate it, by learning how *to make things more rapidly* than nature. Indeed, we are confronted very early with the idea that ores "grow" in the belly of Mother Earth after the manner of embryos. Metallurgy thus takes on the character of obstetrics. The miner and metalworker intervene in the unfolding of subterranean embryology. They accelerate the rhythm of the growth of ores; they collaborate in the work of nature and assist it in effecting a more rapid gestation process. In a word, man, with his various tecnniques, gradually takes the place of time. His labors replace the work of time.[12]

With the help of fire, metalworkers transform the ores, that is, the "embryos," into metals, "adults." The underlying belief here is that given enough time, the ores would have become "pure" metals in the womb of the Earth-Mother. Furthermore, these "pure" metals would themselves become gold if allowed to "grow" undisturbed for a few more thousand years.[13] Such beliefs are well known in many traditional societies and survived in western Europe until the end of the Industrial Revolution. I will quote only one Western alchemist of the seventeenth century, who wrote that

> If there were no exterior obstacles to the execution of her designs, Nature would always complete what she wishes to produce. . . .That is why we have to look upon the birth of imperfect metals as we would upon abortions and

> freaks which come about only because Nature has been, as it were, misdirected; or because she has encountered some resistance or certain obstacles which prevent her from behaving in her accustomed way. . . . For, although she wishes to produce only one metal, she finds herself constrained to create several. Gold, and only gold, is the legitimate child of her desires. Gold is her legitimate son because only gold is a production of her efforts.[14]

The "nobility" of gold is thus the fruit in its most mature state. The other metals are "common" because they are "green," "not ripe." In other words, nature's final goal is the completion of the mineral kingdom, its ultimate "maturation." The natural transmutation of metals into gold is inscribed in their destiny, for the tendency of nature is toward perfection.

Mythologies of Gold

Such an extravagant exaltation of gold invites us to pause for a moment. There is a splendid mythology of *homo faber*. Myths, legends, and heroic poetry reflect the first, decisive conquests of the natural world achieved by early man. But gold does not belong to the mythology of *homo faber*. Gold is a creation of *homo religiosus*. It was valorized exclusively for symbolic and religious reasons. Gold was the first metal utilized by man, although it could be employed neither as a tool nor as a weapon. In the history of technological innovations—that is to say, the passage from stone technology to bronze industry, then to iron and finally to steel—gold played no role whatsoever. Furthermore, its exploitation is the most difficult of any metal. In order to obtain six to twelve grams of gold, one ton of rock has to be brought from the mines up to the surface. The exploitation of alluvial deposits is certainly less complicated but also considerably less productive: a few centigrams from a cubic meter of sand. Compared with the effort invested in securing a few ounces of pure gold, the travail demanded in the exploitation of oil is infinitely simpler and easier. Nevertheless, from prehistoric times to our epoch, men have laboriously pursued the desperate search for gold. The primordial symbolic value of this metal could not be abolished in spite of the progressive desacralization of nature and of human existence.

The Egyptians who, according to Plutarch and Diodorus, hated iron—which they called "the bones of Seth"—considered the flesh of the gods to be of gold. In other words, the gods were *immortal*. That is why, after the model of the gods, the pharaoh was also assigned flesh of gold. Indeed, as the *Brāhmaṇas* repeatedly proclaim, "Gold is immortality." Consequently, obtaining the elixir that transmutes metals into alchemical gold is tantamount to obtaining immortality. I will not discuss here the origins of alchemy nor its development in China, India, and the Islamic, Hellenistic, and Western cultures. In any case, in Eastern as well as in Western alchemy, the transmutation of metals into gold is equivalent to a miraculously rapid maturation. The Elixir (or the Philosopher's Stone) completes and consummates the work of nature.[15] As one of the characters in Ben Jonson's play, *The Alchemist*, asserts, "The lead and other metals would be gold if they had time"; and another character adds, "And that our Art doth further" (Act II, scene ii). That is, the alchemist prolongs the dream and the ideology of the miner and metal worker: to perfect nature by accelerating the temporal rhythm. The difference is that the *aurum alchemicum*—the Elixir—also confers health, perennial youth, and even immortality.

The Origins of Modern Science

By the end of the eighteenth century alchemy was supplanted by the new science of chemistry. But earlier, alchemy knew a short period of fame thanks mainly to Isaac Newton. Although Newton declared that some of his alchemical experiments were successful, he never published his results. However, his innumerable alchemical manuscripts—which were neglected until 1940—have been thoroughly investigated by B. J. Teeter Dobbs in her book, *The Foundations of Newton's Alchemy*.[16] According to Dobbs, Newton probed "the whole vast literature of the older alchemy as it has never been probed before or since" (p. 88). The discovery of the force that held the planets in their orbits did not satisfy Newton completely. He sought in alchemy the structure of the small world to match his cosmological system. But in spite of his intensive experiments from about 1668 to 1696, he failed to find the forces that govern the action of small bodies. When, however, he began to work seriously in 1679–1680 on the dynamics of orbital motion, he applied his alchemical ideas on attraction to the entire cosmos.

As McGuire and Rattans have shown, Newton was convinced that in earliest times God had imparted the secrets of natural philosophy and of true religion to a select few. This knowledge had been subsequently lost but was later partially recovered. After its recovery, it was incorporated in fables and mythic formulations where it would remain hidden from the vulgar. In modern days, it could be more fully recovered from experience.[17] For this reason, Newton usually turned to the most esoteric sections of alchemical literature, hoping that the real secrets were hidden there. It is highly significant that the founder of modern mechanical science did not reject the theology of the primordial secret revelation, nor did he reject the principle of transmutation, the basis of all alchemies. He wrote in his treatise on *Opticks*: "The changing of Bodies into Light, and Light into Bodies, is very conformable to the course of Nature, which seems delighted with Transmutation."[18] According to Professor Dobbs, "Newton's alchemical thoughts were so securely established on their basic foundations that he never came to deny their general validity, and in a sense the whole of his career after 1675 may be seen as one long attempt to integrate alchemy and the mechanical philosophy" (p. 230).

When the *Principia* was published, Newton's opponents emphatically declared that his forces were in fact occult qualities. Professor Dobbs admits that his critics were right: "Newton's forces were very much like the hidden sympathies and antipathies found in much of the occult literature of the Renaissance period. But Newton had given forces an ontological status equivalent to that of matter and motion. By so doing, and by quantifying the forces, he enabled the mechanical philosophies to rise above the level of imaginary impact mechanism" (p. 211). In his book, *Force in Newton's Physics,* Richard Westfall came to the conclusion that the *wedding* of the Hermetic alchemical tradition with mechanical philosophy produced modern science as its offspring.[19]

In its spectacular development, "modern science" has ignored or rejected its Hermetic heritage. In effect, the triumph of Newton's mechanics abolished his own scientific idea. Newton and his contemporaries had expected quite another type of scientific revolution. Prolonging and expanding the hopes and objectives of the neo-alchemist of the Renaissance—that is, the endeavor to redeem nature—men as different as Paracelsus, John Dee, Comenius, J. Valentin Andreae, Ashmole, Fludd, and Newton saw in alchemy the model for a more ambitious enterprise: the perfection of man through a new method of learning. In their view, such a method would integrate a supraconfessional Christianity with the Hermetic tradition and the natural sciences, that is, medicine, astronomy, and mechanics. This ambitious synthesis was in fact a new, religious creation, and one specifically Christian. It is comparable to the results of the previous integration of Platonic, Aristotelian, and neo-Platonic metaphysical constructs. The type of "learning" elaborated in the seventeenth century represented the last holistic enterprise attempted in Christian Europe.

Man, Work, and Time

Although alchemy was supplanted by the new science of chemistry, the alchemist's ideals survived, camouflaged in nineteenth-century ideology. Of course, by that time these ideals were radically secularized, but the triumph of experimental science did not abolish them altogether. On the contrary, the new ideology of the nineteenth century crystallized around the myth of infinite progress. Boosted by the experimental sciences and the progress of industrialization, this ideology took up and carried forward the millenarian dream of the alchemist, radical secularization notwithstanding. The myth of the perfection and redemption of nature survives in camouflaged form in the Promethean program of industrialized societies, whose aim is the transformation of nature, and especially the transmutation of nature into "energy." In the nineteenth century man also succeeds in supplanting time. His desire to accelerate the natural tempo of organic and inorganic beings now begins to be fulfilled. The synthetic products of organic chemistry have demonstrated the possibility of accelerating and even eliminating time. Laboratories and factories prepare substances which nature would have taken thousands and thousands of years to produce. We also know the extent to which the "synthetic preparation of life," even in the modest form of a few cells of protoplasm, was the supreme dream of science from the second half of the nineteenth century to our own time.[20]

By conquering nature through the physico-chemical sciences, man can become nature's rival without being the slave of time. Henceforth, science and labor are to do the work of time. With what he recognizes as most essential in himself—his applied intelligence and capacity for work—modern man takes upon himself the function of temporal duration; in other words, *he takes on the role of time*. Of course, man had been condemned to work from the very beginning. But in traditional societies, work had a religious, a liturgical, dimension. Now, in modern industrialized societies, work has been radically secularized. For the first time in history, man has assumed the task of "doing better and quicker than nature," without the sacred dimension that in other societies made work bearable. The total secularization of work, of human labor, has tremendous consequences, comparable only to the consequences of the domestication of fire and the discovery of agriculture.

But this is quite another problem. What is of interest here is that scientific and technological progress has made it possible to prolong and periodically to regenerate human life (with such indefinite regeneration corresponding to a secularized expression of immortality) as well as to destroy human collectivities, even the whole of humankind.

Are We Condemned to Immortality?

But are these the only consequences envisaged by the great scientists and technologists of our time? I am thinking not of the personal convictions of famous men but of certain significant interpretations of very recent scientific discoveries. I will cite a single example. It is an important example inasmuch as it introduces us to a number of astronomers, astrophysicists, and mathematicians—and such scholars are more open to religious and theological problems than are their colleagues in various divisions of the humanities.

In 1974, a book published in Paris became a best-seller almost immediately and provoked vivid discussion: *La Gnose de Princeton* by Raymond Ruyer. The author, professor of philosophy at the University of Nancy, is well-known for his many works on epistemology, cybernetics, social psychology, and similar topics.[21] While attending an international conference in London, Ruyer discovered the existence of a group of American "gnostics," most of them astronomers, astrophysicists, mathematicians, and biologists from Princeton, Pasadena, and Mount Wilson. Ruyer does not cite names, but he assures us that the manuscript of *La Gnose de Princeton* was read by some of these scholars: "I'm afraid that perhaps they accepted my project [i.e., to publish the book] above all because they do not take the French public very seriously and they count on the power of inattention and on anti-American snobbery in intellectual circles."

According to Ruyer, the group was formed at Princeton in the late 1960s by some astrophysicists and astronomers fascinated by the riddles of cosmology. For these scientists, materialistic explanations of the origin and nature of the universe are invalidated by the most recent discoveries. *Everything* in the universe possesses, like man, a *consciousness*. (This is why they call themselves "Gnostics.") They do not acknowledge a God, but they proclaim the universality of the Spirit, and they believe in a future "super-mankind." They do not publicize their discoveries. For the moment, they prefer to carry on dialogues and discussion within a "discreet" (not "secret") society. Their number has been increasing, to upwards of a few thousands in 1972–1973. Lately, philosophers and theologians have been joining their ranks.

Some critics do not exclude the hypothesis that this "gnostic" organization may be simply a stratagem invented by Ruyer in order to expose the ideas which a scientist-philosopher could hold today concerning the most fundamental problems of cosmology, astrophysics, epistemology, and biology. Every idea presented by Ruyer as belonging to the "Princeton Gnostics" strictly corresponds to the present state of science. But the term "gnostics," whether invented by Ruyer or not, is characteristic. Not only does it indicate the supreme importance conceded by contemporary scientists to human—and universal—*consciousness;* it also reveals a certain nostalgia for a more "discreet" community of scholars, philosophers, and theologians, a nostalgia that reminds us of the "Hermetic Enlightenment" of the seventeenth century.[22]

Now, if everything in the universe possesses consciousness, death becomes irrelevant, and the old beliefs in immortality—"popular" as well as philosophical—appear inadequate if not self-contradictory. Indeed, one can say that we are *condemned* to be immortal or that our old beliefs are, as such, self-contradictory. But it is not my intention here to discuss the metaphysical consequences of the "Princeton Gnosis." (I use this term because Ruyer's book made it famous.) Ruyer presents and interprets for the nonspecialist reader the theoretical consequences of the most recent state of science. As a historian of religions, I am fascinated by the religious "prehistory" of a conclusion such as he portrays, that everything in the universe possesses consciousness; in other words, that everything is aware of its specific quality of life. A historian of religions will recall many similar archaic beliefs and ideas, for example, "animism" (the conviction that everything in the world is alive because it possesses a soul) and certain Indian theologies and metaphysics which posit a universal living matter and a considerable number of states of consciousness and unconsciousness.

I hope that my comments are not misunderstood. I do not situate such archaic beliefs and Oriental ideas on the same theoretical level as the conclusions of certain contemporary scientists. But the recent discovery and interpretation of the universality and perenniality of consciousness may encourage the historians of religions to approach the documents of their discipline with greater sympathy and imagination.

In the last analysis, we discover that the latest activities and conclusions of scientists and technologists—the direct descendents of *homo faber*—reactualize, on different levels and perspectives, the same fears, hopes, and convictions that have dominated *homo religiosus* from the very beginning: the fear of death, and even of the catastrophic destruction of life; the hope of conquering death through a ritually constructed post-existence; and, finally, the certitude that the indestructibility of life and the immortality of the soul are to be accepted as they are, as a series of states of consciousness. Of course, certain *homini religiosi* may add that it depends on every one of us to learn how to reach the highest state of consciousness, namely the awareness of pure Being.

Notes

1. I use the documentation collected by Philippe Manoeuvre, "La rock musique et la fin du monde," in *La Fin du Monde?*, Etudes et Documents présentés par Louis Pauwels, *Question de* . . . 16 (January–February 1977), pp. 210–217.
2. Manoeuvre, p. 213.
3. For instance: "On the Beach" (USA, 1959); "The World, the Flesh, and the Devil" (USA, 1959); "They Are the Damned" (England, 1961); "The Day the Earth Caught Fire" (England, 1962); "Panic in Year Zero" (USA, 1962); "Doctor Strangelove" (USA, 1964); "The Bed-Sittingroom"

(England, 1969); "The Ultimate Warrior" (USA, 1975); "The Apocalypse 2024" (USA, 1975).

4. In *La Fin du Monde?*, pp. 201–209.
5. Ibid., p. 207.
6. In the mid-1970s an international conference was devoted to "The Mediterranean, a Dead Sea."
7. Cf. Langdon Gilkey, *Reaping the Whirlwind: A Christian Interpretation of History* (New York, 1976), pp. 79–80, 81.
8. Quoted by Gilkey, pp. 81–82. See also the entire section devoted to the analysis of the future, pp. 79–96. For a more balanced account of the risks that menace the world in the next two or three generations, cf. Kenneth E. Boulding, *The Meaning of the Twentieth Century* (New York, 1965); *Daedalus* 96, no. 3 (Summer 1967): "Toward the Year 2000: Work in Progress"; Victor Ferkiss, *Technological Man: The Myth and the Reality* (New York, 1969); and Herman and A. J. Wiener, *The Year 2000* (New York, 1967).
9. Teilhard is not quoted in *La Fin du Monde?* among the representatives of "anti-sinistrose." Pauwels and many of his co-workers identify the source of the belief in the imminent end of the world as the Judeo-Christian apocalyptic. See pp. 6ff., 109ff., 131ff.
10. Cf. Lucien Gerardin, "Techniques-Antichrist, Technologies-Messie" (in *La Fin du Monde?*, pp. 173–185), p. 181.
11. After this essay was completed, I came across a stimulating article by Edward A. Tiryakian, "La fin d'une illusion et l'illusion de la fin," in *Le Progrès en Question,* Actes du IXe Colloque de l'Association Internationale des Sociologues de Langue Française: Sociologie du Progrès, Menton, May 1975, vol. 2 (Paris, 1978), pp. 381–403. Among contemporary sociologists, Tiryakian distinguishes two different but dialectically related conceptions of the future: (1) the future as uninterrupted progress from the present situation; and (2) the future as an apocalyptic end of the world. According to the author, the second conception will probably dominate the next phase of Western thought (p. 393).
12. Cf. Mircea Eliade, *The Forge and the Crucible,* 2d ed. (Chicago, 1978), pp. 8f.
13. Ibid., pp. 50f.
14. *Bibliothèque des Philosophies chimiques,* by M. J. D. R., new edition (Paris, 1741), Preface, pp. xxvii-xxix, quoted in *The Forge and the Crucible.*
15. Cf. *The Forge and the Crucible,* pp. 48f., 51f., 160f.
16. B. J. Teeter Dobbs, *The Foundations of Newton's Alchemy* (Cambridge, 1976). See also *The Forge and the Crucible,* pp. 231f.
17. Quoted by Dobbs, p. 90.
18. Quoted by Dobbs, p. 23.
19. Richard S. Westfall, *Force in Newton's Physics: The Science of Dynamics in the Seventeenth Century* (London and New York, 1971), pp. 377f.
20. Cf. *The Forge and the Crucible,* pp. 169f.
21. Particularly important are *La cybernétique de l'information* (1954), *Paradoxes de la conscience et limites de l'automatisme* (1960), *Les puissances idéologiques* (1972), *Les nourritures psychiques* (1975), and *Les cent prochains siècles* (1977).
22. Cf. Francis Yates, *The Rosicrucian Enlightenment* (Chicago, 1972).

The History of Religions and the Phenomenology of Time Consciousness

Paul Ricoeur

I am well aware that I am at best a student of the history of religions and that I would be taking pointless—if not ludicrous—risks were I to suggest new models for the description, analysis, and interpretation of the contents belonging to that field of research. I conceive my task as an attempt to share a kind of second-order meditation about the conceptuality—be it recognized or overlooked, consciously assumed or uncritically taken for granted—that unavoidably underlies any comparative methodology. By a second-order meditation I mean a critical reflection applied to the questions that we address to our documents, rather than to the answers that we get from them. These questions, as we know, are not only not value-free but—more interestingly—not conceptually free. In the very framing of our questions we employ concepts that are those of *our* time and culture and not merely those of the culture submitted to our inquiry. This practice involves no epistemological mistake; it does not indicate a misguided enterprise. It is common to all the human sciences to the extent that they are interpretative sciences, and so must confront the modern interpreter's horizon of thought with—as is usually the case in a comparative discipline—that of a past text of a foreign culture. This permanent need for a reassessment of the conceptual framework of our very questions makes our discipline an inquiry, an inquiry ruled by the logic of question/answer which Collingwood assigned to the human sciences, before Gadamer reasserted its hermeneutical function. This is why we have to put our questions in question in any interpretative inquiry.

I suggest that we apply this critical approach to a specific problem, that of mythical time. More precisely, I suggest that we attempt to disentangle the presuppositions, largely unnoticed if not hidden, that govern our various attempts to characterize mythical time either as cyclical or as linear (more precisely rectilinear). As we all know, this question of the cyclical versus the linear has plagued the comparison between so-called Greek and Hebrew thought, especially after T. Boman's *Hebrew Thought Compared with Greek* (1959), followed unfortunately by O. Cullmann, H. C. Puech, and G. Quispel. In this discussion, the real nature of the question has been overshadowed by hasty conclusions concerning similarities and differences between the so-called Greek thought and the alleged Hebrew thought.[1]

The Contribution of the Phenomenology of Time-Consciousness

Rather than restating or even refining the objections raised against the very purpose of a one-to-one comparison between Hebrew and Greek thought, I propose to discuss two methodological issues. My first section will be devoted to the contribution of the phenomenology of time-consciousness to a critique of the notions of "the cyclical" and "the linear" applied to time. It will pave the way for a study of the many meanings of the same concepts as they are used in comparative religion. This will be our second and more important step.

The most decisive teaching of the phenomenology of time-consciousness from Augustine, through Bergson and Husserl, to Heidegger, is that the concept of time which is tacitly used as a yardstick in the current discussions about cyclical or linear conceptions of time is, on the one hand, an end-product of our scientific culture, but does not, on the other, exhaust the rich plurality of meaning that even now we attach to what we call "time." Let me develop the two sides of the problem before I attempt to show how the intended univocity and the unintended plurivocity of our concept of time affects our reading of texts related to the field of comparative religion.

The first side of the argument goes something like this: As an end-product of our scientific culture time is basically linear, in the sense that (1) like the line in space, it is unidimensional; (2) like a line, it is an endless continuum which can be interrupted at any point—the instant being the temporal equivalent of the point; (3) like a line, it may be divided into intervals, which are parts of one and the same singular whole; (4) these intervals may be compared to one another, in spite of the fact that they are successive, and they may be measured in basic units, thanks to a correlation established between the course of events in public or private life with the movements of bodies in space, which movements are held to be regular. For that purpose, we make use of instruments such as the gnomon, the clock, and the calendar to establish a one-to-one correlation between our sense of the passing of time and the regular motion of the heavenly bodies, mainly the sun and the moon. Finally, (5) we apply numbers to the reckoning of units and intervals in such a way that time is, for us, measured on the basis of the open-ended succession of whole numbers. We may answer, in this way, such questions as, "how long did a period of time last?," by giving numbers of days, months, and years. I want to insist that it is the application of numbers to time that provides the ultimate criterion of open-ended linearity.

This abstract model of linear time is so pervasive that it has been extended little by little from historical to natural phenomena. In *The Discovery of Time,* Stephen Toulmin and Judith Goodfield tell the story of this progressive expansion of a uniform time-scale from human history to geology, to thermodynamics, and finally to the gigantic changes among galaxies. They show how the orthodox Jewish-Christian barrier of 6,000 years had to be progressively broken down to make room for the large-scale phenomena that together constitute the history of mankind, of the earth, of the universe, and even of matter itself.

From this brief survey we may conclude that the pure concept of linear time coincides, for us, with the new time-scale, extended immensely beyond the old 6,000-year history of the universe. In that sense we may equate linear time with this time-scale.

As a corollary to this equation, cyclical time appears paradoxically as a particular case of, and not an alternative term for, linear time. We cannot help thinking of something cyclical except as "a line returning into itself as to form a closed circle" (Oxford English Dictionary). The irony here is that, for our modern Western minds, a cycle is no less linear than the time-scale, except that it returns to its starting point. Several successive cycles merely represent "loops" along the time-scale. Such is the case even with days, months, and years: they are individually cyclical but collectively linear.

Repetition of some pattern, be it natural or social, astronomical or political, is merely, in our modern view, a complexity superimposed onto the linear character of chronological time—a time uniform, homogeneous, and indifferent to the qualitative differences among events. Repetitions, it seems to us, are merely complexities projected onto the abstract concept of the time-scale.

But as soon as this has been said, it must then be acknowledged that, even for us, the sense of time is not exhausted by this abstract, chronological time. It is one of the functions of the phenomenology of time-consciousness to explore a variety of qualitative aspects of time, which could, in turn, pave the way for a fresh approach to the multiplicity of temporal patterns opened up by comparative religion. And here the second part of my phenomenological argument begins. But, let us be clear about what we can expect from it. I do not mean to say that the phenomenology of time-consciousness, which is itself an outcome of Western culture, is by itself able to provide a hermeneutical key for the interpretation of specifically religious patterns of temporality, but rather that it may (1) set our scholarly minds free from the yoke of a unilinear and universal concept of time, and (2) help reveal hidden affinities between some of the most "foreign" conceptions of time encountered in the comparative study of religion, and some of those qualitative aspects of time excavated not only by phenomenology, but by literary criticism, since literature is itself a store of fictional explorations of the depths of time-consciousness. Think only of Virginia Woolf, Thomas Mann, Marcel Proust, James Joyce. Some of these aspects of qualitative time may either shatter the exclusive monopoly of the chronological model or awaken experiences displaying some kinship with various "foreign" religious patterns of temporality.

The first phenomenological feature of time overlooked in a merely chronological account is the distinction between the experience of nowness or presentness and the concept of an isolated punctual instant. Whereas the instant designates any break in the continuity of time and, not being a part of time, has no duration, nowness designates the lived present intentionally directed toward the past through memory and toward the future through expectation. To put it more provocatively: without this nowness, one may have a relation of before and after, but no pastness and no futurity. Furthermore, the complex interlocking relationship between nowness, pastness, and futurity confers a "thickness" to nowness irreducible to the discrete status of the instant as a mere abstract break in the linear continuity. As Augustine first noticed, the *now* is constituted by the very transition and transaction between expectation, memory, and attention. Furthermore, it is transitory in its own way, in comparison with eternity understood as the eternal now of God. This twofold experience of transition as transaction and of transitoriness as lack of perpetuity, of immutability, of rest, of plenitude, cannot be derived from an analysis of linear or chronological time. It cannot be put on the time-scale. Rather, we may suspect quite the reverse: it would seem that the very notion of time-scale is extrapolated from the sense of temporal distance implied in the dialectic between expectation, memory, and presentness. It is only from this latter dialectic that we draw the sense of the pastness of the past, with its degrees of remoteness; then, it is thanks to the mediation of such time-keepers as the clock and the calendar that we are able to extrapolate our sense of remoteness to the various changes affecting the earth, the solar system, and the whole universe.

A paradox occurs here, reminding us that this extrapolation relies on the forgetfulness of the derivation of the very temporal character of the gigantic dimension of universal time from the sense of remoteness rooted in memory and expectation. The paradox is as follows: the inexorable expansion of the time-scale far beyond the traditional 6,000-year barrier makes the span of the human life-time appear ever more insignificant—whereas this same human life-time remains the very source of significance. Put differently, the most insignificant segment of time, in terms of the modern time-scale, is the very place where the question of significance can be raised.

Acknowledging this paradox may awaken us to other aspects of temporality that presuppose a characterization of time in terms of nowness, pastness, and futurity.[2]

I have already alluded to the intentional relationship that obtains between nowness, pastness, and futurity. Husserl described this relationship as one of retention and protention. These intentional relationships allow, in turn, a great diversity of modes of integration. Augustine was once again the first to describe the conflict between our search for concordance and our confession of the basic discordance resulting from the discrepancy between pastness, futurity, and nowness. This dialectic between concordance and discordance is typical of a sense of temporality that exceeds the resources of a linear model of time. It is in turn the source of a wealth of temporal experiences to the extent that this concordance/discordance dialectic may be lived at various levels of integration, ranging from radical dismembering (that is, pure "distention," in Augustinian terms), to the intense thickness of moments of enjoyment or grief, which radiate far beyond the transitoriness of the moment itself. Between disintegration and integration we rely on a great many devices to recapitulate the past in the present, and to secure the rare experience of "repetition" that Heidegger called *Wiederholung,* the same experience that found its aesthetic counterpart in Proust's *Le Temps Retrouvé.* Thus, the pastness of the past is handed down and reoriented toward the future, whereas our expectations are once again rooted in the potentialities inherited from the past.

Temporality appears, in this way, as a multilayered phenomenon, a stratified experience, admitting of various degrees of concordance and discordance. Moreover, this multilayered structure may find varied expressions in the three realms of selfhood, history, and cosmic experience. We may already say, by anticipation, that this variety of ways of interconnecting these three realms provides us with remarkable access to the specific modalities of experience under which religious experience is disclosed and interpreted.

But before taking this step toward an all encompassing sense of temporality in which selfhood, history, and cosmos would exchange their temporal features within an overarching set of intersignifications, let us consider very simply how the realm of history, considered as the midpoint between selfhood and cosmos, makes room for a variety of integrating links—all of which exceed by far chronological order and causal connection.

The relatively recent development of historiography as a science has nearly expelled from our historical sense some *topoi* familiar to Greek, Roman, medieval, and even some modern thinkers—for example, the alternation of order and disorder, of tyranny and liberty, and the allegorical equivalence between several social and political regimes separated by temporal distance. In spite of the collapse of these ancient *topoi,* we cannot help looking for paradigms and precedents even for revolutions that claim to open a new era. Their very newness has to be seen as rejuvenation or regeneration if it is to be recognizable and acceptable.

Relations of analogy are assumed by the use of past experience as exemplar for new historical adventures; the concept of *historia magistra vitae* says nothing else. More esoteric relations of analogy have traditionally been claimed by various eschatological expectations which entertain the hopes that, in turn, sustain our favored utopias. We have a combination of both external analogies and more esoteric allegorical connections in such well-known political phenomena as Caesar repeating Alexander the Great, Byzantium continuing the first Rome, and so on.

These interconnecting links, which are closer to a logic of analogy than to one of causality, give rise, in their turn, to various assessments of the meaningfulness of historical time, ranging from tediousness to unquenchable hope. For some, boredom is generated and confirmed by the return of the same familiar passions, crimes, and sufferings; for others, the cumulative power discerned in the series of significant breakthroughs in the field of freedom, justice, or equality keeps furthering a globally positive image of history as a whole.

Do not these modalities of our historical sense foreshadow the *religious* meaning attached to the repetition of the paradigmatic events as well as to their counterpart, "the terror of history?" It is true, of course, that all of our interpretations of history in general involve borrowings from the religious sphere of experience. By the same token, how could we speak of "the terror of history" in comparative religion as one of the basic experiences that religious symbols and rites are supposed to heal, unless our temporal experience itself does make room for assessments applied to historical wholes, if not to history as a whole?

This last remark, which I deliberately close with a question mark, brings us to the threshold of a new set of reflections bearing on examples provided by the comparative study of religions.

The Plurivocity of the Notions of "Cyclical" and "Linear" Applied to Mythical Time

We are now ready to formulate the following hypotheses: first, inasmuch as the notion of cyclical time, as described in comparative religion, is an undeniable phenomenon, it has to be understood on its own terms, that is, without measuring it against its alleged opposite, our modern concept of linear time. Second, there are undoubtedly noncyclical conceptions of time, but they have to be understood in their own terms, without a hasty assimilation to the abstract linearity of physical time. A third and final hypothesis is that both cyclical and noncyclical models, when released from the yoke of comparison with modern linear time, would display a wide spectrum of modalities, and, more interestingly, numerous overlappings and mixed forms—forms that will look inconsistent only to someone who takes the linearity of chronology as the basic yardstick for the description, analysis, and interpretation of mythical time.

Time has been said to be cyclical in many ways. Let us take as a starting point and basis for comparison the model of mythical time elaborated by Mircea Eliade in *Patterns in Comparative Religion* and in *The Myth of the Eternal Return* (translated into English as *Cosmos and History*). The basic notion is that of a *ritual repetition of a paradigm*: the cosmogonic act of creation. We may call the ritual repetition cyclical to the extent that it follows the recurrent features of some periodical natural phenomenon. But the most basic implication of the model is that of exemplarity (we will see later how the cyclical derives from exemplarity or is grafted onto it). To the extent that every myth has a cosmogonic dimension, it relies directly or indirectly on this model.[3] Now, what is striking in the construing of this model is that we cannot express or describe this most archaic mode of temporality to a learned audience except by using a language that has already been philosophically elaborated; I mean, of course, the Platonic model of exemplarity, transferred to the sphere of the sacred and the profane.[4] In speaking of transfer, I do not want to suggest that the comparison with Platonic exemplarity alters or falsifies the religious content that it seeks to describe. Rather, this way of thinking confirms my initial contention that we have no choice except to admit that the Platonic idiom is the most appropriate to delineate, name, and convey such an experience.[5]

The difficulty, if there is any, has to be located elsewhere than in this recourse to a refined mode of thinking to convey the meaning of a mostly archaic myth. In order to point to the real issue, let us shift from the paradigmatic as such to the cyclical. We leave Plato at this point, since, in fact, there is nothing in his notion of exemplarity that implies periodicity, since the ideal paradigms are held to be supratemporal or atemporal (*in illo tempore*); something periodical and, accordingly, cyclical is introduced in the model only through the mediation of ritual repetition of the theogonic act. Then, a whole range of relationships is opened up between exemplarity and periodicity, allowing numerous variations. In fact only some initiations are cyclical, those whose recurrence is ruled by the periodicity of natural or nonnatural phenomena. We count as natural periodicity the alternation of day and night, the return of the seasons following the equinoxes, and the lunar phases, among many others. In "Temps et mythes,"[6] Georges Dumézil observes that the ritual repetition of a model may take forms other than those ruled by a natural periodicity. He distinguishes between *continuous, occasional,* and *periodical* repetition. Food and sexual taboos fall under the first category (continuous); funeral rites, wedding ceremonies, rituals of birth and initiation, rituals generated by diseases and catastrophes, and commemorative rites are subsumed under the second (occasional). Still following Dumézil, we may say that periodical rituals draw part of their interest from being connected to the institution of the calendar, as primitive as it may be. The study of this institution may, in turn, help us to take notice of the variety of relations that may hold between sacred and profane time, through these three kinds of ritual repetition: continuous, occasional, and periodical.

Of course, this taxonomy remains abstract as long as comparative religion does not support it by the description of the variety of relations that may hold between sacred and profane time through these three kinds of ritual repetition: continuous, occasional, and periodical.

Now, if we take the third category, that of ritual repetition as the paradigmatic case for the repetition of the exemplary, new distinctions have to be made at the conceptual level concerning the meaning attached to the relation between sacred and ordinary time. Once more, a whole range of solutions is displayed in front of us by comparative religion.

Let us assume as the basis for comparison Eliade's interpretation. The main stress in Eliade's work is put on the intention of abolishing time. This he takes to be the natural corollary of the regeneration of time, expected from the repetition of the archetypal cosmogonic act. An important section of *Cosmos and History* is devoted to "the abolition of time by the imitation of archetypes and the repetition of paradigmatic acts" (p. 64 [French]). There is undoubtedly a sense in which any renewal implies the cancellation of a past time. Even today, in our profane culture, the celebration of the New Year involves the feeling that the previous year is buried by the rosy newness of the year to come.

Nevertheless, we may be allowed to qualify this equivalence asserted between the regeneration of time and its abolition. The abolition of time, as understood by Eliade, may be seen as the tragic resolution of the contradiction between sacred and profane time, and we must readily admit that this resolution is far from being exclusively tied with the so-called archaic religious forms. It recurs in the form of highly sophisticated meditations in some varieties of Buddhism, without being associated with the conception of the regeneration of time by ritual repetition of a cosmogonic act.

This is why I am tempted to say that this tragic resolution constitutes only one extreme of the range of solutions provided by religions to the relation between sacred and profane time. (A typology of the range of evaluations attached to this relation would be a worthwhile project. I do not claim to be able to elaborate this typology; only someone well acquainted with the widest possible range of religious practices and conceptions could do so.)

For our more modest purpose it is enough, in insisting on the plurivocity of the concept of mythical time, to draw examples of this plurivocity from the most reliable accounts of religious conceptions.

Still close to Eliade's notion of periodical repetition, we may take into account Dumézil's interpretation of the "Great Time," not only as a wealth of exemplary events ready for reenactment but also as a source of order and, accordingly, of power conferred to ordinary time. According to this view, the basic aim of the institution of the calendar appears to be the establishment of a division between time devoted to religious activities and time assigned to profane behavior. This alternation of times suggests that an important function of primordial rites may be the interruption as much as the abolition of profane time. Thanks to this ordering instituted by festal periods of time, new typical contrasts are introduced within profane time itself, which secures to it a certain amount of meaningfulness, such as the distinction between favorable and unfavorable times for doing or not doing this or that thing. This distinction may be cast in terms of days, lunar phases, months, seasons, or the magical reckoning of time-spans. We may indeed consider this ordering of profane time as an "infiltration," as it were, of sacred time into profane time; but, to the extent that it rules not merely the periodic return of specifically religious festivals but the works themselves, as in Hesiod's *Works and Days,* and besides works, all kinds of ordinary activities such as wishes, oaths, modes of cooking, greeting, and so on, it is profane time itself that is qualified, to use Dumézil's expression.

We have to do here with a new important concept, one which should not be confused with that of ritual repetition. I mean the *rhythmic* structure of time, which relies on the succession of strong and weak intervals and the recurrence of the same patterns on the same occasions. We may hold this rhythmic structure as a modality of cyclical time, although with the reservation that this modality does enrich the plurivocity of the cyclical. A rhythmic sense of ordinary time may or may not be linked to rites of regeneration; it may or may not generate a sense of boredom, or of the meaninglessness of ordinary time. The notion of rhythm deserves to be held as a type of its own in the typology of sacred and profane temporality. There may be a recurrence of rhythmic patterns without circularity, that is, along an open-ended course of time. It is enough that we speak of "recurring" occasions—as expressed in such phrases as, "each time that," "every seventh day," and so on. Our own language offers, thanks to its tense and adverbial systems, ways of expressing the iterative or frequentative aspects of temporality, and allows us to speak of "seizing the moment," and of doing something "at the right time." There is nothing tragic in this qualification of profane time, although a magical conception of fate may be easily grafted onto this notion of the "right time."

At this point a transition is close at hand—one that Dumézil himself suggests—from the notion of the "Great Time" to that of a succession of eras or ages. "There was a time that was blessed," in the sense that everything succeeded, that occasions were all favorable—this was the Golden Age. All succeeding times, and ours more than others, are, by comparison, unfortunate, untimely. As is easily seen, this configuration of the "Great Time" in terms of broad "eras" does not itself entail the notion of periodicity, that is, of the repetition or recurrence of the same sequence of ages. Furthermore, the sequence of ages may constitute a progression or a regression of order and blessedness. I allude here to the sequence initiated by the Golden Age, which thereafter constitutes a series of decadence, with or without recurrence of the pattern. But, in some genealogies of deities, we have an ascending sequence, leading to the emergence of a deity who expresses the triumph of order, justice, and peace over chaotic powers or monstrous Gods. We think of Marduk conquering Tiamat, of Zeus superseding Ouranos and Cronos—but no notion of recurrence is implied in this genealogical model, although it may be coupled with it. And patterns of progressive order must be kept distinct from patterns of decadence.

A new account of the relation between sacred and profane time, still close to Dumézil's "Great Time," is found in the Eastern traditions linked to the notion of *karma*. Instead of seeing ordinary time as a succession of appearing and disappearing instants, we may see time as the medium through which our acts, their effects, and their meaning are preserved in such a way that they constitute a cumulative chain of efficacy. Linked to the idea of reincarnation, we may plausibly conceive of a given destiny as the retribution of actions performed in a previous life. Regarding time, the emphasis is here put on the concatenation of acts generated by the inscription and perseveration of our own time within the Great Time. This conception is not without counterpart in our own phenomenology of time. As soon as we are no longer entranced by the model of linear succession, we are open to modes of thought that involve the opposite presupposition: that of the indestructible concatenation of the traces left behind by previous acts. Without being able to make this belief real for ourselves, we may yet have, so to speak, a marginal understanding of it based on our own sense of responsibility. If the Great Time may still be understood as a store of events whose efficacity is inexhaustible, we may, accordingly, conceive of events in time which enjoy an enduring efficacy overcoming the transitoriness that we naturally ascribe to human actions.

Once more, a new version of the cyclical may emerge from the basic acknowledgment of the cumulative claim of efficacy through time linked to the theme of *karma*. What is endless may be easily seen as endlessly recurring. In the same way, the motto, "Nothing is new under the sun," may be interpreted as a form of eternal return, but with a negative and pessimistic overtone, not as regeneration.

To understand these new figures of the cyclical, it is appropriate to take into account the variety of responses provided mainly by Indian thought to the idea of an endless chain of retributions linked to the theme of *karma*. At one end of the range of attitudes generated by this theme there is the sense of awe, of reverence, of resignation to the ineluctable law of *karma*. At the other end, there is the Buddhist attempt to overcome the torment of retribution by excising the root of endless repetition itself which resides in the power of desire to generate endless suffering.

But, as Eliade underlines in his long article, "Time and Eternity in Indian Thought,"[7] renunciation of the world is not the only consequence an Indian is justified in drawing from the discovery of the infinite cyclical time. In the *Bhagavad Gītā*, for example, Indian thought also maps out a road that does not necessarily lead to asceticism and abandonment of the world. "Renunciation of the fruits of one's actions, of the profits one might derive from action, but not from action itself" is one of the maxims for a hero of practical life who would preserve his identity, but without pride and self-conceit. Keeping in mind the perspective of the Great Time while continuing to fulfill one's duty in historical time, we feel raised by this maxim of wisdom far beyond any simple dichotomy between the cyclical and the linear. The sage is, as it were, sent back by its very retreat from the birth cycles, and all the cyclical aspects of life, including the repetition of suffering, to another linear time, the time of historical involvement.

We see how wide is the range of solutions related to the problem raised by the law of *karma*: from submission, to enlightenment, and to liberation, without excluding a return to the historical field of action under the maxim of "renunciation of the fruits of one's actions."

Seen from the point of view of the awakened or enlightened spirit of the sage, this deeply rooted connection between desire and suffering may still be expressed in the vocabulary of the cyclical. But the circle established by the chain of retributions has almost nothing in common with the periodicity from which we started—that is, with the regeneration of time by periodical rites. The return of suffering is not itself regulated by natural periodicity, such as that of the lunar phases or the daily or yearly cycles of the sun. This return has a purely existential meaning, loaded as it is with cosmic overtones.

Furthermore, the same conception of time, which may still be called cyclical, with the reservations just made, entails noncyclical aspects, which in turn are far from complying with the abstract criteria of abstract linearity that govern a large part of Western thought concerning time. (This is why I speak with great caution of noncyclical conceptions of time. It leaves room for many more solutions to the problem of the relations between sacred and profane time.)

In fact, we have already met forms of noncyclical time in the notion of divine genealogies, in the succession of ages, ranging from the Golden Age down to our present hard time; the myth of Great Time may generate the conception of eras, following one another, each of gigantic lengths, and offering no other connection, besides these individual qualitative specificities, than their pure sequence, and some numeric proportions which say something about their relative importance. Here, it seems that the magnitude of time is exalted, its capacity to enclose cosmos, history, and selfhood in all encompassing and overarching totalities. In "Time and Eternity in Indian Thought," Eliade underlines the vastness of even the smallest unit of measurement, the *yuga*, or age. "Each *yuga*," he says, "is preceded by a 'dawn' and followed by a 'dusk' which constitute the transition between them. A complete cycle, or *mahāyuga*, consists of four ages of unequal length, the longest occurring at the beginning of the cycle and the shortest at its end" (p. 177). I chose this quote because of its use of the term cycle, not in a sense for which periodicity is the key characteristic, but to express the completeness of a closed era. Nothing forbids that we use the term cycle to express nonperiodical completeness or closedness, for the reason that the circle is the most appropriate symbol of what is closed and complete. But we must not be the prey of the image and must remain attentive to both qualitative and even numeric relationships which belong to nonlinear features of time. "The names of these *yugas*," Eliade writes, "are borrowed from the names of the 'throws' in the game of dice." Four, the winning throw, is reserved for the perfect age; three, for the next one; and then two and one; the figures 4, 3, 2, 1 denote then both the interesting length of the *yuga* and the diminution of the *dharma* prevailing in them. Equally interesting in this schema of time is that the relative duration of each of these four *yugas* is reckoned in terms of divine years, each of which embraces 360 human years. But nothing would be more wrong than to compare this fabulous computation of years in terms of what we called at the beginning time-scale. When we read that a thousand such *mahāyugas* constitute a *kalpa,* and that a *kalpa* is equivalent to a day in the life of Brahmā, another *kalpa* to a night, we surmise that the purpose of this monstrous amount of numbers is to defeat our reckonings and compel us to rebuild at a much higher level of vastness our initial modest model of the cyclical based on the periodicity of ritual imitation of a paradigm. Eliade may write: "the essential element of this avalanche of figures is the cyclical character of cosmic time . . ."; one of the main ideas "that stand out from this orgy of figures" is "the eternal repetition of the fundamental cosmic rhythm, the periodic destruction and re-creation of the universe" (p. 180). But, as is easy to see, the meaning of the words cycle, period, repetition, have been considerably enriched. The question is no longer that of the regeneration of time by ritual but a call for an act of spiritual freedom, for a deliverance from the cosmic illusion.

Allow me to introduce one more example to support my initial hypothesis that the cyclical allows such a wide plurivocity that it overlaps with quasi-linear aspects of time (which in turn share a merely apparent kinship with our modern concept of linear time). I borrow this example from Granet's *La Pensée chinoise.* Needless to say, I have no way of assessing the validity of Granet's interpretation. My remarks are nothing more than questionmarks and notes. I introduce them here because they have to do with some quasi-linear aspects of time.

The outcome of Granet's analysis is twofold: on the one hand, the temporal features of Chinese thought deserve to be called quasi-linear because—at first sight at least—they present none of the modalities of periodicity or circularity. But on the other hand, they bear only slight resemblance to what would count as linearity for us, that is, a unique and universal time-scale. In fact—still according to Granet—time is initially represented by grafting new modalities of the cyclical onto a definitely noncyclical conception of time.

Concerning the first aspect of the problem, Granet emphasizes the idea of a series of eras, seasons, and epochs, closely correlated with a complex of domains, climates, and orientations characterizing space. This qualitative diversity common to both space and time is reinforced by emblems such as colors, animals, etcetera, which, in turn, are taken to represent affinities with specific temporal eras and spacial orientations. We are prevented from identifying the series of eras simply as segments of a linear time by the interactions obtaining between the emblems themselves. As Granet puts it: "Time and space are never conceived apart from the concrete actions that they display as connections of appropriate emblems, apart from the actions which can, in turn, be applied to them thanks to emblems underscoring their singularity" (pp. 88–89). This is why Granet prefers to speak of occasions and rites, following the modes of thought applied to time and space by the Chinese thinkers themselves when they aim at classifying rites and occasions in terms of their specific efficacy. At first sight we seem to be brought closer to what Westerners call linear time in that time is divided according to political rather than natural periods: "the annual cycle of seasons," says Granet, "is not the prototype of the Chinese representation of time." The beginnings of new dynasties, reigns, and portions of reigns determine the qualitative distinction between eras. For example, one of the inaugural gestures of a new reign is the promulgation of a new calendar, implying the abolition of the old order as well as the creation of a new one. Nothing about this description fits in our abstract notion of linearity and its corollary, the unique time-scale. The promulgation of a new calendar alone is a political act which precludes linking the regeneration of time to the natural periodicity of the year or seasons.

But, if it is true that we do not find in this Chinese conception of time the kind of cyclical recurrence generated by the ritual reenactment of the cosmogonic act, some other modes of periodicity may be grafted onto the conception of an apparently open-ended series of eras, dynasties, and reigns. Granet characterizes as rhythmic the distribution of ceremonies around a central gesture, according to some harmonic numerical reckoning. If we think of rhythmic as (1) "any process marked by the regular succession of strong and weak elements or of opposite or different conditions," or of any "due correlation and interdependence of parts producing a harmonious whole" (Oxford English Dictionary), then a culture so typically framed by a ceremonial order as the Chinese assumes some cyclical character—due precisely to the rhythmic nature of its numerous ceremonies.

Moreover, some further traits allow us to speak of the "return of the cyclical" in spite of the quasi-linear character of a time whose significant divisions are not based on natural periodicity. According to some Chinese thinkers, the virtues displayed by an abolished era are not strictly annihilated but, as it were, "stored" somewhere and allowed to return later—just as the name of an ancestor may be allowed to return, after, say, four generations. Granet writes: "In the same way, when they write history and introduce order into the past, the Chinese assume that dynasties alternate, each with its own virtue, and succeed one another in a cyclical way" (p. 100). In this context, as well as within that of the cyclical return of the Five Virtues described by Chinese scholars of the fourth–third century B.C., the term cyclical carries one of its basic meanings, that of the return of the same in the succession of time. And yet, the notion of cyclical time has very little to do, in this context, with the regeneration of time by the ritual repetition of a paradigm, especially when this repetition is ruled by the natural periodicity of days, lunar months, or solar years. This reckoning of eras or ages is disconnected from any considerations of natural periodicity, and is situated between two opposed uses of the cyclical: that of the ritual repetition of a supratemporal model, and that of a cycle of ages. As such, it underlines the plurivocity of the term cyclical, no longer defined by comparison to what we now call linear, or rather, rectilinear time. This plurivocity does not, however, prohibit analogies and borrowings of all kinds amongst the most extreme modes of cyclical return, in spite of the quasi-linear sense of temporality which is, as it were, interpolated between them.[8]

In this quick survey I have not borrowed from the two cultural and religious worlds, the Greek and the Hebraic, whose comparison has determined the alleged dichotomy between cyclical and linear conceptions of time. My strategy has been, rather, to set examples related to cultural worlds other than those out of which our Western culture has emerged, in order to pave the way in the field of comparative religion for a fresh approach to the tedious discussion about Greeks and Jews. What has been already started in comparative historiography by scholars like Momigliano should be followed up in the same critical spirit.

We need the long detour through the various forms of cyclical time in order to make a fair assessment of the so-called Jewish conception of time. Then its alleged linearity would no longer be derived from its superficial similarity to what we now call linear time, that is to say, the abstract time-scale of the scientific universe. Thanks to this long detour, we will no longer be surprised to find side by side, within the vast variety of Hebrew writings, both striking examples of one of the several modalities of cyclical time, mainly exemplified by festivals and ceremonial rites, and clear examples of linearity, mainly among the narrative parts of the Hebrew Scriptures—under the condition, however, that biblical narratives keep being defined in their own terms. Between these two poles of "cyclical" festivals and "linear" narratives, there are all kinds of intermediary cases. The Sinai Covenant appears as an enduring rather than a repetitive event; hence, the solemn call of Deuteronomy "to remember" and "to retell"; hence, also the unique connection between a strong sense of tradition and memory, and a future-oriented sense of time initiated by the prophetic writings; hence, finally, the innumerable analogical links connecting history-making events in spite of temporal distance (the new Sion, the new desert, the new covenant).

Eliade is not the last to underscore the specificity of this Hebrew sense of time, which is better characterized by the exchange between traditional memories and prophetic (and later eschatological) expectations than by its affinity with our linear time. The section devoted to history as the epiphany of God, in *Cosmos and History,* is all the more precious because it is written by Mircea Eliade, the scholar and poet of the eternal return. This section suggests that it is less the annihilation of history than its redemption that makes the difference between Hebrew and Eastern religions. But, if we want to keep the concept of linearity to express this specificity, we should have to reformulate it in such a way that it conveys the belief that the expected Kingdom of God means more than the lost Paradise. Then nothing prevents us from disentangling from this superficial rendering of the sense of time in terms of linearity a new, highly sophisticated form of repetition, that of the *Urzeit* within the *Endzeit.*

Conclusion

Let me draw some conclusions from this critical survey of a puzzling methodological problem in the history of religions. What gain can be expected from the introduction of hermeneutical-phenomenological considerations into this field? My conviction is that the exchange may be beneficial for both parties. On the one hand, a hermeneutical phenomenology of time consciousness may liberate our thought from the exclusive model of time as a pure succession of neutral instants metaphorically represented by a line—a line indifferent to the events that punctuate it. Thanks to this liberating action, phenomenology can draw attention to some nonlinear aspects of temporality, and, in so doing, clear the ground for conceptions and speculations, and above all for experiences of time foreign to our Western minds.

On the other hand, the description of the conception of time generated by religions other than those that have shaped our own culture may enrich and enlighten some features of temporality which no phenomenology could discover or describe without the help of the various symbolisms displayed by these religions. And this is as it should be. For what would be the use of comparative religion if it did not aim at producing an echo in the midst of our own experience, and if, at the price of some painful tensions and conflicts, it did not enlarge our own self-understanding, by contrasting what we understand with what we do not understand of the religions of others?

Notes

1. Professor A. Momigliano has exposed the wrong assumptions held by the opponents of this fierce battle. First, on the Greek side, one tends to forget that Homer, Hesiod, and the Tragedians display several implicitly different worldviews and offer no theoretical statements about time comparable to those professed by Plato, Aristotle, Democritus, the Stoics, and Plotinus. On the Hebrew side, one underestimates the conflicting implications concerning time connected with rituals and festivals, the Deuteronomic ideology, prophetic sayings, and eschatological movements. Only Hebrew historiography in Samuel and Kings could be usefully put side by side with Greek historiography. Ironically, no significant differences concerning the treatment of time can be ascribed to these well-delineated works. Above all, biblical writings contain no systematic speculation about time worthy of being compared with that of Greek philosophers (A. Momigliano, "Time in Ancient Historiography," in *Essays in Ancient and Modern Historiography,* Middleton, Conn.: Wesleyan Univ. Press, 1977). In concurrence with Momigliano, see James Barr, *Biblical Words for Time,* London, 1962; P. Vidal-Naquet, "Temps des dieux et temps des hommes," *Revue de l'histoire des religions,* 1960, pp. 55–80.
2. The various modalities of narration, which all cultures display, imply an ability to construe stories as meaningful temporal wholes, within which beginning, middle, and end are interconnected in such a way that we may not only survey these temporal wholes, but may interpret their endings in terms of the initial circumstances and intervening peripeties. This ability to elicit patterns from sequences, configuration from succession, constitutes, as I have shown elsewhere, a basic feature of narrative time. I shall dwell no further on the narrative quality of experience, in order to focus on some other properties of temporality which may point in the direction of conceptions of time displayed only by religious texts belonging to a wide variety of cultures.
3. "The cosmogony . . . provides a model, wherever there is a question of doing something" (*Patterns,* p. 411).
4. "Hence it could be said that the primitive ontology has a platonic structure and in that sense Plato could be regarded as the outstanding philosopher of primitive mentality" (*Cosmos,* p. 34).
5. In *Cosmos and History,* Eliade claims only to be providing "a mere exegesis of the general meaning that all these ceremonies display . . . our ambition is to understand their *meaning,* to try to see what they may show to us, with the reservation that it is the task of further inquiries to provide a particular—whether genetic or historical—description of each mythico-ritual ensemble" (pp. 73–74).
6. Georges Dumézil, "Temps et mythes," in *Recherches philosophiques* 5 (Paris, 1935/1936), pp. 235–251.

7. "Time and Eternity in Indian Thought," in *Man and Time*, ed. Joseph Campbell (New York, 1957), pp. 173–200.
8. Granet suggests that the emblematic function assigned to the seasons may have contributed to the conception of a cycle of ages, similar to the return of the seasons. A certain analogy between the cyclical return of the virtues of abolished eras and the spectacle of natural periodicity may ultimately obtain, in spite of the obvious disparity between the two kinds of return. This analogy may be further reinforced by the character of decay and renovation common to both natural and political models of periodicity. The notion of a Great Time, in Dumézil's sense, may well lurk behind both senses of cyclical return.

From the History of Religions to Religious Anthropology:
A Necessary Reappraisal

MICHEL MESLIN

Many books have been written and many things said about the history of religions in the nearly 120 years since it gained its autonomy.[1] Nevertheless, it is necessary at the present time to reevaluate the discipline. This reevaluation is all the more urgent because in our highly technicized world—a world which we have described, perhaps a bit prematurely, as completely secularized—we are now witnessing a resurgence of interest in religious problems. Like every human creation, the history of religions has been subjected to the erosive effects of time and has been forced to change. The time has come to reexamine the values proper to the discipline in order to determine what remains of the hopes to which it gave rise and the principles that have guided its development. At the same time, we may see whether the problems that arose when it won its autonomy and asserted its coherence have all been satisfactorily resolved.

The fundamental problem of how to view the relationships between man and the divine is an old one. Fascinated by these relationships, men in nearly every generation have formulated a number of theories to explain them. In the process they have built up a discipline that has increasingly sought independence from metaphysical and theological attachments. But our reassessment must not merely exhume, in the manner of a history of ideas, certain instances, more or less intense, of man's reflection on his fellow men. If we turn our attention for the moment to the internal development of the history of religions, we do so in order to remind ourselves of its originality, to recognize the mistakes it has made and the wrong turns some have naïvely taken, and especially to reject methodological pretensions that would reduce the explanation of religious phenomena to the mere formulation of a causal series. If a more exact knowledge of the theories of the human sciences has brought to the history of religions only one thing, it has brought a sensitivity to the relative and complementary importance of different, systematic means of explaining and understanding religious realities.

The first part of this chapter will aim not at drawing up a list of prize-winning men and works but at drawing out some basic methodological questions. The names of the masters who have preceded us and who have made us who we are will be with us only in our thoughts. My hope is that this sort of methodological reflection will allow us to envisage more clearly the future of our inquiries. Then we must ask ourselves honestly whether the impact of the human sciences has not altered the fundamental perspectives of the history of religions to the point of divesting it of its originality. An examination of the discipline's past—a past that makes up for its brevity with its richness—should bring to light the new problems that historians of religions face today. It should also point up the need for a greater openness in, and perhaps a profound transformation of, the history of religions.

The Constitution of an Autonomous Discipline

The history of religions is relatively young. We can only begin to speak of it in a technical sense with F. Max Müller, who laid the foundations for a *Religionswissenschaft* in the comparative mythology he had developed from philological techniques. A few years later, in 1870, E. Burnouf, one of the earliest exegetes of the sacred texts of ancient Iran, called for the establishment of a "science whose elements are still widely scattered, a science which is not even defined and which we call the Science of Religions, perhaps for the first time."[2] The influence of positivist philosophy and the hard sciences led many at the time to speak not of the science of religions but of the history of religions or *Religionsgeschichte*. Thus, since the last quarter of the nineteenth century the vocabulary used to denote this young discipline has revealed a tension, if not a conflict, between two conceptions. The choice in favor of "history of religions" followed from a clear desire to study only religious elements in themselves as they might be grasped through their diachronic development. Conceived as the study of the varied forms of religious transformations, that is, of the existence of religion, the history of religions stands naturally in opposition to a *Religionswissenschaft* that devotes itself to the study of religion's essence. A historical approach would view itself as critical and objective. It is, in fact, absolutely essential to defining the relationships that unite humanity with the divine, an element that we constantly rediscover in the history of human reflection on religious phenomena.

This constant of our discipline—the necessary distance between the observer of religious phenomena and the object of his study—appears already in ancient Greece. In Greece the absence of any divine revelation and of all theological dogma made human representations of the divine the only source of religion. The religion of the polis attached its approving seal to the human representations, but its approval did not make the representations any less subject to a free-ranging critique by reason. In formulating a critique of psychological representations of the divine, Xenophanes attached great importance to the resemblance between man and the representations he makes of the gods.[3] Heraclitus showed that myths should be perceived as symbols of the truth that designates the hidden essence of the divine without exhausting it.[4] In the end, the break with official religion resulted in the euhemerist interpretation of mythology. In a quite similar way, the fracturing of Christian unity in the sixteenth century emancipated the believer from a religious system that was judged too exclusive and constraining. Religious individualism set itself up against all doctrinal, ecclesiastical institutions, and reason became the criterion for appreciating and judging human attitudes in the face of the divine. Since that time, man as a reasoning subject has adopted a more subjective attitude toward problems of the sacred. His ideas about such problems have been subject to variations in human understanding itself. Simultaneously, through a sort of psychological compensation, he has considered the phenomenal structure of religion to be essential. More important than the intangibility of dogma has been an increasingly historical conception of a sacred that is lived.

From this brief excursus one can understand how in the nineteenth century, under the influence both of rationalism (which was still vigorous) and of the development of the positive sciences, those who sought to deal with religious matters scientifically thought it necessary to distance themselves from metaphysics and from any form of doctrinal orthodoxy. The young field of the history of religions could not assent to being the humble servant of theology, nor could it assent to being the instrument of a more or less naïve apologetics. Theology and the history of religions are fundamentally different. In effect, theology is human discourse on God. Its object is the essence of a religion that is deemed the only true and authentic religion. Its primary task is to describe to that religion's followers the object of their faith, to conceptualize it rationally, and to develop an ethics in correlation with what it judges to be the truth. Thus, every theology is a normative science. Its procedures are conditioned by faith in its own truth. It is exclusive and unitary, and it answers the question, "What should we believe, and why are we to believe it?" It is precisely this normative character that the history of religions wished to oppose. Out of a desire to situate itself at the level of human conduct, the history of religions voluntarily distanced itself from metaphysical speculations and theological systematizations. Thus, it declared from the start that it firmly intended to steer a laicizing course. At the same time, in order to attain complete autonomy from theological discourse, it strove to define its object and its methods of investigation and analysis. From the outset, it asserted that it was history.

Is not this assertion simply the application of a positivist view of history to the sphere of religious acts, a view of history that, in the second half of the nineteenth century, had just gained full mastery over its own techniques and, so to speak, won its wings? I believe it is. In its beginnings, the history of religions applied itself quite narrowly to describing the various religious experiences of man's past, to retracing the evolution of beliefs and rites, and to analyzing the links between them. It presented itself as the study of the religious universe of a humanity multiplied into as many particular realities as there are human cultures and societies. It did so after the fashion of a series of mirrors which, set according to slightly staggered perspectives, reflect back a nearly infinite multiplicity of images of one and the same object. For example, Chantepie de la Saussaye's very important *Lehrbuch der Religionsgeschicte,* which first appearred in 1887–1889, organizes the analytic study of religions by classifying them according to geographical, ethnological, and cultural categories. In doing so, Chantepie asserts his firm intention to avoid all rapprochement between different religious experiences and to respect their originality by considering each in its own context. His *Religionsgeschichte* takes the form of a history of natural religions, of the religions of peoples and of churches, as if the sweep of human history had never embraced anything other than a plurality of collective religious experiences. Even the concept of religion can be apprehended scientifically only through its human realizations, which are bound to particular historical and cultural conditions. Thus, through its difficult efforts to establish its autonomy, the history of religions sought to furnish a positive, scientific knowledge of the sacred as it is lived in all human cultures open to historical study.

Such a program presupposes an optimal empirical knowledge of religious realities. This presupposition immediately presents a problem. What is a religious reality? The history of religions has tended to answer the question from a standpoint strongly loyal to a primary principle of positivist history: a historical reality is a dated event that has causes and that continues in time through its effects. In taking this stance, the positivistic history of religions thought it could separate its analyses from all manifestations of a world of the fabulous, of which the historian could not, *stricto sensu,* take account. But such a world is nothing other than a manifestation of supernatural and mythic worlds, both of which are important witnesses to collective beliefs and world-views. In taking the stance it did, the discipline voluntarily limited itself to analyzing religions on the basis of documents capable of being dated, classified, and interpreted by scholarly specialists, each using his or her own scientific gifts but all sharing a common disdain for generalizing syntheses. The ideal was to be able to read a text or analyze a document in order to extricate from it what was significant from the religious point of view. This ideal made it absolutely imperative for historians of religions to master the solid techniques of philology, paleography, and ethnology. But it also produced a certain heterogeneity and diversity in methods applied to the common object (religions) because of the varying nature of the documents that were used. The influence of a philosophical postulate and technical requirements of a history that claimed to be scientific led certain historians to surmise that when they found themselves taking an interest in religious problems that did not fall into objectively analyzable categories, they were going beyond their role, stepping outside the laws of their discipline. The historical nature of a religious reality, which could be considered solely in terms of its positive, datable, and phenomenal aspects, was distinguished from interpretations attainable only through faith, about which the historian was obliged to remain silent. Merely recall the enormous effort expended to oppose the historical Jesus to the Christ of faith, to recover a historical Buddha or a pre-Qur'anic Muhammad.

We understand today more clearly than half a century ago the exaggeration and the danger in opposing a so-called objective reality of the past, which the historian can reconstitute integrally through his craft, to a kerygmatic interpretation of the same reality. Such an attitude disdained the kerygmatic interpretation, which it relegated to the mere theologian. Yet it is clear that these realities and their interpretations constitute an irreducible whole in the lived religious experience. The same is true of myth, which a positivistic history of religions all too easily disregards. If the truth of myth does not appear to be rational and scientific to modern eyes—if its stories cannot be taken to be historical in the strict sense of the word—nevertheless it is totally impossible for the historian of religions not to integrate myth as a fundamental document into his analyses. The problem lies in knowing what to retain of the mythical and fantastic material that can be recovered by the historian. I believe that in myth the most intimately religious is precisely that which those living the myth understand to be a manifestation of the sacred and which, because it is understood to manifest the sacred, also informs human ritual and legitimates various forms of social and ethical conduct.

Clearly we can only grasp the sacred where we encounter it, that is, in human existence itself. In the diverse religions and multifarious religious experiences of humanity we perceive that the sacred is lived historically in a given time and space and that its expressions derive, to a great extent, from their cultural milieu. All religious experience, as it expresses itself in myths, rituals, symbols, and sacred scriptures, is caught up in diachrony. It becomes historical from the moment that an individual becomes more or less clearly conscious, through it, of a relationship that unites him with a reality which he judges to be transcendent. But however great the constraining power of religious traditions may be, the content of the experience that they transmit is condemned to suffer, to some extent, the wear and tear of time. Time erodes the sacred's various modes of expression and occasionally alters quite profoundly the objective view that a culture possesses of religious reality. For these reasons, the analysis of religious phenomena should be conducted from a historical and cultural standpoint. The history of religions is first of all history.

But it is the history of *religions*. By insisting on classifying religious realities on a diachronic basis, does not the discipline refuse to consider the function every religion serves at the heart of some human society? By resolutely asserting religion's plural character, the history of religions does more than voice its defiance of any theology. It renounces any possibility for an enlightening analysis of the concept of religion. Archeology, ethnology, even history itself show clearly that from the earliest evidence of religious practices some 100,000 years ago up to the most recent events seized upon by the mass media, we must take account of the roles religious activities play in human society. The multitude of religions that we know and can analyze seem to be experienced by their adherents as references to a reality higher than human reality at the same time that they are experienced as a means for monitoring the world in which the adherents live from day to day. Through religion man defines himself in the world and with regard to his fellow humans. We may thus start with the hypothesis that all religion, whatever its particular historical form, functions to explain man and the world and to justify the place man occupies in the world. In religion, man comes to possess a wisdom that undergirds and determines particular activities and that maintains and justifies a particular order of things. That religion performs such a function points out just how wrong it is to separate in analysis religious realities from their religious interpretations. Every religion stirs its adherents to assure themselves of the coherence of their being and the cohesiveness of the group in which they live.

Recent analyses have shown that religion's fundamental role is not that of a social regulator, as Marx and Durkheim asserted. Nor is religion merely a characteristic of what it means to be human. Rather, religion arises primarily for existential reasons. All religion appears to be founded on the consciousness of human finitude. This consciousness impels man to search out the deepest sources of his own limits. Religion cannot help but manifest itself constantly in novel forms, for it is man's questioning of himself about himself and the place he occupies in the world.[5] Contrary to what was asserted for so long, then, a religious reality cannot be taken to be a mere historical event, even if it is located in time. A religious reality is not, in fact, determined solely by the political, economic, and cultural circumstances with which it is contemporaneous. "Its substance neither arises from nor totally exhausts itself in the event and its manifestations."[6] A simple comparison of various religions shows clearly that the historical forms with which religious phenomena are clothed correspond to types and presuppose specific structures. These types and structures are encountered again and again. They are more or less identical and constant in every religious experience that history might discover and study. Despite variations in detail, which result from history, the permanence of types and structures fully warrants disengaging religious phenomena from diachrony in order to recombine them for comparison and analysis outside the historical perspective. The phenomenology resulting from this procedure is not only another way of arranging religious realities along a structural as opposed to a diachronic axis. It is also necessary for clarifying and clearing away materials we are able to grasp only from their entanglements in the empirical data of history. I do not wish to belabor the point. We can see now how indispensable it has become to broaden an overly historical conception of the history of religions, a conception that, whatever its merits, cannot cover and explicate the entire field of human religious behavior. The encounter with the human sciences should occasion this necessary broadening of horizons.

The Impact of the Human Sciences and the Conflict of Interpretations

As the history of religions was taking shape, there appeared alongside the hard sciences other disciplines which shared the study of human behavior. The study of religious behavior could not remain aloof from these currents. In an extraordinary expansion, unprecedented in history, Western thought of the last part of the nineteenth and the first decade of the twentieth centuries developed—through working hypotheses, practical observations, and new theories—many new perspectives on humanity. The encounter with a "savage" humanity thought still to have been close to the primitive purity of human beginnings, together with a great increase in ethnographic investigations, fueled an entire dialectic, the dialectic of the self and the other. In turn, the dialectic fed the animist theories and the evolutionary schemas of E. B. Tylor, A. Lang, and J. G. Frazer. In France, E. Durkheim and his successors reaped the philosophical heritage of A. Comte. They showed that society was a tremendously important factor in the development of religious realities. Under the influence of Feuerbach and Schleiermacher, the psychological causes of religious phenomena were seen more and more clearly, even if certain outrageous theories on the pathological origins of religion tended to make *Religionswissenschaft* a mere appendage of medicine. W. James criticized this medical materialism in the name of a religious pragmatism that strongly stressed the influence of the individual temperament in the development of a particular religious experience.[7] Simultaneously, other theories were explaining that religion could only be held to be true to the extent that the individual felt the need for it to be true.[8] Before long a Viennese doctor would bring to light the process by which relationships of man with the divine were mediated by the father and show that nothing was to be gained in studying religions by denying human desires. Freud also showed that myths are nothing more than twisted remains of the imagination and desires of different peoples—"man's time-honored dreams"—and, from the phylogenic point of view, that myth is for a people what dreams are for the individual.[9] When he applied this hermeneutical template to ancient mythology, Freud found his most celebrated illustration, the myth of Oedipus. For him, the Oedipus myth represented the manifestations of infantile desire, the desire of the son for the mother and against the father, against which the incest prohibition is imposed.[10] The force of Freud's thought impelled O. Rank, E. Jones, and especially Geza Roheim to develop consecutively Freud's new technique for investigating mythic thought by linking it with the psychology of the individual's unconscious. But in founding a psychoanalytic anthropology, these thinkers did not reject traditional sociocultural hermeneutics. They merely asserted that psychoanalysis situated myth at the juncture of two mechanisms, the mechanisms of social situation and of the complexes of the libido. The disciple whom Freud despised all the more because he had once been so fond of him, C. G. Jung, constantly emphasized the revolution psychoanalysis had produced in the interpretation of mythology. For Jung, myths were revelations of the unconscious soul, involuntary affirmations of unconscious psychical realities. He deveoped a *Tiefpsychologie*—a depth psychology—which opened new perspectives on the understanding of religious symbols. His research showed that there were certain psychical types and that these types were analogous to religious representations. By knowing and experiencing internal archetypal images, a person could better comprehend, both rationally and emotionally, the meaning of the symbols human beings use in their various religious languages as well as the meaning of the representations religions offer their followers as bases for reflection and action. Finally, the philosophy of E. Husserl and especially Max Scheler's greatest work, *Das Ewige im Menschen* (The Eternal in Man), endowed the analysis of religious realities with the indispensable tool of phenomenology. In effect, Scheler showed the very particular character of any religious act by stressing the intentionality animating it and relating it to a transcendent entity. Scheler asserted the closed character of religious experience. He insisted on the absolute necessity of knowing and understanding the meaning of the phenomenon that reveals itself to the subject's consciousness. He showed the extent to which every religious belief led the believing subject to identify with the being he or she believed in. In all these ways, the different sciences of man, which emerged in less than a generation, profoundly modified the idea one might have had of religious realities. They could not help but influence the development of the history of religions.

One of the most important cultural phenomena of the past decades has undoubtedly been an increasingly frequent recourse to the various human sciences in an attempt to understand both existence itself and the causes of religious phenomena. At first sight, such a move is completely understandable. The hard sciences have given no answers to any of the questions in the whole problematic field traversed by a single religious faith and practice; indeed, they are clearly not interested in such questions. The sciences of man, by contrast, would seem to offer very accurate answers. They propose a mode of explanation that permits the mysteries surrounding the relationships between man and the divine to be resolved and certain irritating questions posed by our critical spirit to be satisfied. As a result, their operative validity seems all the more solid. Every religion presents itself as a system constructed by a long tradition of thought about fundamental human problems—life, love, good, evil, death. Through pedagogy and catechesis every religion is established as a system of beliefs, myths, and rituals which function in precisely delimited ways, at the same time that it reflects clearly its historical, cultural, and social contexts. However, there is a second level of systematization alongside this primary level, the interpretation of each religion by its devotees and its students. How can we understand the meaning of a religious experience defined by such a network of symbols, rites, images, and dogmas? How can we distinguish the acts of an individual from collective behavior? Does one's capacity to transpose one's self into another in order to grasp what the other sees and believes define what it means to understand a religious reality? Who would not grant that such a transposition is not an easy task, perhaps, in fact, an impossible task? How can one be oneself with the other? In pursuing better understanding, how does one leave oneself in attempting to outstrip one's own intellectual finitude, in accepting the mediating roles of sacred texts and symbols, and in making the ritual's intentionality one's own? One must explain and understand at the same time, even though one knows full well that there is no explanation that is not first grounded in understanding. But can I really understand a religious phenomenon itself, or is my understanding merely a projection of myself?

To be sure, in the course of their development the human sciences have developed tools that are well-adapted epistemologically, tools that allow the researcher to refine his analyses so that they can claim ever greater comprehensiveness and the ability to measure with the greatest exactitude sociocultural, psychological, and political influences on religious representations and the moral conceptions of believers. Their answers are technical in the sense that they always locate themselves at specific psychological, economic, political, or sociological levels. Inasmuch as they follow from an analysis of facts which are examined with all the trappings of scientific reasoning, they would seem all the more to be expressions of the truth. But what sort of truth do we have when the answer varies according to the perspective one takes from the start? Every interpretation of a religious phenomenon will only find what it is looking for, and the plurivocity of answers which the human sciences offer runs the risk of ending in an ineluctable conflict of interpretations.

Sacred and Profane

The dialectic of the sacred and the profane, so common in the history of religions, is a particularly topical example of how the human sciences have transformed this discipline. The notion of the sacred used by anthropologists, phenomenologists, sociologists, historians of religions, and by theologians as well, is so general as to be wholly ambiguous. Since Durkheim, the semantic field of the sacred has been greatly broadened. Under the influence of a phenomenology that would not allow the sacred to be located solely in social structures, various theologies have applied the notion of the sacred to many religions. Thus, one must carefully distinguish two camps: those who base themselves on ethnological, historical, and sociological findings in an attempt to define the sacred while searching for a concrete knowledge of its scope, and those who use the term "sacred" at the level of religious discourse in order to engage in theological or pastoral reflection. Yet this distinction is not sufficient. In every religious experience the dividing line between the sacred and the profane is always empirically fixed by man, and it always changes. It is inserted, more or less, into everyday life; it connotes both the great moments of cosmic time—seasons, day, night, fertility cycles—and the high points of human existence—birth, puberty, marriage, death. Thus, the sacred consists first of all of observable and analyzable realities. If we seize upon them in the context of life, we do so because the sacred structure is an *ordo rerum,* an order in which there is a dialectical opposition between complementary notions arranged in a series, such as

sacred–holy–pure/profane–defiled–impure,

or

sacred–taboo–impure/profane–licit–pure.

Only through historico-cultural analysis can we understand how these pairs of oppositions function in any given religious experience.[11] But all historico-cultural analysis leads to the idea that even if we encounter the pair "sacred/profane" or "pure/impure" everywhere, we can in no way infer that the contents of these notions are identical. The concrete and exact signification of the sacred becomes transformed under the influence of the evolution of ethics, law, language, and the concept of the divine itself. This evolution in fact consists of connecting the profane to the impure and of identifying the sacred more or less with the pure. In the end, the situation is completely the reverse of that in the archaic religions, in which the sacred is assimilated most often to the impure.

How can we escape from this apparent labyrinth? Rather than attempting to force a definition of the sacred upon the varying realities established by the historian of religions as ethnologist, would it not be better to try to understand how the categories of sacred, profane, pure and impure function? In other words, instead of trying to construct a morphology of the sacred, perhaps we should reflect on its syntax. It is obvious that a being, or an animal, or an object possesses a specific and immutable nature. A stone is always a stone, a tree a tree, a sheep a sheep. Only something else—an external power, a force, a desire foreign to the being or object—can enter it, render it sacred, and make it pure—or impure. This syntax reveals a constant dialectic between a principle of separation—a taboo or prohibition—and possession by a power, a being, or an object that acts as a principle of conjunction or cohesion. It has often been noted that the sacred attracts and repels at the same time. Man fears it but he makes use of it. *Et inhorresco et inardesco,* in the words of Augustine. R. Caillois emphasized strongly that dialectic of the sacred in which two terms, in opposing one another, automatically defined an active nothingness which constituted the profane.[12] Holiness and defilement oppose themselves to the profane, and holiness, like wholeness—the very state that defines the sacred—fears both defilement and the profane. As a result, a pair may be made from any two of the terms pure, impure, and profane, and then placed in opposition to the remaining term.

But if the sacred is that which is forbidden to the profane, and if the profane may be defined only in relationship to a sacred which it must avoid, how is contact between the sacred and the profane brought about? Is there not a danger that the former will disintegrate when it is brought into contact with the latter? Here lie the roots of the moral and theological notion of sin. Sin is conceived as an attack upon (sacred) wholeness and as a rupture in the order upon which (sacred) wholeness is founded. We can thus distinguish three classes: that which is natural and profane and which ritual can render sacred; that which is reputed to be impure and which cannot become truly sacred except by the mediation of magic, a caricature of the sacred; and that which one culture considers sacred but which other religious experiences hold to be either impure or profane. The profane must, in fact, be understood less as a basic antitype to the sacred than as its complement. The dividing line between the sacred and the profane is mobile. It is guided by an individual's desires and by the choices made by the society in which he lives.

The mobility of the sacred–profane demarcation allows us, I believe, to place the common definitions of sacrifice in a new light. Recall the theory Robertson Smith elaborated by drawing on the religious experience of the ancient Semites. Basing himself too narrowly on the recently discovered idea of totemism, Robertson Smith believed that the sacrificial killing had the consumption of the sacred animal as its only end. From this arose the prohibition against normal and ordinary food. Because the taboo is transgressed, rites of expiation must follow the rite of communion in order to reestablish the broken covenant. In the beginning, Robertson Smith asserted, the sacrificial animal was eaten. But as the sacrificial victim became increasingly sacralized, its consumption was first limited to priests alone. Then it was burned up completely as a holocaust to a jealous god. The extreme holiness of the victim in the end rendered it impure for men. Such, Smith explained, is the ambiguity of the sacred.

A better knowledge of historical facts has allowed for refinements in the theory. Marcel Mauss formulated a somewhat more precise notion. In his view, sacrifice "consists in establishing a means of communication between the sacred and the profane worlds through the mediation of a victim, of a thing that in the course of the ceremony is destroyed."[13] The word "sacrifice" itself implies the idea of a consecration, and Mauss greatly emphasized that the sacrificial victim or object does not possess the sacred nature in itself but that the rite confers this nature upon it. For him, sacrifice is the means man employs as a profane being whose nature is radically opposed to the sacred to obtain something from his god. But contact with the divine is fatal, and so the victim must be immolated. Actually, all of our analyses show very clearly that the victim is put to death only as a practical means of causing it to pass from the world of men to the world of the gods to whom it is offered. It is not contact with the divine that is fatal, with the danger being attached to the victim by the sacrificer; still less is an exchange (of death for life) effected by the sacrificial gift. There is a real symbolic operation in which the death of the victim signifies its passage from the world of men to the world of the gods. Through this act of crossing over communication with the divine is established. Thus sacrifice is by no means "a sort of sacrilege," as Marcel Mauss declared it to be. When man sacrifices (*sacrum facit*), he does not cause a victim to pass from a profane region, the world of men, to a sacred region, the world of the god. He transposes a victim or an offering from his day-to-day world to a place where he encounters the divine, the region of the sacred itself. Far from being in opposition, the world of the sacred and the world of the profane are in permanent and complementary contact. Whatever form it may take, sacrifice is the means by which man participates in that which is greater than himself, and the sacred is not limited to the place where, through this voluntary participation, man perceives the divine. We can no longer be content to oppose the sacred to the profane in sacrifice. The sacred exists only in relation to the divine. Thus it is necessary to connect the notion of sacrifice with a mode of the human experience of God. In this way we will be able to consider the sacred to be something profane which, by mediating meaningfully and expressively, joins man to the divine and in doing so becomes sacred itself.[14] In the so-called primitive religions, to be sure, the divine and the sacred are sometimes confused. The mediating element is often the place at which divine power becomes incarnate, and hierophanies do not always distinguish clearly between the god and the element charged with divine power. Conversely, in other religious systems the sacred disappears almost completely in the interest of divine transcendence. But the sacred remains, nonetheless, the mediator between the profane and the divine because it is, as it were, the reverberation or the reflection of the divine in the profane. "The science of religions may well group rites, myths, places of worship, times of the year, objects and characters under the rubric of the sacred, but it cannot so group the transcendent reality to which religious man more or less confides himself through the mediation of the sacred."[15] The sacred results from man's will to bind himself to a transcendent reality that will always remain partially hidden from him. Man associates this part of the world more or less symbolically with the experiences of the divine he is capable of having.

Religious Symbols

The impact of the human sciences on the historical view of religious realities has also made itself felt clearly in the study of the symbolic language in which every religious experience, whether communal or individual, is expressed. In one sense it is possible to think that no religious experience is truly spontaneous or ineffable, inasmuch as it must be formulated in order to be transmitted to others. Even in religions that consider themselves to have been revealed, revelation is given for man. It is conditioned by the capacity of human consciousness to grasp it. It can only express itself in human language. Hence arises the problem of symbolic language. Every time man wishes to express the nature of his relationship with the divine, every time he wonders about the nature of higher beings or about the world that surrrounds him and the place he occupies in it—in his mythic accounts, in his supplications to his gods, and also in his dreams and visions—he uses symbolic language. This is not because symbols possess, by their very essence, some kind of sacralizing value or a nature that is religious in itself and makes them the tool most suited to speaking about the divine. As Nietzsche wrote in *Ecce Homo,* it is not because (in the words of Zarathustra) "things come to us desiring to be symbols." We must be extremely clear. No symbol, not even a religious symbol, exists outside of humanity or outside of a particular discourse, so that it could, of itself, confer a new signification upon something or someone. Things possess hierophanic value only through the human word. Nature, of itself, is mute. The only voice it can ever have is the one man lends it. It can never reveal the divine except to one who is already acquainted with the divine and who can insert and incarnate the divine into the world of his day-to-day existence as well as into the cosmos. Only through man can the religious symbol reunite, in one instantaneous and intuitive understanding, a spiritual reality and a perceptible phenomenon.

Centuries of rationalism had hidden the importance of the symbol. One of the most positive contributions of the human sciences was to reintroduce it into our mental universe. Since Marcel Mauss the French school of sociology has insisted strongly and with reason on the social role of the symbol. Its primary function is to establish particular relationships between beings who recognize an identical meaning in the same sign and who interpret it as the bearer of a secret meaning, a veritable cypher of apparent mystery. Symbolic language connects the person who understands it to a vaster intended community, whether that community be merely sociopolitical or also spiritual. The historico-cultural hermeneutics of religious symbols points out the degree to which most people have acquired their own religious significations through a cultural and doctrinal overdetermination conforming closely to an established and fixed religious tradition. Because of the internal coherence of each religion, the meaning of the symbols each uses can be univocal only for the followers of that religion. Thus, historico-cultural analysis leads to the recognition of the exclusiveness of religious symbols. There is no symbolic cohabitation that is not sacrilegious: crucifixes are never found next to the Torah, nor Śiva in a mosque, nor a Buddha on the high altar of a Christian church! But historical analysis also reveals another important fact which seems to contradict the exclusiveness of religious symbols. The very nature of the symbol implies that it always retains a secret aspect inside itself and that that which "falls within its meaning" is not always capable of translating completely the religious reality it is meant to signify. P. Tillich showed clearly how the religious symbol can surpass the reality of the sign in signifying another reality that would otherwise be inexpressible.[16] In revealing the inexpressible, in expressing the unspeakable, the religious symbol seeks to facilitate a passage from the world of the imagination to ontological reality. It is easy to see that in doing so, symbolic language is evoked first by an obvious desire for communication. A most profound source of symbolic language is the desire to reconnect oneself with a totality in which one believes one sees a sign of the divine and which one cannot express in any other manner.

But how do such symbols root themselves in the totality of human experience, from which they draw their richness and their effectiveness? Depth psychology has revealed the incessant eruption—conscious and unconscious, individual and collective—of images, symbols, and modes of representation which are, so to speak, the dreams of historic humanity. According to Jung, religious experiences of the initiatory, ritual, or mystical kind take root in the symbolic structure of an unconscious that is much more extensive than the unconscious defined by the Freudians. The symbolic images man uses are both projections of unconscious desires and carriers of an innate religious meaning determined by a particular tradition. They connect every human individual or group with the reality of the divine, as it can be perceived through these images. In his incessant search for psychological equilibrium, and even beyond his own internal conflicts, man tends to realize his being fully by adhering to a religious system that expresses what he sees as the truth. Moving from phantasm to symbol he strives to possess the truth that will bring the full flowering of his being, his happiness, and his salvation. A history of religions conscious of the complex totality of the human being cannot neglect the hermeneutic of the hidden underlying the representations of the sacred which the world of the imagination greets as manifestations of a transcendent Wholly Other.

Analysis of such symbolic types as Water, Center, and Father[17] shows that man takes recourse to symbolic language only when he has no other, more suitable language for signifying what he wishes to evoke. He uses symbols to bring out a meaning that is partially hidden but that always extends the symbol's established meaning. The signified reality is always of greater scope than the signifier, and the symbol thus gives rise to a sort of induction of meaning. But symbolic language is also a "bound language," to borrow an expression from P. Ricoeur.[18] Every symbol takes root in fields of meaning which are different and of varying level, a fact that warrants the more or less rival historico-cultural, linguistic, and psychoanalytic hermeneutical approaches. For example, the type of the Father, the Mother, or the Wife tends to express privileged interpersonal relations. It is undeniably weighted with affective attitudes, but it also takes its meaning from an entire cultural and religious tradition which partially insures its efficacy. The symbol cannot take effect unless it relates to some experience. In every symbolic equation, what is symbolized always stands at the center of some human interest. In the case of religious symbols, the necessity for personal appropriation is all the more powerful, since every religious symbol is connected with a fully integrating experience that unites with the divine. Thus, one can never separate the cultural from the existential context in symbolic analysis. The prime error becomes the reduction of religious symbols to mere manifestations of a "psychological calculus," to natural psychic functions.[19] It is precisely by virtue of the existential correspondences upon which symbolic language is based that the religious symbol can act both within and upon the psychical material. To the extent that a religious symbol aspires to express a higher reality to man, a reality he deduces from a lived experience, it becomes engaged in the existence of the person who uses it by opening the human and internal reality upon which it is founded onto an eternal and transcendent dimension.

I could easily offer other examples to show the extent to which the strictly historical perspective found at the beginnings of the history of religions have been modified considerably over the past two generations. One might well wonder what could remain of a *history* of religions in the wake of the investigation of religious realities by the social sciences. The first half of the twentieth century was marked by the rise of religious phenomenology and the renewal of theology under the impulse of hermeneutical studies. Today two systems for interpreting man, both tied to the linguistic sciences—structuralism and psychoanalysis—propose a systematic reduction of religious realities into cultural phenomena. Yet the question of the meaning, if not the essence, of religious phenomena has yet to be answered. Can the history of religions interpret and explain the genesis and the dynamic of socioreligious realities without moving outside the historical realm? Or should the discipline content itself with collecting series of past phenomena, phenomena methodically gathered and carefully inventoried as if they were so many yellowing butterflies, to collect dust in so many drawers?

Toward a Religious Anthropology

Our object of study, the religious phenomenon, compels us to go beyond the necessary but insufficient dimensions of mere historical research. In the sense that we are exploring a human dimension that is quite constant yet often mysterious and extratemporal, we cannot content ourselves with a *history* of religions. Out of a desire for balance and for understanding, we become disposed to join the historical with the social, the psychological with an analysis of the structures of language and of symbols. I have already stated that every religion first offers itself to us as a human phenomenon. An anthropological view of religious reality becomes the only scientific approach, and it is possible only on the condition that, in order to understand the object of research as well as possible, the hermeneutic that is applied to this object respect it. Because man understands himself through what he says about his own religious experiences, he becomes conscious of his own existence when he is challenged by the sacred.

Joachim Wach, for example, integrated the sociology of religion with the most encompassing view of religious realities that he thought possible. He constructed a balanced system which integrated both the contributions of a history of religions attentive to the myriad realities of past religious experiences and the contributions of the comprehensive sociology of M. Weber and E. Troeltsch. Wach's work was a pioneer effort to construct a unitive science founded on understanding and on the meaning of human religious activity. Granted, the idea of understanding (*Verstehen*), on which Wach began to publish in 1926, is ambiguous. Nevertheless, it opens our eyes to a whole series of meanings. Under the combined influence of Hegelian philosophy and Rudolf Otto, Wach's religious anthropology forged a synthesis between the religious and the social, the individual and the collective. For this reason it remains a model upon which our discipline would do well to reflect. If we must remain conscious that mystery occupies an ineluctible place at the heart of every individual religious experience, we must also relate the experience of mystery to the diverse social and cultural systems which human societies have developed, the systems in whose context mystery is experienced. "[What] we need" Wach wrote, "[are] precise definitions . . . and methods and limits of interpretation comparable to the great theological, philosophical and legal systems of hermeneutics."[20]

Indeed, to acknowledge the universality of religious experiences in human culture by asserting that man is naturally religious and to be satisfied with that assertion is to be satisfied with saying and explaining nothing. A religion is not merely a code, a law, or a book that is held to be sacred because it reflects the beliefs of a human community. It is at the same time an ensemble of ritual practices inserted into the fabric of day-to-day society. The task of a religious anthropology is to analyze both these aspects of religion. Victor Turner's approach seems to have much to teach us in this regard. Turner was trained in social anthropology at Manchester under Max Gluckman. He had been taught to distinguish carefully between process and structure in traditional societies through the meticulous observation of a series of privileged cases (the extended-case method). But in his fieldwork he felt the need to go beyond Gluckman's overly functionalist position. Concentrating on the society of the Ndembu, Turner perceived that certain rituals, the life-crisis rituals, revealed and integrated society in important ways. In analyzing the symbolic structure of other rituals, Turner realized that they, too, operated as cathartic processes that freed societies of their internal tensions, that is, that they operated as "rites of affliction."[21] In his work among the Ndembu, then, Turner pointed out in quite a remarkable fashion the efficacy of religious ritual in social life. More precisely, he defined the close relations that exist between Ndembu religious symbols and social activity. Religious rituals appear to reflect social structure and social antistructure simultaneously. They function as dynamic factors in the social process. This is the reason that the observer must grasp and perceive the symbols and metaphors people use from within the concrete sociocultural situation. Symbols and metaphors are never extratemporal systematizations.

Turner, a specialist in East African ritual, did not hesitate to focus his analytic methods on the problem which the *aggiornamento* of Vatican II posed to Roman Catholic liturgy.[22] For Turner, the recent liturgical reform "which is occurring in a major historical religion" is marked by a "structural functionalism" founded on the close relationship between liturgy and society.[23] Applying his concepts of *communitas* and liminality with a measure of success, he asserts that it is necessary not to lose sight of "the pervasive, repetitive, formal quality" of all ritual.[24]

We may well ask ourselves what might be the pertinence of this highly suggestive comparison between the workings of rituals in traditional societies and the Christian liturgy. May the same questions be posed in the same way to both situations? Does not the concept of liminality, upon which Turner's model for explaining the ritual process within the social process is based, highlight in the final analysis that which is marginal or has become perverted in Christianity? Whatever reservations one may have, this approach, which starts from social anthropology and arrives at a religious anthropology concerned with drawing out the ontological value of symbols and ritual acts, is of great interest.[25]

But this religious anthropology constitutes only the first stage in understanding and unifying a wide diversity of theories attempting to explain religion. It is not possible to dissociate the sociological awareness of religious phenomena from a hermeneutics based on the comparative method and still remain attentive to the inner structure of religious experience. It is necessary to take account of the entire culture and society in which religious realities are lived. As Wach affirmed, there can be no understanding except in terms of the human density of *Zusammenleben,* of "living together." This sense of internal relationships seems to me to be the sense most important to the history of religions. If human religious experiences, past and present, are nothing more than human transcriptions of a reality which itself remains more or less hidden from man but upon which he bases his behavior, it is also true that the sacred defines itself primarily as a relationship. For this reason, I find those hermeneutics reductionistic which occupy themselves with explaining origins and essences instead of with analyzing relations established between man and the divine in the sphere of the sacred. Even if religion and the forms in which it is lived are mere illusions or epiphenomena, as certain psychoanalytic and sociological theories would have us believe, still, the lived relationship between the believer and his gods is partly unexplained. For the person who believes in a power superior to the human condition, that is, for *homo religiosus,* the object of our study, transcendence is not an illusion. Thus, it is quite important that we distinguish two different modes in every religious act: first, the recognition by man of a sacred which he holds to be an objective reality transcending his own condition and defined through ritual, symbolic, and affective experiences; and second, the expression which man gives to this reality perceived as immanent. The expression of a religious experience does not describe a sacred external to man. It witnesses to a reality lived between man and something other than himself which informs and modifies his behavior. Consequently, we should conduct our investigations on several levels. We should move unceasingly from the historical and social to the deep structures of thought and of language and even to what is unconscious and latent in thought and speech. Multiple levels of awareness set up a plurality of hermeneutics which often conflict. Every analysis that would be content to apply a single hermeneutic to religious realities necessarily disfigures them in its reductionism. We must work to elaborate a unitive religious anthropology. To be sure, it should not be conceived as an all-encompassing metaphilosophy which would determine in advance the central guidelines for research and the status of results. Rather, it should be an accounting of the key points by which we are able to apprehend and understand the sacred as man lives it: the identity that allows an individual to say "I" and a group to say "we," the social bond in its varied forms, the relation of man to cosmos and the way in which he symbolizes the universe in order to place himself in it better, and so on. Many researchers feel that the interdisciplinary approach, so much in vogue now, is truly necessary. The revival of interest in work in epistemology and the philosophy of the sciences bears witness to their feeling. But only to the degree that studies undertaken with the greatest scientific rigor converge toward man will the contributions of the different social sciences be able to throw light on our religio-anthropological approach. Between the study of the religious object and the signification of a sacred lived by man, a wide field of individual and collective intentionalities opens itself to our investigations. Here the true strength of our discipline must lie, since it is open to the four winds of the spirit and concerned above all with understanding, in the diversity of historical experiences, the deep unity of man's religious behavior.

By employing such an approach one can hope to exorcise for all time the old and often reawakened fear of a history of religions made the servant or instrument of theology and to confirm the absolute autonomy of our discipline. The frequent attempts at dialogue between religious anthropology and theology seem to have posed the basic question of a hermeneutic suited to several different religions. A simple phenomenological approach makes clear that all religions are bearers of a certain salvation, and that this revelation is received by men in terms that are tied to his finite condition. In a theological perspective various religions may be considered worthy of the attention of anyone searching for God. Indeed, all religious traditions have come to terms more or less exactly and completely with the individual and collective hope for a future salvation. In the eyes of the theologian they enter into an economy of salvation and an ecumenical perspective. But must we assume that other religions, located outside the brightened circle of the Judaeo-Christian revelation, are capable of throwing only a dark reflection of this revelation? Is this the case with the revelation of the Qur'an? Or should we not take a more favorable stance and consider all religious experiences to give off the brilliance of a light that is shed equally upon all human beings but which is especially focused, with Thaborian intensity, on biblical revelation alone? Once again, we must be aware of which salvation this is, and from what in particular men hope to be saved. Precisely in the face of this double question religious anthropology takes on its fullest hermeneutical value.

If our discipline must never judge the progress of the human mind toward some absolute religious truth, it must, nevertheless, go beyond the empirical data of religious facts in order to understand a sacred as lived by man. It does so by analyzing the fundamental structures of the various religions. It considers the materials of a particular religious tradition to be woven, as it were, by existential experience. But it must analyze with enough critical detachment to understand the level and the occasion in the life experience of both individual and group at which the properly religious intentionality situates itself. Here is where our discipline differs greatly from theological discourse. Theology is more normative. It is always conditioned by faith in its own truth. But we are interested in all that men believe and in all that they define and experience as sacred. Our interest arises neither from mere curiosity nor from a comparatist approach. Both these motivations are capable of dissolving religious values by reducing them to the level of merely relative representations. By taking all of man's religious experiences into consideration, religious anthropology is first and foremost an opening onto the Other in its spiritual dimension. The meaning of the sacred and the perception of the divine are awakened, enriched, and reinforced—in short, better understood—by such a multidisciplined approach.

In the end, what we label our work—history of religions or anthropology—matters little. It is most important that we respect and be attentive to mankind's diverse religious creations and perceptions. In this way our work produces a conception that is newer and more comprehensive than any conception a single religion can portray to its followers. By carefully gathering together the varied signs of an economy of salvation which are distributed through historical time and across the whole human race, and then by carefully comparing them with each other to understand them better, our discipline could form a basic foundation for any theology of religions. But dialogue can be fruitful only if all recognize from the outset the autonomy of each discipline and if each of us keeps in mind the inherent limits of all human analysis before the mystery of the divine plan.

Notes

1. See, e.g., Mircea Eliade, "Crisis and Renewal in the History of Religions," *History of Religions* 5 (1965): 1–17; and Joseph M. Kitagawa, ed., *The History of Religions* (Chicago: University of Chicago Press, 1967).
2. Eugène Burnouf, *La science des religions* (Paris, 1870), p. 1.
3. Fragments 11, 14, 15.
4. Fragments 32, 57.
5. D. Bill, "The Return of the Sacred?," *British Journal of Sociology* 28 (1977); and Mircea Eliade et al., in *Revue internationale des sciences sociales* 29, no. 2 (1977).

6. H.-Ch. Puech, ed., *L'Histoire des religions,* vol. 1 (Paris: Bibliothèque de la Pleïade, 1970), Preface, p. xiv.
7. William James, *The Varieties of Religious Experience* (1902).
8. H. Leuba, *A Psychological Study of Religion* (1912).
9. Sigmund Freud, *Die Traumdeutung* (1899), and *Totem und Taboo* (1912).
10. C. Downing, "Sigmund Freud and the Greek Mythological Tradition," *Journal of the American Academy of Religion* 43 (1975): 3–14.
11. For ancient Israel, see the pioneering work of W. Robertson Smith, *Lectures on the Religion of the Semites* (1889, reprint ed. 1894, 1927), which has been taken up again and placed on a new foundation by Mary Douglas, *Purity and Danger: An Analysis of Concepts of Pollution and Taboo* (London, 1966). An analysis of the vocabulary of the subject is very enlightening. See Emile Beneveniste, *Le vocabulaire des institutions indo-européennes* (Paris: Editions de Minuit, 1950), vol. 2, pp. 179–207 [Eng. trans., *Indo-European Language and Society,* trans. Elizabeth Palmer (London: Faber, 1973, pp. 445–69)].
12. Roger Caillois, *L'Homme et le sacre,* 3d ed. (Paris: Gallimard, 1950) [Eng. trans., *Man and the Sacred,* trans. Meyer Barasch (New York: Free Press, 1960)].
13. Henri Hubert and Marcel Mauss, *Sacrifice: Its Nature and Function,* trans. W. D. Halls (Chicago: University of Chicago Press, 1964), p. 97.
14. H. Bouillard, "La categorie du sacre dans la science des religions," *Le Sacre: Etudes et recherches,* Actes du Colloque, Centre International d'Etudes Humanistes et Institut d'Etudes Philosophiques de Rome, Rome, 4–9 January, 1974 (Paris: Aubier, 1974), pp. 33–34.
15. Ibid.
16. *Symbol und Wirklichkeit* (1966), pp. 4–5; see also Antoine Verte, *L'Interpretation du langage religieux* (Paris: Seuil, 1974), pp. 59–72.
17. Michel Meslin, "Plenary Address," Thirteenth International Congress of the History of Religions, Lancaster, 1975; and "Dieu et père," *Impacts* (1983).
18. J. E. Menard, ed., *Le Symbole,* Colloque de Strasbourg (1974), p. 158.
19. As did Paul Diel, *Le symbolisme dans la Bible, sa signification psychologique* (Paris: Payot, 1975); cf. my critical comments in *Les Quatre Fleuves* 7 (1977): 120 ff.
20. Joachim Wach, *Sociology of Religion* (Chicago: University of Chicago Press, 1944), p. 6.
21. Victor Turner, *The Forest of Symbols: Aspects of Ndembu Ritual* (Ithaca, N.Y.: Cornell University Press, 1967), *The Drums of Affliction* (Oxford, 1968), and *The Ritual Process: Structure and Anti-Structure* (Chicago, 1969).
22. Victor Turner, "Passages, Margins and Poverty: Religious Symbols of Communitas," *Worship* 46 no. 7 (1972): 390–412 and no. 8 (1972): 482–494.
23. Ibid., p. 390.
24. Ibid., p. 392. For Turner the prime example of liminality in Christian ritual is transubstantiation, which creates a "pure Christian communitas." Cf. "Religion in Current Cultural Anthropology," *Concilium* 136 (1980): 70.
25. Consider V. Turner, *Revelation and Divination in Ndembu Ritual* (Ithaca, N.Y.: Cornell University Press, 1975), p. 31: "I learned from the Ndembu that the ritual and symbolism . . . have ontological value, in some way related to man's condition."

Current Methodological Issues in the History of Religions

Ugo Bianchi

It is difficult, I realize, to make an exhaustive formulation of the major methodological issues facing the history of religions at the present. Religion as a subject for comparative study is too much in flux, too problematic in itself. A very large number of scientific enterprises have studied religion: anthropology, sociology, psychology, the phenomenology of religion, *Religionswissenschaft,* the history of religions, and "comparative religion," whose place among religious studies is no less of a problem than its name is a matter of course in English-speaking countries.

At the same time, I am aware that I belong to a tradition of study, begun in Italy by Raffaele Pettazzoni, which definitely favors a history of religions comparative-historical and culture-historical in character. This methodological setting does not intend to undermine the validity of other approaches or to be imperialistic, but at the same time it is confident that it can meet the demands of a scientific, humanistic approach to religion, above all, the demand that it be concrete and holistic.

I will try to discuss some of the current methodological issues from the point of view of my particular understanding of the history of religions. In particular, I will discuss the approaches commonly labeled "systematic" or "phenomenological" and "historical." Let me begin with some general considerations.

No methodological approach, it seems fair to state, can be entirely wrong, provided it is not explicitly paradoxical or sectarian. But a methodological approach *can* be "reductive," not in Husserl's sense, but in the sense that it is not adequate to its subject matter, that is, that it is incomplete. An approach can be reductive for two reasons. Some approaches to the positive study of religion are programmatically selective for philosophical reasons.[1] Others are only implicitly reductive. They simply intend to concentrate on a particular aspect of the relevant issues, as may occur in the sociology, the psychology, or the anthropology of religion.[2] One danger looms especially large here, the danger of improper generalization or "projection" from the results of research that does not extend beyond particular cases, particular societies, or particular groups of individuals and that even avows that it concentrates only on a particular aspect and has no interest in the polymorphous universe of religion and religions. Or the researcher may combine general, explanatory theories of culture and religion with his particular findings and their subsequent, "philological" elaboration. This very peculiar approach can be seen—though not exclusively[3]—among social anthropologists who are committed both to being participant-observers for a limited period in the field and to continually elaborating their data by confronting them with major, general interpretive theories developed in the past, for example, that of Durkheim.[4]

The need to avoid reductionism does not require a "religious" hermeneutics of things religious, if by "religious hermeneutics" one intends to contrast "religious" and "cultural" or to distinguish them absolutely. From the point of view of the history of religions, religion is a part of culture. Not that it can be reduced to culture. It is culture, and it shares in culture's creativity and variety. On the other hand, religion's specificity depends not so much on theoretical presuppositions as on its being intercultural, that is, its specificity depends on the (partial) intercultural continuities that allow *Religionswissenschaft* to speak of "religion" in the singular. Consequently, in the history of religions, the struggle against a priori reductionism, whether theoretical, ideological, or programmatic, is fought not so much with contrary assumptions as with sound, comparative, cultural-historical research. Once the issue of the relations between religion and other cultural elements is posited in the ambit of comparative-historical research, it reveals clearly the full, specific "weight" of religion, both phenomenological and historical, and as a result discourages overly bold attempts to explain away or to reduce, that is, to formulate incomplete interpretations. The polymorphous and circumstantial patrimony of culture—that is, the fact that different cultures are historical realities with different patterns or inspirations—is in its turn so articulated and protean that no sociological analysis of a particular human group or of a particular religious manifestation can legitimately support reductive generalizations about religion and its connections with culture—structural, functional, and so on. If we are to avoid arbitrariness and, perhaps, the so-called hermeneutical circle, we will not be able to verify a general theory of religion by resorting to a coherence of symmetry of elements within a particular structure or to a functional balance in the organizational network of a society and the behavior of the individual in it. On the other hand, as Pettazzoni said, the study of religion is essential to the study and the understanding of culture(s). No particular culture can be understood unless the religion active within it is understood, that is, among other things, unless its religion is not programmatically reduced. The historian of religions himself will be committed both to understanding a particular religion in the context of its specific culture and to exploring the more or less extended continuities, both of contents and of functions, which that religion shares with other manifestations and on account of which he is entitled to term the other manifestations "religious," albeit provisionally and problematically.

I might point out that not every functional or operative definition of religion is reductive, provided it is confined to a specific milieu and set of circumstances. There is a third possibility as well: definitions of religion may be tautological, as when, for example, a definition of religion as ultimate concern is taken to be a functional definition.[5] (One could, by the way, also consider this definition to be ostensive, that is, as expressing the content itself of the *definiendum*.) Whether the definition of religion as ultimate concern is considered functional or ostensive, if it is to be effective, it must be backed by an exhaustive, comparative-historical analysis of all possible religious meanings of "ultimate," of all its religious "contents" that lie beyond tautology. Otherwise, one could agree with M. Spiro's paradoxical observation that someone's ultimate concern might be baseball or the stock market, to say nothing of the terminological confusion which another of Spiro's examples, militant political commitment, might cause.[6] The historian of religions cannot fail to notice that, from the point of view of both the phenomenology and the psychology of religion, the "ultimate concern" of a sportsman or of a capitalist or even of a militant communist is far from univocal with the "ultimate concern" of a religious person, whether a Christian or a Buddhist, although already in the case of a Buddhist qualifications would need to be made. This realization is not a matter of sensitivity or intuition on the part of the historian of religions. The historian of religions cannot but conceptualize, and so Spiro's objection to the definition of religion as ultimate concern is paradoxical to the same degree that it is "materially" anthropological. It reduces the undeniable, strong attraction felt by any religious person, as well as by any nonreductionist student of religion, to the "ultimate." But insofar as the religious "ultimate" is conceived inadequately—or not conceived at all—and insofar as any identification of religion with "ultimate concern" which is too immediate and noncircumstantial is tautological, Spiro's objection is sound. One can raise the charge of tautology also against any definition of religion aiming at being "ostensive" or even merely "operative" and based on an articulated description that is not without value but that, at the same time, contains in some sense the *definiendum* in the *definiens*. Of this type are all definitions of religion that contain terms such as "the holy," "the sacred," "ultimate," or "fundamentally important aspects of existence"[7] without referring to their contextual, historical conceptualizations. Finally, another definition which aims at being "functional," albeit in the context of a vigorous orientation toward historical comparison, was put forward by my late colleague, A. Brelich.[8] According to Brelich, religion intends to make it possible for persons to come to terms with that which they are not able to control by ordinary means. But compelled by his tendency to think in functionalist terms, Brelich added that in other cultural and historical circumstances, the controlling function of religion might be exercised by other cultural expressions—a statement which seems to entail a contradiction.

From the above remarks on the requirements of the history of religions and its "privilege" over against the sociological, psychological, and anthropological approaches, we can see that the history of religions must be holistic in two senses. It must study religion—a particular religion or a particular religious phenomenon—within the context of culture, that is, within the context of that culture or set of cultures to which it belongs. At the same time, it must be prepared to hold together the threads, that is, the morphological or historical continuities that link the particular religion or some of its elements to the polymorphous and problematic world of religion. Some scholars express the commitment of the history of religions to being comparative with the terms "systematic" or "nomothetic." The first sense of "holistic"—religion studied in all its aspects within a particular cultural context, which context is in turn studied in all aspects that connect it with religion—could be termed "idiographic," provided the adjective is not understood merely to mean "descriptive."

One danger with this nomenclature, it seems to me, is that it might imply that all historical problematics reside in idiographic research and that the systematic or nomothetic aspect of the history of religions is not historical. This implication would plainly contradict the essential requirement that our discipline be comparative and historical. Involved in this discussion is the more general question concerning the nature of the phenomenology of religion, to which the past decades have given conflicting answers. It is well-known that Pettazzoni criticized Gerardus van der Leeuw's phenomenology of religion and his extreme statements that "die Religionsphänomenologie ist nicht Religionsgeschichte" and that "von einer historischen 'Entwicklung' der Religion weiss die Phänomenologie nichts."[9] I will have more to say later, but for the moment it is sufficient to observe that, as Pettazzoni himself recognized, the best phenomenologists of religion, such as van der Leeuw and C. Jouco Bleeker, have not intended to free their enterprise from the control of "philological-archaeological hermeneutics," as van der Leeuw put it.[10] Consider, for example, Bleeker's appeal at the methodological conference in Turku, 1973: "retournons à la philologie et à l'histoire."[11]

Merely to juxtapose the "systematic"/"phenomenological" and the "idiographic-historical" approaches will not meet the need for a coherent methodology in the history of religions. We need urgently to link and to harmonize the two approaches. If van der Leeuw's drastic statement were followed and the two approaches simply ignored one another, the needed linking would be impossible. We must commit ourselves to discovering or rediscovering the link in order to make our discipline comprehensible. Otherwise, it will split into two different and to some extent mutually exclusive methods and areas of research.

Before proceeding further, however, let me emphasize that it is not necessary to identify "systematic" with "phenomenological." For example, no one would want to substitute "phenomenological" for "systematic" in such expressions as "*systematische Religionswissenschaft*" or, even more clearly, "*systematische Religionsgeschichte,*" for to do so would engender an epistemological monster with the name of "*phänomenologische Religionsgeschichte.*" We have already seen that although for some major phenomenologists phenomenology is subject to the control of history (that is, philology), it is at the same time an alternative to history. It is sensitive to the religious element in religions as well as to the religious element in the basic constituents of the religious structures—or the phenomenological, religious categories—of mankind. Thus, the phenomenology of religion could be called the scientific formalization of the religious self-consciousness of humanity. Precisely on this basis it would be "comparative" and as a result distinguish itself from both a *vergleichende Religionswissenschaft* and a *vergleichende Religionsgeschichte.*

Clearly, historians of religions use the term "phenomenology of religion" in other senses as well. Recall, for example, the meanings attached to the term by Th. P. van Baaren, Geo Widengren, Åke Hultkrantz, and, earlier, by Pierre Daniel Chantepie de la Saussaye, to say nothing here of a philosophical phenomenology.[12] With these scholars we come nearer to a *systematische Religionswissenschaft* in contrast to *Religionsgeschichte.* Van Baaren equates the term *vergleichende*

Religionswissenschaft with the term *Phänomenologie der Religion*. He then suggests that the latter term—and, by implication, the former—should be abandoned in favor of the designation *systematische Religionswissenschaft*. Widengren, on the other hand, preserves the traditional designation, *Phänomenologie der Religion*, in the general context of an objectivistic, at times even a positivistic, outlook on the relations between knowledge and religion. Other scholars, such as Kurt Rudolph, engage in polemics against phenomenology as practiced by van der Leeuw but favor a *systematische Religionswissenschaft*. For my purposes it is necessary to distinguish "systematic'" from "phenomenological" and to discuss separately the positions of the various scholars I have mentioned.

I begin with phenomenology of religion in the first sense mentioned, the phenomenology which appeals to a special religious sensitivity on the part of the phenomenologist. Not long before his death, Pettazzoni wrote an essay entitled, "The Supreme Being: Phenomenological Structure and Historical Development."[13] His position in that article, as well as in another article, published in 1959, "Il metodo comparativo,"[14] differed somewhat from his views in the early decades of his scholarly activity. He concluded:

> Phenomenology and history complement each other. Phenomenology cannot do without ethnology, philology, and other historical disciplines. Phenomenology, on the other hand, gives the historical disciplines that sense of the religious which they are not able to capture. So conceived, religious phenomenology is the religious understanding (*Verständnis*) of history; it is history in its religious dimension. Religious phenomenology and history are not two sciences but are two complementary aspects of the integral science of religion, and the science of religion as such has a well-defined character given to it by its unique and proper subject matter.[15]

I have already commented elsewhere on this statement by Pettazzoni. What troubles me is that I cannot see why the historian, particularly the historian who is interested in religion and ready to do extensive, holistic research in religion and religions, should be given, from outside his *Fach* and scientific training, a sensitivity, a capacity to grasp the specifically religious contents of a document or a historical phenomenon.

As for van Baaren and the "Groningen Working Group," I have already mentioned this Dutch scholar's criticism of the phenomenology of religion in its classical form (Rudolf Otto, G. van der Leeuw). To my mind, van Baaren's contribution to a "new phenomenology"—in his terms, to *systematische Religionswissenschaft*—is sound.[16] I agree particularly with his position on questions of definition and the limited validity of some terms, such as *tabu,* which have been common in the comparative study of religion. He rightly insists that definition proceed by means of *"beschreibende Umschreibung."*[17] This procedure, which excludes a priori categorization and simplistic conceptualization, can be termed "inductive." It is in direct touch with the "cultural" nature of religion as the object of a study which is neither theological nor antitheological in character. At the same time, provisionally "listing" major features of religion in order to reach an *"Umschreibung"* (circumscription) comes very near to the inductive, dialectical procedure founded on *historical* comparison which I will propound toward the end of this essay. In criticizing some classical terms in the phenomenology of religion, van Baaren suggests that "on the basis of an accurate analysis of the numerous, comparable, but not identical phenomena, the history of religions proposes to us," historians of religions should adopt new expressions (*Ausdrücke*) which are not so easily liable to be misunderstood. Here van Baaren expresses, more or less consciously, the opinion that *systematische Religionswissenschaft* amounts in concrete terms to that discipline which is, or should be, comparative and historical programmatically, that is, the history of religions. For this reason I find less intelligible his statements that "history of religions is nothing else than a part of history . . . ," that it "can be divided into special and general history of religions," and that "the ideal of general history of religions is to write a history of religions as such," an ideal which "lack of material makes . . . impossible."[18] As we shall see, the inner, dialectical and "extensive" dynamism of the comparative, historical history of religions is completely different from this improbable mirage which is totalistic rather than truly holistic. (By "extensive," used here in its active sense, I mean to indicate that this dynamism always extends its effect to new areas of research and ever increasing knowledge.)

Geo Widengren's strong stance in favor of philological and historical research is too well known to be belabored here. It will suffice to quote the opening sentences of his "La méthode comparative: entre philologie et phénomenologie," read at the Rome methodological seminar in 1969 on the occasion of the tenth anniversary of Pettazzoni's death:

> It is well-known that the present time is characterized by a reaction to the historicism which was typical of the period preceding our own. In our discipline, which is even called "the history of religions," this tendency has resulted in a predilection toward a sub-discipline which is systematic rather than historical, the phenomenology of religion. One understands quite well why those with a particular interest in historical research on religious topics have followed this development with a great deal of discontent, especially since those who have promoted phenomenology often began their careers

> as historians and have continued to write as historians of religions. This explains why they have felt it necessary to try to preserve a connection between history and phenomenology.[19]

According to Widengren, this was the case with Pettazzoni.

I also quote from Widengren's opening address at the International Congress for the History of Religions held at Stockholm in 1970:

> It has always been taken for granted (and how could it be otherwise?) that the phenomenology of religion takes its material from the sister, or rather mother, discipline, the history of religions. Is it possible to understand the phenomenology of religion, and especially the phenomena of a given religion, without knowing its history?[20]

These considerations, of course, do not prevent Widengren from being interested in the phenomenology of religion, as we see from his book, *Religionsphänomenologie*.[21] In his methodological discussions of phenomenology and history Widengren draws some conclusions which seem unnecessary about the categorical opposition between historical and comparative methods, between history and phenomenology. But in his Rome paper he also writes:

> But if the phenomenologist wishes to hold firmly to this concept [historical development], he must take account of the respective ages of the cultures which he studies. Above all, he must pay attention to problems of genesis. Nor can he afford to neglect the historical connections which link certain cultures and peoples. These connections are very easy to demonstrate thanks to the historical method.[22]

Widengren seems to come near to an organic, historical typology of religion in which the sense of "organic" is equally removed from any "organicistic" conception of the history of human culture and from the cold stasis of "system."

K. Rudolph's more recent statement concerning the systematic and historical setting of *Religionswissenschaft* include his articles, "Das Problem der Autonomie und Integrität der Religionswissenschaft" and "Die Problematik der Religionswissenschaft als akademisches Lehrfach,"[23] as well as his contribution to the Fourteenth International Congress for the History of Religions at Winnipeg, Canada, in 1980, on the theme "Basic Positions of Religionswissenschaft."[24] In his Canadian remarks Rudolph quoted strong statements by A. Dieterich and H. Usener propounding the soundness and, as Usener put it, the "self-authenticating security" of the philological method amidst all historical methods and the "delicacy of philological sensitivity." To be honest, one should not forget some of the shortcomings of philology as practiced by Reitzenstein, to say nothing of the extreme comparatist R. Eisler. Rudolph then proceeded to affirm the validity of a further "mode of working, namely the comparative or systematic." To Rudolph "*Religionswissenschaft* is an historical systematic discipline having as the object of its reflective and reconstructive investigation sets of circumstances which are parts of human culture in the sense of tradition, modes of behavior and ideas." Rudolph's terminology seems to oscillate here. He introduces new qualifications, speaking of the "application of this comparative method, which itself can be either systematic (synchronic) or historical (diachronic) in accordance with the purpose of the investigation and the changes of historical viewpoint." According to Rudolph, this study can "bring wider relationships into view," so that "*Religionswissenschaft* represents therefore not merely a pragmatic but a necessary linkage, indeed an interlocking or a 'dialectic' of the historical and the systematic (comparative) way of seeing." The reader will find in the second article mentioned above an exposition of Rudolph's views on synchronically and diachronically oriented research, or, in Wach's terms, research oriented horizontally or latitudinally (*querschnittmässig*) and research oriented vertically or longitudinally (*längsschnittmässig*).[25] In the end, Rudolph, too, seems to approach a history of religion conceived holistically as a discipline that expresses itself in historical comparison when he writes that this "comparative or systematic study of religions—which is not, according to Wach, normative—is proper to *vergleichende Religionswissenschaft* ["the comparative science of religion"], *or better,* to *vergleichende Religionsgeschichte* ["the comparative history of religions"]."[26] Given Rudolph's premises and distinction between a general and a special history of religions which he shares with van Baaren, the adjective "comparative" is unnecessary.[27]

In the discussion about the systematic and historical aspects of the history of religions, two interconnected topics call for urgent clarification: the question of definition—that is, the meaning of our categories ("religion," "deity," "ritual," "myth," and so on) and the process by which they are formed—and the question of comparison, particularly *historical* comparison, as a path that will enable historians of religions to enucleate categories which, far from establishing a limit, may serve as tools for the study of the fundamental dynamisms in the religious history of mankind. The study of such dynamisms is, clearly, the basic aim of our discipline. Only the "historicization" of our problematics—but not "historicization" in the sense of philosophical historicism or of anthropological "cultural relativism"—will allow us to overcome the difficulties to which van Baaren points and which are intrinsic to a phenomenological nomenclature (e.g., *tabu*) developed within the strictures of unsupported and unsupportable generalizations and, I might add, within the cold rigidity of a "system." It can overcome these difficulties because it is open to both continuity and novelty.

Only historical comparison, a comparison not limited to "facts" arbitrarily isolated from the historical contexts and processes that give them meaning and life, will avoid killing those "facts," that is, will avoid transforming them into "phenomena," fascinating and repelling phantasms in a lodge of disincarnate ghosts. Only a comparison extended to contexts and processes, only a comparison that is historical and holistic, will be creative and scientifically sound. Only such a comparison will guarantee that research remains objective and will avoid the reductionism which ironically threatens the phenomenologist of religion and the student of the "sacred" as well as the anthropologist or the sociologist of religion. Reduction stands opposed to religion as a proper object of study, but it is also opposed to history and to the "ideological-critical function of the history of religions" which Kurt Rudolph has analyzed in a recent article.[28] In human history religion's "work in progress" is not limited to a continual reshaping of itself over against the profane, although of course this reshaping can and does occur. A sympathy and an empathy does reside at the heart of the world of religion, and studying the modalities and the typological and historical implications of these continuities is of great scientific interest. But in human religious history religion also reshapes itself in front of, or over against, religion. Religious revolution, religious novelty, indeed a whole series of religious dynamisms are of equal interest, old and new reshapings which have culminated, to give only a few example, in the "mysterio-sophic revolution" (Orphism) against the ideology and the practices of the fertility cults, or the biblical message of the one God in heaven, or the Gnostic revolt against the archons of this material world, or the universalism of the Christian Messiah and his Gospel, or the sealing of the "Glorified" as the last of the prophets, or the implacable "deconstruction" of existence in the message of the "Enlightened."

Within this living history of religion, what are our "phenomenological" categories and our "systematic" terminologies? Paradoxical as it may seem, we do not need to lose our interest in them, or even our scientific faith in them, provided they are flesh and blood. Elsewhere, I have theorized about the dynamism of the comparative-historical approach to religion and religions.[29] The procedure is "dialectical." It is anchored in the concreteness of the old, of what is already known (that is, the scholar's experience and cultural milieu). At the same time, it is open to the new (that is, the new "religious" worlds which the scholar analyzes and compares).[30] The dialectics of the already "digested" philological and historical experience of the scholar and the progressive, coherent, philological, and historical examination of new materials have nothing in common with the dialectics between ideological presupposition, or rigid and programmatic conceptualization, and an alleged "verification" from an analytical study of the evidence.

The legitimate dialectics that govern comparative-historical study find their use already in the realm of concepts. In Aristotelian terms, "religion" and other principal categories of religious phenomenology are not univocal but analogical notions. To move from the concept to the "thing," we may say that the world of religion(s) cannot be adequately expressed as a "system" or by relating it to a "grid" intended to reveal its structures and functions. Rather, it resembles a mountain-complex of varying formations—not all equally old or impressive—which culminates in several peaks and consists in some places of parallel or convergent valleys, in others of irregular ridges. To speak without metaphors, comparative-historical problematics are open to the alternative historical processes of diffusion and parallel development. "Parallel development" should be understood not on the basis of evolutionary or archetypal presuppositions but as a specific kind of historical problematic. It attempts to discover some sort of "analogy" between different but partially comparable historical processes, an analogy that is founded on the cultural-historical premises of those processes and on the historical-cultural options available to groups of societies. In other words, a comparative-historical approach seeks to formulate a "historical typology" of both culture and religion.[31] Of course, it is not always possible to envision the object of our study as "pictures in motion," to borrow the expression of Bleeker and Widengren. We will photograph it as "arrested pictures." But it is important to remember that the subjects of the pictures are, or were, in motion, that the phenomena are, or were, in Pettazzoni's terms, genomena; that these "wholes," even comparable wholes, are formations, often inventions, not "brute facts" or pale "phenomena."

According to some philosophers, the historian of religions is committed only to establishing and describing facts, not to understanding them. Once the intuitionist flavor of "understand" is bracketed or eliminated from our discourse, we cannot but oppose such philosophers as well as others who support an alleged "metascience" that is not metaphysics.

Mircea Eliade speaks here for our entire discipline.

> Western philosophy cannot contain itself indefinitely within its own tradition without the risk of becoming provincial. Now the History of Religions is able to investigate and elucidate a considerable number of "significant situations" and modalities of existing in the world that are otherwise inaccessible. It is not just a matter of presenting "raw materials," for the philoso-

> phers would not know what to do with documents that reflect behavior and ideas too different from those familiar to them. The hermeneutical work ought to be done by the historian of religions himself, for only he is prepared to understand and appreciate the semantic complexity of his documents.[32]

I am not personally fond of the word "hermeneutics," in part for reasons removed from the general problematics discussed here, but I find these comments illuminating. It would be difficult to underline more effectively what Eliade calls the creative role and the responsibility of the history of religions.

Before World War II, talk of culture and cultures was quite unfamiliar to educated Europeans. After the war such talk became commonplace, in some cases trivial and even dangerous to certain individuals' spiritual equilibrium. To face culture and cultures and survive, to understand them and to understand oneself—that is, to be "creative"—is indeed an exciting prospect for the history of religions today.

Postscript

To the essay printed above, which reproduces in substance the account of my views presented at the Chicago conference in May 1983, I would like to append here a few further remarks to expand my position. First, I would suggest that it is impossible to distinguish adequately, much less to contrast, the historical and systematic approaches to the study of religion and religions, a study that must be conducted with positive and inductive methods. Another distinction can be made more easily, a distinction between idiographic study—a study that concentrates on a particular fact or set of facts (for example, a religion) considered in itself and in its specific context and apprehended as a *genomenon,* that is, as a process of becoming—and comparative or comparative-historical study—a synoptic consideration of two or more distinguishable facts or sets of facts in the world of religion(s); in the widest sense, a synoptic consideration of all analogous distinguishable facts and sets of facts. More precisely and more historically, comparative-historical study also includes a synoptic consideration of the contexts and the processes of becoming in which religious facts and sets of facts exist. Both idiographic and comparative studies are primarily historical. They consider their respective subject matters holistically; that is, they concentrate on cultural contexts and processes of becoming. As a result, I do not like to use "systematic" as an alternative to "comparative-historical." "Systematic" connotes a striving for completeness and order. Therefore, it is too abstract, too phenomenological, not sufficiently factual. Comparison—historical, not phenomenological comparison—is the synoptic study of religious dynamisms or *genomena;* thus, it possesses a definite, historical dimension, whether its working hypotheses are diffusionist or parallelistic. One of its first tasks is to perceive the precise limits to any unreflective or unqualified use of the general and problematic term "religion" for cognitive purposes, as well as to perceive the limits of any similar use of most categories of religious phenomenology.

The idiographic and comparative approaches are dialectically linked; that is, they generate each other. No idiographic study can do without a more or less extended comparative outlook. Otherwise, it would not be able to perceive, to circumscribe, and to characterize the fact or set of facts it is considering. Similarly, comparative study cannot do without idiographic study and the philological experience of the scholar. Comparative study results in a "historical typology" of religion. It studies religion as a "concrete universal" (not in the Hegelian sense) on the basis of a methodology that is positive and inductive, not deductive or normative. It does not aim to be systematic in the sense of nomothetic or taxonomic. Moreover, the history of religions should not reason *per genus et differentiam specificam,* that is, by means of "categories," as if religion "in general" were a *genus* whose characters were wholly represented in each of the *species* subordinated to it, or as if religion were an *essence* that underlies the *accidents* represented by the differences inherent in the different "historical" religions.

The difficulties surrounding the "extension" and the "intention" or *comprehensio* of the term "religion" should be made easier by considering religion, as concept and fact, and most religious categories—such as myth, ritual, sacrifice, priesthood, salvation—to be analogical rather than univocal or equivocal. This view does not imply philosophical relativism or nominalism. It merely seeks to guarantee that the *Religionswissenschaftler* remain constantly in touch with the inherent variety of concrete religious facts and complexes of facts.

A statement by E. E. Evans-Pritchard highlights clearly how difficult it is to harmonize positive, inductive research with "generalization": "One must not ask 'What is religion?,' but what are the main features of, let us say, the religion of one Melanesian people?" Only then, Evans-Pritchard maintains, can the scholar pass on to "generalizations about a Melanesian people *in toto*." What is at stake here, it seems to me, is precisely how the scholar can approach the religion of a particular Melanesian group *qua* religion in an exact sense, as distinct but not separate from other aspects of the entire culture to which it belongs. Paradoxically, my example, which is taken from the writings of an anthropologist who, unlike the majority of his colleagues, expressly favored a historical setting to anthropological study, shows that any mere "generalization" or theoretical categorization is useless in the comparative study of religion. We need to understand and to be guided in our research by the connection between the two different senses of the term "holistic" applied to historical study. "Holistic" refers both to the study of a particular religious phenomenon within its particular cultural context and to the study of the continuities between a particular religious fact or set of facts and others occurring in other cultural and historical milieus. In different cases these continuities result from cultural diffusion, convergence, and parallel development, although the latter should not be understood in the sense of unilinear evolution. It is on the basis of (partial) continuities that we are even able to term facts or sets of facts "religious."

The approaches to which the two senses of "holistic" refer relate dialectically and function reciprocally. They generate each other and progress together. The more conscious a student is of the ways in which a particular religious complex is connected with its cultural context, the less apt he will be to (mis)interpret the particular complex in terms of another. Conversely, the more conscious he is of some widespread continuities in the phenomenology of religion—continuities that are not always the same—the less apt he will be to be reductive or parochial. The more conscious he is of the reciprocal functioning of the two holistic approaches, the less apt he will be to formulate not only reductive definitions of religion, whether ostensive, functional, or merely conventional and operative, but also the sort of falsely general, univocal, and rigid definitions of religion that frequently arise in the history of religions, only to pass away quickly when their day is past. A rigid definition of religion will be tenable at most only in idiographic research as the notion of religion proper to its cultural context. It is certainly unsuited for comparative work.

It was not my aim to resolve the difficulties surrounding the definition of religion. I only wished to make several methodological remarks concerning the possibility of formulating a definition. Formulating an actual definition is not itself so urgent a task. It is, of course, not irrelevant, but it is more urgent to understand the dialectical procedure by which comparison can achieve its purposes. This dialectic is not between preconceived "theory" and concrete "verification" but between already "digested" philological knowledge, both idiographic and comparative-historical, and progressively extended knowledge of the partial but not constant continuities which, together with peculiarities, constitute the broken and moving territory of religion as it emerges in space and time. Consequently, the history of religions cannot be content with phenomenological categorization, "ideal types" (which are preeminently mental), archetypes, or *eide* which result from philosophical "reduction." In the objective study of religious dynamism, we are not in a position to assign a privileged place to divergence or to convergence as a consequence of an a priori theoretical option. Only historical comparison will progressively detect the "historical universal" which we call "religion."

I must add that although I advocate a methodology open to variety and "analogy" in the world of religion(s), I do not preclude the possibility of discovering structural similarities ("univocity") where they exist and the concomitant possibility of constructing well-delimited definitions. As examples of such structural similarities I might cite Eliade's understanding of the structure of initiation or of the *axis mundi*. Both are widespread and very homogeneous. Another example is the strict definition of dualism as "the doctrine of the two principles, whether eternal or not," that is, as a series of particular options within the field of doctrines and myths concerned with "origins" or creation. Still, no religious fact or phenomenon can be reduced to its bare structure, and this irreducibility must affect its meaning in the field of the historically concrete.

Notes

1. See my remarks in U. Bianchi, *The History of Religions* (Leiden, 1975), pp. 201–220.
2. See the discussion in L. Honko, ed., *The Science of Religion: Studies in Methodology*, Proceedings of the Study Conference of the International Association for the History of Religions, Turku, Finland, 1973 (The Hague, 1979), pp. 299–321.
3. Jacobsen's *The Treasures of Darkness* combines an evolutionary, naturistic explanation of the oldest Mesopotamian gods with a searching analysis of the figure of Dumuzi which should be of great interest to the historian of religions.
4. See my observations on V. Turner, *The Forest of Symbols* (Ithaca, N.Y., 1967) in Honko, ed., pp. 302–306.
5. See R. D. Baird, *Category Formation and the History of Religions* (The Hague, 1971). I can agree with Baird's criticism of the usefulness of "real definitions" for the purposes of the history of religions, particularly the following observation: "if whatever implicit definition [the historian of religions] operates under is treated as a 'real definition,' i.e. a statement (implicit or explicit, vague or clear, defined or intuited) that gives the 'essence' of the thing religion, then one is assuming that all the applications of 'religion' are univocal" (p. 15). This is precisely my point. At least at the present stage of research, we should treat the concept of religion as analogical, not univocal (see below). But I do not see Baird's proposed solution as a real alternative.
6. M. Spiro, "Religion: Problems of Definition and Explanation," in M. Banton, ed., *Anthropological Approaches to the Study of Religion* (London, 1966), p. 90. See also U. Bianchi, C. J. Bleeker, and A. Bausani, eds., *Problems and Methods of the History of Religions*, Proceedings of the Study Conference organized by the Italian Society for the History of

Religions on the occasion of the Tenth Anniversary of the Death of R. Pettazzoni, 1969 (Leiden, 1972), pp. 16ff.

7. For the last phrase, see M. Pye, *Comparative Religion* (Newton Abbot, 1972).
8. In H.-Ch. Puech, ed., *Histoire des religions,* Encyclopédie de la Pleïade, 29 (Paris, 1970), pp. 26 and 35.
9. See R. Pettazzoni, "Il metodo comparativo," *Numen* 6 (1959): 10, as well as Pettazzoni's article in the first issue of *Numen* (1954), pp. 4–5. For van der Leeuw's comments, see his *Die Phänomenologie der Religion* (Tübingen, 1933), pp. 650 and 652.
10. Van der Leeuw, p. 642.
11. Honko, ed., p. xxv. For Bleeker's position, which balances his concerns as a phenomenologist of religions and as an Egyptologist, see his "The Contribution of the Phenomenology of Religion to the Study of the History of Religions," in Bianchi, Bleeker, and Bausani, pp. 35–45, as well as his "The Phenomenological Method," *Numen* 6 (1955); "Methodology and the Science of Religion," in E. J. Jurji, ed., *Religious Pluralism and World Community* (Leiden, 1969), pp. 237–247; and "Comparing the Religio-Historical and the Theological Method," *Numen* 18 (1971): 9–29.
12. Consider Åke Hultkrantz's statement in "The Phenomenology of Religion: Aims and Methods," *Temenos* 6 (1970): 74–75; "The phenomenology of religion is thus the systematic study of the forms of religion, that part of religious research which classifies and systematically investigates religious conceptions, rites, and myth-traditions from comparative morphological-typological points of view."
13. R. Pettazzoni, "The Supreme Being: Phenomenological Structure and Historical Development," in M. Eliade and J. M. Kitagawa, eds., *The History of Religions: Essays in Methodology* (Chicago, 1959), pp. 59–66.
14. See n. 9, above.
15. Pettazzoni in Eliade and Kitagawa, p. 66.
16. See Th. P. van Baaren, "Systematische Religionswissenschaft," *Nederlands Theologisch Tijdschrift* 24 (1969): 81–88; and "Science of Religion as a Systematic Discipline: Some Introductory Remarks," in Th. P. van Baaren and H. J. W. Drijvers, eds., *Religion, Culture and Methodology: Papers of the Groningen Working Group for the Study of Fundamental Problems and Methods of Science of Religion* (The Hague, 1973), pp. 35–56.
17. Van Baaren, "Systematische Religionswissenschaft," p. 83.
18. Van Baaren, "Science of Religion," pp. 44f.
19. G. Widengren, "La méthode comparative: entre philologie et phenomenologie," *Numen* 18 (1971): 161–172 (also published in Bianchi, Bleeker, and Bausani, pp. 5–14). See also his "Some Remarks on the Methods of the Phenomenology of Religions," in *Acta Universitatis Upsaliensis* 17, *Universitetet och Forskingen,* pp. 250–260.
20. In C. J. Bleeker, G. Widengren, and E. J. Sharpe, eds., *Proceedings of the Twelfth International Congress of the International Association for the History of Religions, Stockholm, 1970* (Leiden, 1975), p. 20.
21. G. Widengren, *Religionsphänomenologie* (Berlin, 1969).
22. G. Widengren, "La méthode comparative," p. 164.
23. K. Rudolph, "Das Problem der Autonomie und Integrität der Religionswissenschaft," *Nederlands Theologisch Tijdschrift* 27 (1973): 105–131; and "Die Problematik der Religionswissenschaft als akademisches Lehrfach," *Kairos* 9 (1967): 22–42. See also his "Das Problem einer Entwicklung in der Religionsgeschichte," *Kairos* 13 (1971): 95–118.

24. K. Rudolph, "Basic Positions of *Religionswissenschaft*," *Religion* 11 (1981): 97–107.
25. See K. Rudolph, "Die Problematik," p. 29; Åke Hultkrantz, "Über religionsethnologische Methoden," in G. Lansczkowski, ed., *Selbstverständnis und Wesen der Religionswissenschaft* (Darmstadt, 1974), pp. 360–393. For Wach's terminology, see J. Wach, *Religionswissenschaft: Prolegomena zu ihrer wissenschaftstheoretischen Grundlegung* (Leipzig, 1924), p. 21.
26. K. Rudolph, "Die Problematik," p. 29; emphasis added.
27. Å. Hultkrantz also insists on the distinction between "systematic" and "historical," or "horizontal" and "vertical" methodologies, respectively. He classifies the first as "systematic-functional," or, alternatively, "systematic-phenomenological." Interestingly, he adds that "monographic as well as comparative research can make use of both types of methods, the 'horizontal' systematic and the 'vertical' historical" (Hultkrantz, "Über religionsethnologische Methoden," p. 377). On the other hand, he expresses the opinion that "normally the comparative approach to research in the history of religions can advance no more than probabilities" (p. 388). In the essay cited, Hultkrantz limits his consideration to nonliterate cultures. In a view that encompasses a broader range of cultures, his reserve seems excessive. As we shall see, the older, practical identification of "diffusionism" with the cultural-historical method, to which Hultkrantz properly refers, does not hold true for what I call the "historical typology of religion." Especially in certain cases it is possible to find on the basis of sound evidence a parallelism, to be sure a partial and historically conditioned parallelism, between two or more cultural-historical and religio-historical "processes" or "developments" that are mutually independent. A classic example is the parallel development of polytheism in the high cultures of antiquity, as well as the parallel development of the high cultures themselves (cf. A. Brelich, "Der Polytheismus," *Numen* 7 [1960], pp. 113ff.). Another example is Karl Jaspers's well-known "axial-age." No abstract phenomenology could account for the vividness and historical "reality" of the various polytheistic religions or, in the case of the "axial-age," of the prophets and reformers. Hultkrantz does not, it seems to me, do justice to the concept of (historical) typology (cf. his "Phenomenology of Religion," p. 79). The study of "types of typologies of religion," which Hultkrantz attributes to me, requires a comparative, historical outlook (cf. my *Probleme der Religionsgeschichte* [Göttingen, 1964]). In "Über religionsethnologische Methoden," Hultkrantz makes some interesting observations on the "new evolutionism" of White and Stewart. In his opinion, "the 'new evolutionism' is no substitute for the historical method but its completion." Unlike the old evolutionism, it is empirical, and its evolutionary pattern can be conceived as an "abridged" history. But to speak of regularities, or even of laws, seems to me more than a historical sensitivity can bear.
28. K. Rudolph, "Die 'ideologiekritische' Funktion der Religionswissenschaft," *Numen* 25 (1978): 17–39.
29. See "The Definition of Religion: On the Methodology of Historical Comparative Research," in Bianchi, Bleeker, and Bausani, pp. 15–26, reprinted in U. Bianchi, *The History of Religions*, pp. 201–220.
30. Cf. G. Lanczkowski, *Religionswissenschaft als Problem und Aufgabe* (Tübingen, 1965), p. 30: "All understanding of that which is unfamiliar

displays above all a relating of the unfamiliar to that which is already known. The possibility of understanding in the human sciences derives chiefly from comparison. Thus, we have no prior understanding which evades our possibility of comprehending as a 'totally other.'" See also O. Fr. Bollnow, "Religionswissenschaft als hermeneutische Disziplin," *Zeitschrift für Religions- und Geistesgeschichte* 31 (1979): 233–235; K. Rudolph, "Die Problematik," p. 29; and J. de Menasce's review of Bianchi, Bleeker, and Bausani in *Revue de l'histoire des religions* 182 (1972): 187–191.

31. See my "The Definition of Religion."
32. M. Eliade, "Crisis and Renewal in the History of Religions," *History of Religions* 5 (1965): 9, reprinted in M. Eliade, *The Quest: History and Meaning in Religion* (Chicago, 1969), p. 63.

Supplementary Bibliographical Note

In addition to publications quoted in the text and footnotes, essential literature concerning recent debates on methodological issues in the history of religions includes:

CLAVIER, H. "Résurgences d'un problème de méthode en histoire des religions." *Numen* 15 (1968).

COLPE, C., ED. *Die Diskussion um das Heilige*. Darmstadt, 1977.

CROSBY, D. A. *Interpretive Theories of Religion*. The Hague, 1981.

CULIANU, I. P. "History of Religions in Italy: The State of the Art," *History of Religions* 20 (1981): 253–262.

———. "History of Religions in Italy: A Postscript." *History of Religions* 20 (1982): 191–195.

DA SILVA, A. BARBOSA. The Phenomenology of Religion as a Philosophical Problem: *An Analysis of the Theoretical Background of the Phenomenology of Religion in General, and of M. Eliade's Phenomenological Approach, in Particular.* Dissertation, Uppsala, 1982.

DESROCHE, H. AND U. SÉGUY, EDS. *Introduction aux sciences humaines des religions.* Paris, 1970.

DRIJVERS, H. J. W. "Theory Formation in Science of Religion and the Study of the History of Religions." In Van Baaren and Drijvers, eds., *Religion, Culture, and Methodology*. The Hague, 1973, pp. 57–77.

DROBIN, U. "Social Anthropology and Comparative Religion." *Temenos* 8 (1972): 118–128.

Ecole Pratique des Hautes Etudes, Section des Sciences Religieuses. *Problèmes et méthodes d'histoire des religions*. Paris, 1968. General methodological issues are not treated.

EDSMAN, C. M. "Theologie oder Religionswissenschaft?" *Theologische Rundschau*, n.s. 35 (1970): 1–32. (Also in Lanczkowski, ed., *Selbstverständnis*, pp. 320–359).

ELSAS, CHR., ED. *Religion: Ein Jahrhundert Theologie, Philosophie, Soziologie, und Psychologie: Interpretationsansätze*. München, 1975. Particularly the Introduction: "Problemgeschichtliche Einleitung," by Elsas.

GALLOWAY, A. D. "Theology and Religious Studies: The Unity of Our Discipline." *Religious Studies* 11, no. 2 (1975): 157–165.

GEERTZ, C. "Religion as a Cultural System." In M. Banton, ed., *Anthropological Approaches to the Study of Religion.* London, 1966.

HULTKRANTZ, Å. "Anthropological Approaches to Religion (a Review)." *History of Religions* 9, no. 4 (1970): 337–352.

———. "The Phenomenology of Religion: Aims and Methods." *Temenos* (1970): 68–88.

———. "History of Religions in Anthropological Waters: Some Reflections against the Background of American Data." *Temenos* 13 (1977): 81–97.

KITAGAWA, J. M. *Gibt es ein Verstehen fremder Religionen?* Leiden, 1963.

———, ED. *The History of Religions.* Essays on the Problem of Understanding. Chicago, 1967.

———. "Humanistic History of Religions and Theological History of Religions." General address to the 14th International Congress for the History of Religions, Winnipeg, 1980. In Peter Slater and Donald Wiebe, eds., *Traditions in Contact and Change: Proceedings of the 14th International Congress of the International Association of the History of Religions.* Waterloo, Ontario, 1983.

LANCZKOWSKI, G. *Einführung in die Religionsphänomenologie.* Darmstadt, 1978.

———. *Einführung in die Religionswissenschaft.* Darmstadt, 1980.

———, ED. *Selbstverständnis und Wesen der Religionswissenschaft.* Darmstadt, 1974.

MESLIN, M. *Pour une science des religions.* Paris, 1973.

OXTOBY, W. G. "Religionswissenschaft Revisited." In J. Neusner, ed., *Religions in Antiquity* (Studies Goodenough). Leiden, 1968.

PENNER, H. H. "The Poverty of Functionalism." *History of Religions* 11 (1971).

PENNER, H. H. AND E. A. YONAN. "Is a Science of Religion Possible?" In *Journal of Religion* 52 (1972).

PLATVOET, J. G. *Comparing Religions: A Limitative Approach.* The Hague, 1982.

PUECH, H.-CH., ED. *Histoire des religions,* vol. 1 (Paris, 1970), Preface, pp. vii–xxvii.

PUMMER, R. "Recent Publications on the Methodology of the Science of Religion." *Numen* 22 (1975): 161–182.

RATSCHOW, C. H. "Methodik der Religionswissenschaft." In *Enzyklopädie der geisteswissenschaftlichen Arbeitsmethoden,* 9th Installment. Munich-Vienna, 1973.

Religion. Special Issue, August 1975: "The History of Religion: An International Survey." On the study of religion in different countries.

Religion und Religionen (Festschrift Mensching). Bonn, 1967.

RINGGREN, H. "Die Objektivität der Religionswissenschaft." *Temenos* 6 (1970): 119–129.

RUDOLPH, K. *Die Religionsgeschichte an der Leipziger Universität und die Entwicklung der Religionswissenschaft.* Berlin, 1962.

RUPP, A. *Religion, Phänomen und Geschichte.* Prolegomena zur Methodologie der Religionsgeschichte. Saarbrücken, 1978.

SHARPE, E. J. *Comparative Religion: A History.* London, 1975.

———. "Some Problems of Method in the Study of Religion." *Religion* 1 (1971): 1–14.

SCHLETTE, H. R. *Einführung in das Studium der Religionen.* Freiburg-Breisgau, 1971.

SCHMID, G. *Principles of Integral Science of Religion.* The Hague, 1979.

SEIWERT, H. "Systematische Religionswissenschaft: Theoriebildung und Empiriebezug." *Zeitschrift für Missionswissenschaft und Religionswissenschaft* 61, no. 1 (1977): 1–17.

SIMON, M. "The religionsgeschichtliche Schule, fifty years later." *Religious Studies* 11, no. 2 (1975): 135–144.

SMART, N. *The Phenomenon of Religion.* London, 1973.

———. *The Principles and Meaning of the Study of Religion.* Lancaster, 1968.

———. *The Science of Religion and the Sociology of Knowledge: Some Methodological Questions.* Princeton, 1973.

SMITH, W. CANTWELL. "Comparative Religion: Whither—and Why?" In M. Eliade and J. M. Kitagawa, eds., *The History of Religions: Essays in Methodology.* Chicago, 1959.

TWORUSCHKA, U. "Integral Religionswissenschaft. Methode der Zukunft?" *Zeitschrift für Religions- und Geistesgeschichte* 26, no. 3 (1972).

WAARDENBURG, J. *Classical Approaches to the Study of Religion.* 2 vols. The Hague, 1978.

———. *Reflections on the Study of Religion: Including an Essay on G. Van der Leeuw.* The Hague, 1978.

———. "Religionswissenschaft in Continental Europe, excluding Scandinavia." *Numen* 23, no. 3 (1976): 219–238.

WERBLOWSKY, R. J. Z. "On Studying Comparative Religion: Some Naive Reflections of a Simple-Minded Non-Philosopher." *Religious Studies* 11, no. 2 (1975): 145–156.

WIEBE, D. *Religion and Truth: Towards an Alternative Paradigm for the Study of Religion.* The Hague, 1981.

The History of Religions and Its Conversation Partners

NINIAN SMART

Who are we and with whom do we converse? Questions about identity and relationship haunt us, in part because we recognize that the web of human learning and understanding is as seamless as the world about us and within us. Yet we work—most of us—on campuses where divisions are endemic and departments are the norm. There is a secret feeling that there is not, despite the rhetoric of academe, a one-to-one match between discipline and department. We recognize thus that there are tensions between institutions and logic, and we may regret, as persons involved in the history of religions, that our field of religion is often located in a framework of learning around us. We are often placed on the edge of a Christian faculty of theology or divinity, as if the study of all religions were a special case of the study of one. Sometimes we are cut off from divinity by institutional boundaries, as when religious studies are considered an arts or humanities discipline in a division different from the school of divinity. Neither subordination nor alienation helps our conversation with Christian theology. And when we look in the direction of the social sciences we may observe anomalies too: the history of religions proceeds along its path often removed rather far, institutionally, from the sociology of religion, or from anthropology, and still farther from psychology. With philosophy there is sometimes a mood of mutual suspicion, as though the religionist and the philosopher reflect competing worldviews—which indeed happens, though it is not logical that it should. So we might go on, for our field travels along paths that wind into and among the whole gamut of cultural studies from Australia to Siberia and from France to Japan; and it has relationships to the sciences as well.

Apart from the problems of institutional unease and alienation, there are the definitional and methodological questions that have been so much debated during the last quarter-century and more: the limits and use of the very word "religion" and its plural "religions"; the possibilities of bracketing and the question of how the outsider gets inside the insider; the tensions between historical research and dialogue among the living; the fascination and seeming unattainability of objectivity. Of all these areas of debate the question of definition is perhaps the most substantial, because it raises the issue of whether the distinction between a *religion* and a secular *ideology* is itself not an ideological distinction of our contemporary world. Had the history of religions grown up in a Confucian environment would it have made so much of the division between Christianity and secular humanism or between Islam and Marxism? Would it not have looked upon them as different paths for the organization of society, the cultivation of the individual, and the interpretation of the cosmos? There is a case for thinking of the study of religions as the study (more broadly) of worldviews. I shall come back to this point for it helps to indicate some fruitful overlaps between our field and some of the conversation partners. This broader perspective gives us a new vocabulary: the history of worldviews, the analysis of worldviews, worldview evaluation, worldview construction, living a worldview.[1] However, though logic and often our practice point in this broader direction, the tradition we inherit is of the history of religions and of *Religionswissenschaft* or of the comparative study of religion. And whatever we say about the need to broaden out to worldviews, the heart of our work lies in the traditional faith traditions. Indeed, I suspect that it is from there that we can derive the resources through which the broadening becomes fruitful: for it is through the analysis of the symbols of traditional religion that we can come to understand the secret symbolism of secular worldviews. It is thus important that we should continue to draw sustenance from our roots, in the traditional conception of the field.

I began with a reference to the institutional placing of our field. There are other institutional oddities that need to be observed. For historical reasons that are easy to understand and trace, the dominant religions of Western society, namely, varieties of Christianity and Judaism, are studied in ways thought relevant to the seminary and the training of sacred specialists. However, this leads to the entrenchment of academic divisions, such as Old Testament, New Testament, Church History, Dogmatics, and so forth (in the case of Christianity), which carve up the religion in ways we might find odd if it were applied to other faiths. Our practice tends to be much more holistic and organic in dealing with other religious traditions. But the imprint of the Christian schematism remains. For one thing, because Christianity is well studied in Western institutions there is a slide into thinking of the history of religions as being all religions but Christianity (or Judaism). Since both the tradition of classical scholarship and that of religious concern in the West are text-oriented, a similar text orientation is often applied to other traditions, while religions with oral and no written texts are left somewhat to the methods and purview of anthropology.

Actually, the history of religions, through the wider notion of the study of religion, or religious studies, becomes identified with its conversation partners. The sociology of Buddhism in Sri Lanka is part of the study of Buddhism; the political ideas of Shi'i Islam today are part of the subject-matter of political science; the history of Hellenistic religions is part of the classics; the exploration of the Nuer and their religion is part of anthropology; the theories of Freud or Jung or Fromm about religion are part of depth-psychology.

And yet historically historians of religion have sometimes tried, by contrast, to draw a rather sharp line between themselves and others, and this above all in the matter of theological or value judgments. Thus at the Marburg conference of the International Association for the History of Religions a statement was signed by a variety of scholars defining the subject as belonging to the humanities, not to theology, etc. As Eric Sharpe points out in his history of the field,[2] a very strong stand on this was taken by Zwi Werblowsky, who drew up the statement and who later published an even more incisive expression of this point of view in *Numen*. It is, of course, very important for us to realize when we are being descriptive and theoretical on the one hand—when we are being involved with traditions analysis—and when we are presenting or evaluating a religious or other worldview. Obviously, though, the Christian or Jewish or other theologian is primarily concerned to construct or reconstruct or otherwise present a worldview. She or he is in this respect part of the ongoing phenomenon called Christianity or Judaism or whatever.

The situation is complicated by the fact that the history of religions may itself be part of the material that the theologian reflects about and uses in his constructive work: conversely, some ideological theory, such as Marxism, may give insights into certain aspects of religious development, and these may be woven into the fabric of the historian of religions' account. Nevertheless, it is very important to keep the descriptive or analytic aims and the normative distinct. Why? Because the intention of the historian must in some sense be to show things as they are and were, without passing judgment on them; and all he or she needs is the confidence that it is possible to delineate the phenomena of faith and the feel of belief without venturing into affirmations for or against the truth or value of such faith or belief.

Sometimes the slogan of objectivity is used, and sometimes it is said that objectivity is impossible or misses the point. I think it is an unfortunate slogan. If I feel sad, but do not show it, then it might be thought that my sadness is not objective or objectively verifiable. But of course my sadness is as much a fact as the shape of my nose: it is simply more difficult to find out about and to describe. Since objectivity often is contrasted to inwardness, the slogan leaves out of account the inner facts which we always have to get at in human affairs and above all in matters pertaining to religion. I think it would be better if we were to speak not of objectivity but of degrees of descriptive success. What we aim for in delineating religious events is the highest possible degree of descriptive success. What we then say normatively is another matter.

If, then, theology is one of the conversation partners, what does each side have to say? I shall return to this; but it might be wiser if we were to look first to those fields that share more closely the descriptive concerns of the historian of religions, such as anthropology, sociology, literature, and area studies. Here I can do little but mention what seem to me to be some of the most important remarks to be made in the various conversations, in each direction. But before I get to this, let me deal with one further complication in the geography of disciplines. Between the descriptive and the normative lies a mysterious and ambiguous realm, that of theory. Anthropologists do not just describe peoples and the interconnections within societies: they also create theories to account for recurrent patterns, and so do other disciplines. And this is true no less in the history of religions. One of the chief reasons for the great influence in the last quarter century of the Chicago school is the theoretical power of Mircea Eliade's work. Theories may conceal norms and metaphysical presuppositions: but they are at least on the surface in the business of generalizing and explaining or providing modes of exploration, of describing and delineating structures. Even a comparison is a part of a typology, and a typology is a (rather low-level) theory. The history of religions cannot evade some degree of theory. So we can ask, in regard to the conversations between disciplines, what are the descriptive and what are the theoretical contributions from each side?

Of all the conversation partners I suppose anthropology maintains the most animated interchange with our field. The comparative study of religions was born and nurtured between philology and anthropology. What anthropology supplies descriptively are two main things. First, there is the wonderful array of ethnographic studies which bring the smaller-scale societies to the attention of historians who because of their craft tend to home in on the great traditions of the literate religions. Second, anthropologists remind the historian of the dimensionality of living religions: it is a tendency of the scholar to overestimate ideas and symbols and to overlook the dense social ambience of all spirituality and ideology. Conversely, the modern history of religions can help supply wider perspectives of context and change. Let me furnish here just two examples. One is the study of new religious movements in the Third World (I especially think of the encyclopedic work of Harold Turner[3]): here the historian of religions can decipher and illuminate the life of symbols as they help to reintegrate lifestyles put in question by the advance of the "White Frontier." Another example is the supply of materials from the past (for example, ancient Greece) which the anthropologist or sociologist cannot directly explore by her usual methods.

As for theory, I suppose in modern times there has been more import than export, that is, the religionist has been prone to accept more from the anthropological theorist than conversely. Consider the influence of Lévi-Strauss, Victor Turner, Mary Douglas, and others. Eliade's symbolic analyses, however, have considerable heuristic value for much small-scale material, and of course his theory of shamanism gives a synthesis that, though debatable, helps to illuminate a vital phenomenon in a broad range of societies.

It is worth noting that the historian of religions' traditional interest in texts and doctrines may help to provide a counterweight to a purely mythic analysis of religious beliefs. One of the functions of doctrines is to enable myths and symbols to "hook on" to the transcendent. Whether there is anything transcendent is, of course, open to debate, and it is not necessary for us to think (as Joachim Wach seems to have done[4]) that some such belief in a transcendent holy is a presupposition of *Religionswissenschaft.* But belief in its "reality" to those who believe in it is a necessary presupposition of our field. It is part of the phenomenological approach that the believer is in this as in other respects right: that is, right about his own beliefs. Anyway, the phenomenology of *doctrines* is an important part of our field—the consideration of the function of doctrine in various religions and of the reasons why some religions are relatively undoctrinal; the exploration of the variations in doctrine and their relationship to varieties of experience, ritual, and so on (consider, for example, the correlation between *bhakti* and doctrines of grace and between the contemplative life and the *via negativa*).

The varied contributions of the sociology of religion to our field are great. At the descriptive level it has helped especially in Western countries to give a strongly empirical dimension to Christian, Jewish, and related studies. The fact that Christianity is so often studied theologically (as a set of normative ideas and practices within a strongly intellectualist and text-oriented framework) gives sociological studies, especially by those who have written "ethnographically" of forms of Western Christianity—Bryan Wilson,[5] David Martin,[6] and Hans Mol,[7] among others—the role of contemporary historians of religion in the Western context. Second, and overlappingly, sociology has taken a strong interest in new religious movements, and this hooks in with the comparable endeavors to explore new religions in Africa, Japan, and elsewhere. All this can promise the rise of a dynamic phenomenology, that is, a phenomenology of religious change. Just as there are recurrent patterns of religious experience and practice, so there are recurrent patterns of change.

What of the history of religions' descriptive exports to sociology, beyond those already mentioned in relation to anthropology? I would add to those (equally relevant to sociology) a sense of the contingently Western character of the evolution of the field—the rather "culture-bound" characteristics of the thought of even so cross-cultural a figure as Max Weber.

At the theoretical level, recent decades have seen much concern with moving toward a theory of secularization: here some vital issues are posed to the historian of religions, and their treatment is adumbrated in some of the reflections about the modern condition expressed in Eliade's writings.[8] For if archaic and older mythic forms of belief and symbolism are vanishing from whole segments of modern Western and other populations, what effect is this having upon the "spiritual" life of our contemporaries? Is religion driven underground to reemerge as art? Also at the level of theory, Weber's great work remains as a challenge. Times have changed, and our knowledge of the history of religions has advanced immensely since his death. But the whole question of the dynamic role of deep cultural (and thus religious) ideas and social structures has reemerged in a new form, as the globe becomes a single competitive marketplace and political arena.

The historian of religions can offer the social sciences two important theoretical insights. One is that for various historical reasons, themselves bound up with comparative religion's placement alongside theology in many institutions, our field has paid much attention to the theory and practice of *epochē*. This "methodological agnosticism" is important for the social sciences, but practiced only intermittently, especially in theoretical contexts. My own work, *The Science of Religion and the Sociology of Knowledge,* arising from concerns with the polymethodic and cross-cultural study of religion, contains a critique of Berger in this regard and a theory of *epochē* that steers that golden middle path between reductionism and dogmatism.[9]

Another area in which the history of religions has to offer insights is the one of civil religion: there is a whole swath of suggestive material for dealing with the symbolisms of secular ideologies and institutions, including nationalism, which can be drawn from recent writings in the history of religions.[10] To put it another way: symbolic analysis can be fruitfully applied beyond the traditional religious context and in that very fact there lies a possible theory of syncretism between sacred and secular, of which civil religion is but one manifestation.

Symbolic analysis takes us into the field of depth psychology. There is no doubt that Jungian analysis of myth has contributed greatly to the vitality of modern concerns with comparative work on myth and symbolism, from Eliade and Joseph Campbell through Kerenyi and other members of the Eranos group. The new structuralism of Claude Lévi-Strauss superficially is at odds with the Jungian approach: but the slants are by no means on a collision course, however different the metaphysical underpinnings.[11]

Though Jung has been a good stimulant, it cannot be said that in general the psychology of religion is or has been lately in a healthy condition. But there are areas within it of vigorous research, notably in the psychology of religious development, influenced by and reacting against Piaget[12]: this work has occurred at the borders of education, since it is very relevant in application to programs in education in world religions and confessional contexts. Here the interest is deeper in parts of Europe such as Britain and Scandinavia, where a pluralistic approach to religions in school instruction is common.

Psychological data about dreams, altered states of consciousness, and types of religious and ethical development provide suggestive material for the historian of religions in her or his treatment of such phenomena as shamanism, initiation, the life cycle, and so forth. Psychological research can also supply us with other material, such as orientation in space and interpersonal psychology, which can be synthesized with work on the symbolism of space, communication, and so on. Conversely, the history of religions has by now assembled a lot of biographical and other data in connection with mysticism and conversion experiences, among others, and a phenomenological ordering of such data may help toward a more balanced appreciation of depth experiences. Moreover, both the history of religions and anthropology are putting together a range of interesting data on "indigenous psychologies," that is, the psychological theories implicit in various cultural and religious traditions. The fact that these theories often draw conceptual lines in different places can be suggestive more widely to those interested in the philosophy of mind.

I now turn briefly to classical and modern studies in the various cultural regions of humanities. It is obvious that the classics, Western history, and Asian, African, and other studies are closely related to, and overlap with, the history of religions. The period since World War II has seen amazing advances in most of these areas of research and understanding. Let me briefly point to ways in which our field can help these others, and conversely. It is obvious that comparative work can help the understanding of a particular culture. Thus cross-cultural studies of mysticism suggest certain essential patterns which help to generate questions about what shapes the particularities of each tradition. Again general analyses, for example, of the sacred city, can help to illuminate some features of a particular society, as in David Carrasco's recent work on the Aztecs and their response to Cortez.[13] Conversely it needs no emphasis that much of the substance of the history of religions is drawn from the textual, historical, archeological, sociological, and other work of area specialists. But it is worth pointing out that as area studies are polymethodic, using the various disciplines of history, sociology, and political science, they should take seriously the study of religions and more generally worldviews as part of their approach. Both worldview analysis and symbolic analysis are necessary ingredients in the understanding of cultures and their histories and contemporary state.

This is where it does seem to me particularly desirable that our field and that of political science should come together. It does not make sense to discuss modern religion in Poland, Israel, or Iran without seeing how various blends and tensions have developed between religions and ideologies. Thus worldview analysis seems a more appropriate way of approaching most areas of human political and religious activity than is the present tendency to divide off religion from secular philosophy. Again the political work of Weber is worth attending to. I shall not here elaborate on the actual and possible imports and exports between the fields, partly because such trade is more a promise of the future than an actuality of the present.

Cultural and area studies of course range between the humanities and the social sciences. If political science and economics lie at one end, then literature lies at the other. Here there has been much theoretical interplay, because of a joint interest in hermeneutics. But there has been relatively little concern with the use of literary and other artistic means of expressing the findings of the history of religions. (Eliade, of course, has in his own way always been an exception to this.)

There are normative, as well as descriptive and theoretical, aspects of most of the fields we have touched on so far. Some psychology includes a philosophy of health; some sociology touches on social engineering, and this needs underpinning in some social philosophy; political science sometimes is involved in constructing politically oriented worldviews or in implementing them; some cultural studies are aimed at justifying a set of cultural values. Similarly some exponents of the history of religions are also directly involved in such activities as cross-cultural dialogue, the promotion of religious toleration, the working out of a religious philosophy or theology. But before commenting on this more normative side of things, let me say a word or two about the export and import of data and ideas at a more descriptive and theoretical level between our field and philosophy and the various theologies, Christian and otherwise.

In the case of philosophy there has of course been a notorious split, until recently, between the Anglo-Saxon and the European existentialist and other traditions. The latter (particularly the thought of Heidegger) has fed into Christian theology and theological hermeneutics. Often the former has been perceived as hostile to or skeptical of religion. However, philosophy of religion has flourished in the analytic tradition. In this mode it has something important to contribute to our field, though this has not as yet been very widely appreciated. The methods of linguistic analysis (for instance, the doctrine of performative uses of language) can be used to shed light on ritual and other religious phenomena. The use of conceptual analysis is relevant to the formation of theories of such widespread notions as sacrifice. Conversely the philosophy of religion cannot respectably afford to be so crudely culture-bound as it has typically been in the English-speaking world, and the varieties of religious tradition transmitted to its consciousness by the history of religions are vital to its health.

Analysis is, in theory at least, metaphysically neutral. Much of technical philosophy at this level can be used, so to speak, as a tool for sorting out the concepts and contexts of religion. But some analytic philosophy and most of the existentialist tradition, together with Marxist philosophy (for example, the Frankfurt school), seem to me to be more in the business of worldview construction or worldview expression. They go well beyond analysis. This is in its own way traditional: treating philosophy as a process of arriving at a worldview, which may or may not be compatible with traditional religions. Thus some of Heidegger's thought turns out to chime in with Zen. A. J. Ayer's logical positivism of his early days was rather aggressively antireligious. Sartre's position was a kind of religious atheism. And the neo-Marxists try to reformulate the Marxian worldview in the light of recent history and experience. So here the history of religions itself confronts something in the nature of a theology: and when what is primarily descriptive and theoretical meets that which is axiological it begins to generate an axiological message of its own by paying attention to the pluralism of human cultures and to the quest for transcendence which is to be found in so many of the religious phenomena we study.

But modern philosophy has some interesting methodological and theoretical remarks to make to the history of religions. First, there is the possibility of using analytic methods in the "search for essences"—the typology which is part of the phenomenology of religion. Second, philosophy is one of the directions from which are emerging new approaches to hermeneutics, semiology, etcetera, all of which are relevant to the enterprise of symbolic analysis as part of the history of religions.

Conversely, our field can contribute something to philosophy. Here it is necessary first to be somewhat speculative. As comparative religionists we have a certain higher-order commitment to the importance of religious phenomena. In this we tend to take a particular approach to the world, which may be worthy of philosophical consideration, for it incorporates an embryonic philosophy. This approach is to see the human being as *homo religiosus* or as *homo symbolicus.* Thus we see the human being as framer of meaningful values, which often take mythic and ritual form and which are often experienced in ways oblique to the common-sense world of ordinary perception which has so exercised Western philosophers since Descartes and the empiricists. Thus we as religionists tend to be somewhat "mentalistic" in our philosophy: emphasizing the mental sets and symbolic attitudes that suffuse our world. This side of life has to be incorporated into any comprehensive account of human nature. We share this attitude with anthropologists, and like them we see patterns of symbolism as well as great cultural relativities. Second, it seems to me that we have something to contribute to the philosophy of the social sciences, with the whole doctrine of relational bracketing, as when we bracket Vishnu in the *Gītā* or the historical dialectic in Soviet thought, and thus contribute to the theory of a value-free science of human actualities. But even to say this is controversial, since the debate continues within the study of religion about the possibility and desirability of this approach. For me, it is a question primarily of getting at the facts of human life before we decide on what is true about the next.

And now I come to the theologies—Christian, Jewish, Islamic, Hindu, Buddhist, and other, that is, to the processes of reflecting and building upon the ideas and experiences of the various traditions from within those traditions, or at least adjacent to those traditions. There are religious thinkers who may be somewhat ambiguous as to their institutional or traditional placement, but even so they follow in the footsteps of the thinkers of their tradition. For convenience I shall use Christian theology as the chief example.

It is of course an obvious point that the history of religions has supplied much material for theological reflection. Once it breaks free of the assumptions that the categories of Christian belief and doctrine are adequate to describe the phenomena of other religions, history of religions becomes, as it were, the diplomatic corps of world religions at the court of Christian theology. It represents other traditions to the one that considers itself the normative tradition. Some of the great figures of our field have tried to perform the functions of both ambassador and judge and interpreter. I am thinking of Archbishop Nathan Søderblom and Rudolf Otto above all, but we can point to many others.

In addition, the history of religions has revealing comparisons and contrasts to offer, which help to illuminate the "normative" tradition. These comparisons can offer points of contact in the dialogue of religions. Such dialogue I take to be primarily a kind of plural, many-cornered theologizing, a cooperative attempt to find as much common truth as possible. As such it is not in the strict sense part of the history of religions as a descriptive and theoretical inquiry. (It is, of course, necessary to have dialogue with persons of a tradition in order to understand it and get its "feel"—and such dialogue is part of the methodology of doing the history of religions; but this is not dialogue in the pregnant sense of the term.)

Conversely, the theologies supply the history of religions with evidence of the trends of religious belief at the interface between their traditions and the modern world. Moreover, they are living commentarial heritages, which thus give access to a range of hermeneutical data that are a key part of the historian's field of inquiry.

As for theory, on the side of the theologies the often Angst-laden concerns of apologetics and of systematic theology produce concepts that are useful in historical analysis. Thus Hendrik Kraemer was right to stress the "totalitarian" (that is, organic) character of a religious tradition in his *The Christian Message in a Non-Christian World,*[14] and so to emphasize the aspect of contextual particularity in religious ideas and phenomena. His aim was to stress the uniqueness of Christianity in a rather (I would judge) exaggerated way which narrowed the sights of mission for the generation it influenced: but that is beside the point in relation to his methodological insight. Another useful lesson to be learnt from Christian theology is in the area of religious ethics. The attempt to frame an account of the relation between faith and ethics in one tradition has been a major source of the foundation of the relatively new field of comparative religious ethics, which has at least one foot in the history of religions and which is, as a descriptive and analytic exercise, indeed a branch of comparative religion.

On the theoretical export out of history of religions to the theologies, I would suggest that two items are especially important. First, it provides an analysis of symbolism and myth that is significant for the self-analysis of the traditions. The concept of myth, which has figured so prominently in the whole demythologization debate, needs reappraisal in the light of the history of religions. Second, the methods of our field might be brought to bear upon the question of compatibilities and oppositions of religious doctrines, thus reinforcing some of the conceptual analysis in the philosophy of religion, and reflecting, too, the fact that the question of such compatibilities and oppositions is in part an empirical one. The topic is an important one, because it bears closely upon the epistemology of interreligious dialogue and reflection, and in a globe in which the religions, ideologies, and cultures are in such close interaction, clarity itself is a means toward a realistic appraisal of what would need to be done to achieve greater spiritual harmony.

These, then, are some of the remarks that might pass to and fro and have passed to and fro between the history of religions and its conversation partners. There are other partners that I have not alluded to: geography, where the mapping of human value systems contributes to the mental geography of the planet; business studies, where the skills we cultivate could be of relevance to the illumination of economic development and patterns of exchange; linguistics, where religious iconography has some vital things to say about nonverbal communication; and the sciences, where we can shed light on the symbolic weights that impede the reception of new theories in cosmology and about living forms, and on those that may be suggestive of new theory in other directions.

But I hope that my sketch of the conversations helps to place our field in wider endeavors and to prepare the way for thinking of fruitful developments. There are many fine possibilities through which our field can make its central contribution to the understanding of human feelings and society and of what lies beyond and around them. The last quarter-century has been a marvelously fruitful time for the history of religions, and more generally the study of religion. We have seen an amazing explosion of cross-cultural studies in depth of the varied spiritual traditions of the human race. We have acquired much greater sophistication in worldview analysis than the human race has ever possessed. There have been great advances in thinking about methodology and the significance of symbolic life. If at times we think that we have a long way to go to persuade our colleagues and the wider community of the fecundity and importance of our field, we should by no means be dispirited, for we have much to be proud of in the advances of the last twenty-five years.

Notes

1. I have elaborated on this conception in my recent *Worldviews: Cross-Cultural Explorations of Human Beliefs* (1983).
2. Eric J. Sharpe, *Comparative Religion: A History* (1975), p. 276.
3. See, for instance, Harold Turner's *Encyclopaedia Britannica* article (1975) on new movements in tribal religions. *E. B.*, Macropaedia, Vol. 18, pp. 697ff., "Tribal Religious Movements, New."
4. See especially his "The Meaning and Task of the History of Religion," in Joseph M. Kitagawa, ed. *The History of Religions: Essays on the Problem of Understanding* (1967).

5. Bryan Wilson, *Magic and Millennium* (1978).
6. David Martin, *A General Theory of Secularization* (1975).
7. Hans Mol, *Religion in Australia: A Sociological Investigation* (1971).
8. See Eliade's essay in the Kitagawa volume cited above.
9. *The Science of Religion and the Sociology of Religion* (1973), esp. Chaps. 1–4.
10. See articles by N. Smart, R. Panikkar, and K. Bolle in Peter Merkl and Ninian Smart, eds., *Religion and Politics in the Contemporary World* (1983).
11. See Edmund Leach, *Culture and Communication: The Logic by Which Symbols Are Connected* (1976), Chap. 1.
12. E.g., the work of Goldman, Brian Gates, and others; see N. Smart and D. Horder, *New Movements in Religious Education* (1975).
13. *Quetzalcoatl and the Irony of Empire* (1983).
14. Prepared for the missionary conference in Tambaram, South India, published 1938.

A Look at the Chicago Tradition in the History of Religions:

Retrospect and Future

CHARLES H. LONG

Discipline and Dilemma

It has been noted that the scholars at the University of Chicago have a penchant for developing schools of thought. Remarking on this tendency William James wrote the following to his friend F. S. C. Schiller: "The best of the lot was reading up on the output of the 'Chicago School of Thought.' . . . A real school and real thought. At Harvard we have plenty of thought, but not a school. At Yale and Cornell, the other way about."[1]

This predisposition, which, indeed, is a part of the tradition of the University of Chicago, expresses a concern for method and methodologies within the several disciplines of academic life. Schools of thought and methodological discourse are not expressions of the desire for ideological purity but rather a concern for self-conscious reflection about what one is doing and why.

It was therefore not strange that in 1983 we gathered in Chicago to discuss methodological issues in the history of religions. The last Chicago Conference devoted to method in the history of religions was held in 1966. These conferences are, however, only symbolic and public expressions of a historical tradition: the concern for method is characteristic of this discipline at this university. George Stephen Goodspeed held the first chair of comparative religions in the university. Upon his retirement Albert Eustace Haydon taught comparative religion between 1919 and 1945. I begin this history with the career of Haydon. Haydon, Joachim Wach's predecessor, published two articles devoted to methodological issues in 1922 and 1926, respectively. The first one was entitled, "From Comparative Religion to History of Religions," and the second, "Twenty-Five Years of History of Religions."[2] We shall return to these later. Even before the time of Haydon, I have learned from the oral tradition through Bernard Meland that Gerald Birney Smith had expressed similar methodological concerns. From Goodspeed to Haydon to Joachim Wach to the arrival of Mircea Eliade on to the present, methodological discourse has continued unabated. One could put together a quite distinguished anthology composed of methodological articles from the Chicago school.

I have chosen the Chicago school as a basis for my remarks for several reasons. It constitutes a long and consistent discussion of the meaning of the discipline on the American scene, and it is a tradition that has produced an overwhelming number of the historians of religions in this country; this tradition has been equally the locus and entrée for methodological concerns of this discipline in other parts of the world. In my remarks concerning the leading figures of this tradition I shall not attempt to give a complete analysis and description of their work; rather I shall highlight certain tendencies regarding method that I consider basic for discussion of future developments in this area.

Given this tendency for the discussion of method it is appropriate to ask, what was or is at issue in this discussion? What is there to be talked about in the study of religion? Let us examine the record of this discussion.

Haydon's article of 1922, "From Comparative Religion to History of Religions," undertakes a critique of the notion of comparative religion as a disciplinary orientation for the study of religion. It is clear that this discussion accepts as a critical norm the notion of "religious sciences," or "science of religion" as the basis for analysis: "Critical, objective interpretation of the religions of the world is one of the new fruits of modern scholarship. Only students of this last generation use the terms 'science of religion' without a sense of strangeness."[3]

Two tendencies come under attack in this article. First of all, the assumptive notions that there is a kind of fundamental law of religious development, and second, that this law leads to a demonstrable superiority of Christian faith. The case rested upon three further assumptions.

> First, that religion is a certain basic thing in all religions and that phenomena are therefore similar everywhere leaving the investigator only the task of

> discovering the order of their arrangement. Second, that human nature is a unit producing similar forms when brought into contact with external nature. Third, that religious ideas and forms are capable of being gathered under universal terms owing to their similarity.[4]

Haydon finds the orientation represented by comparative religion incapable of rendering plausible premises for these assumptions, for unless comparative religion already possesses some preconceived ideas about the standard of religious excellence or some philosophical presuppositions as to a single cosmic power at work, its leading assumptions are not provable from the internal structure of its method.

For Haydon, the history of religions represents a way out of this impasse. It is a way out because it gives up or sets aside these kinds of issues. Now by history of religions, Haydon has reference to the specific study of empirical religious traditions. He does not intend history of religions as the English equivalent of *Religionswissenschaft*—the systematic inquiry into the nature of religion itself. He makes this clear in his statement that "Its [history of religions'] task is to deal not with religion but *religions*, each of them the product of a human group and claiming to be interpreted in all its richness and individuality."[5] For Haydon history of religions is an inquiry into specific religious traditions.

Four years later, Haydon returned to the problematic nature of the history of religions in his article, "Twenty-Five Years of History of Religions." In this article he reviewed and praised the advances in research devoted to a wide range of religious traditions—Chantepie de la Saussaye's *Lehrbuch. . . ,* van Gennep's study of totemism, Skeat's *Malay Magic,* Webster's *Secret Societies,* Breasted's works on Egyptian religion, Noeldeke's studies of Islam, etcetera. He is indeed pleased with the work over the last twenty-five years; it represents precisely the advance beyond the old notion of comparative religion he had criticized.

But he also notes that these specific works reveal another kind of problem in the area of method. The historian of the last quarter-century has, in his words, "escaped the revelation dogmas of the theologian only to yield to more subtle influence of philosophies with the resultant warping of method and coloring of interpretation."[6] These philosophies are those of Hegel, Schleiermacher, and Comte, who represent different understandings of religion, and Kant, Ritschl, and Spencer, who express three ways of harmonizing religion with science.

This is not the only problem revealed from these empirical studies. He further notes that the studies referred to in his survey represent five distinct schools, each with its own method: the philological school, the anthropological school, the sociological method, the method of *Völker-*

psychologie, and finally, the continuation of the tradition of the historical school of Albert and Jean Reville, Chantepie, and Tiele.

He must therefore admit, he says, that

> the method of history of religions is no longer the simple historical method used by the founders of the science before the opening of the century; it is an aggregate of all the sciences whose domains cover data which the historian must use. The success of history therefore depends upon the adequacy of the methods and findings of the various sciences involved. During the last twenty-five years these allied sciences have been struggling for a satisfactory method. The materials of religion often held the primary place. *The story of the various methodological drifts is also the story of method in the history of religions.*[7]

As far as I can discern, this was the situation in regard to method when Joachim Wach came to Chicago as professor of history of religions. Haydon, while aware of the status of the various studies within the history of religions, was wary of systematic and philosophical approaches to the entire range of data and materials characterized as religious. The methodological issue was for him located within the various methods that were used to study religion and not oriented to systematic schemas.

It is interesting to note that neither in his 1922 nor in his 1926 article does Haydon mention Rudolf Otto's *Das Heilige,* published in German in 1917 and translated into English in 1923. For that matter, Nathan Søderblom and G. van der Leeuw are also missing. The review of Otto's classic was published in the *Journal of Religion* in 1925, and the author of that review was Gerald Birney Smith, not Eustace Haydon. Smith's review, which appears in a review article with three other works, is sympathetic in its understanding and appreciation. He says at the end of this review that

> Professor Otto in our day, as Schleiermacher in his, has brought us face to face with that infinite cosmic mystery which supernaturalism made so real, but which most modernist interpretations of religion have so rationalized as to eliminate all sense of holy fear. Perhaps, after all, religion exists not so to promote social programs, not to give pleasing explanations of creation and providence, but to bring men honestly face to face with the awe-inspiring and dreadful non-human universe in which we humans count for so little, and to initiate us into an experience of oneness with the mystery in which dread and awe shall merge into worshipful trust.[8]

Before arriving at this conclusion, G. B. Smith had chided Otto for failing to show the correlation of religion to other aspects of life. This kind of critique seems to be a standard one for the members of the Divinity

School faculty of that time. It is found throughout Haydon's evaluation of Hasting's *Encyclopedia of Ethics and Religion,*[9] and it is also found in a review of Wach's *Sociology of Religion* (the first appearance of Wach's name in the *Journal*) in 1945, the year before he came to Chicago. The reviewer, in this case Edwin E. Aubrey, calls the work "a comprehensive and erudite work in the German manner." Its greatest weakness is that "it fails to give adequate treatment of the dynamic processes which make up every religion and that it will thus tend to reinforce the declaration of Ruth Benedict, which he means to refute, *that because religion is no longer a living issue, it can now be studied objectively.*"[10]

Wach's appearance at Chicago marks the beginnings of systematic approaches to the study of religion. Wach recognized, as did Haydon, that a general science of religion covered various disciplines: phenomenology, history, psychology, and sociology. This general science of religion differed from theology, which was for him a normative discipline concerned with the analysis, interpretation, and exposition of a particular faith. The difference is quantitative and qualitative; the general science of religion covers a variety of empirical religions, whereas theology is limited to one. The philosophy of religion is similar to theology in its normative dimension but akin to the science of religion in its subject matter.

But the matter is not quite as simple as Wach states it in the first paragraph of his *Sociology of Religion.* In carefully nuanced statements in the first three chapters of this work, he continuously points to the primacy of religious experience and expression as those marks to be recognized in all of the data, methods, and disciplines that constitute the science of religion.[11] On the one hand, he follows Hegel's intuition that religion is an aspect of absolute mind and, like economic systems, works of art, laws, and systems of thought, is an objective modality of culture to be distinguished from "organizations of society" such as marriage, friendships, kin groups, associations, and the state. This latter group he will later designate as "natural groups." He did not go the whole way with this interpretation because he realized that religious expressions are ambiguous, less objectified than a law or a product of industry.

The ambiguity of religion, its comparable lack of clarity to other cultural forms that are more objective, is finally interpreted in a positive sense. The "holy" is not so much another value to be added to the Good, the True, and the Beautiful, but is the matrix from which they are derived; religion is not a branch but the trunk of the tree.

Wach's orientation might be characterized in the following manner: (1) A concern for a systematic method for the study of religion. In this regard he always felt that the proper translation of *Religionswissenschaft* into the English "history of religion" should be adopted. The student of the discipline was interested in understanding the nature of religion and not simply particular religious traditions. (2) An emphasis on the phenomenology of religion as expressed by Rudolf Otto. This meant that in the tradition of the South German school of Kantianism the epistemological issue was always to the fore. (3) The context of method was always hermeneutics and the understanding of religion was part and parcel of the more general problem of hermeneutics in the modern period. (4) Thus historical method, while based upon philology and a careful assessment of data, was completed only in hermeneutics. Ancillary to this understanding of history was his concern for typologies as defining the basis for selection and discrimination of historical evidence. (5) An interest in methodologies and data from philosophy and all the human sciences as the basic intellectual context for the discipline expressed its humanistic meaning.

Related to the above but not forming a part of his formal schema was Wach's interest in Christian history and theology. From one perspective this stemmed from personal faith and his intellectual traditions. In another sense it formed part of the data of religion itself; the spread of Christianity and its relationship to the modern period was an important dimension in the understanding of the modern world.

But given this emphasis on systematic method and the autonomy of the discipline of history of religion, he did not think that the discipline had arrived at this kind of unity—what he often referred to as an *integral* understanding of religion. This is best stated in the epigraph before the first chapter of Wach's *The Comparative Study of Religion,* where he quotes E. Burnouf's prediction in *La Science des Religions:* "This present century will not come to an end without having seen the establishment of a unified science whose elements are still dispersed, a science which the preceding centuries did not have, which is not even yet defined, and which, perhaps for the first time, will be named science of religion."[12]

This is the second time we have heard this refrain echo from this tradition. It was first expressed in Haydon's dissatisfaction with a spurious comparative religion and later in his quandary regarding an integrative structure for the various historical studies of specific religious traditions. Wach, for quite other reasons, raises the same refrain. In one sense Wach felt that some aspects, if not the core of the problem, had to do with an uncritical acceptance of the interpretation of the religious life that came from the ancillary disciplines—the other human sciences. His problem could be defined as a conflict of interpretation. He thus wanted his students to undertake critical analyses of the other disciplines and also the explication of the specifically religious element and structure in the exemplars of *Religionswissenschaft.* Thus, one of the best dissertations on Bronislaw Malinowski at the University of

Chicago was written by one of Wach's students; there were also dissertations on Gabriel Marcel and Nathan Søderblom, as well as studies of mysticism. The Wachian heritage made this tradition highly self-conscious about the problem of method, its dilemmas, and its creative possibilities.

Those of us who were students of Wach in the early 1950s had read Mircea Eliade's *Traité d'histoire des religions,* and his *Le Mythe de l'éternel retour,* and the *sangha* (Wach's name for the community formed by students and friends of the history of religion) had discussed the possibility of his visit as Haskell Lecturer and visiting professor in 1956. The arrangements were made but Wach's death in August 1955 prevented us from witnessing the "conversation" that could have taken place.

For those of us who had studied with Wach and who then listened to the lectures of Mircea Eliade, there were scholarly continuities and discontinuities. The intense concern for method was continuous but it was expressed in a very different manner; one might say that in Eliade's lectures and writings, the methodological dimension was implicit in comparison to Wach's explicit expression. Kees Bolle correctly points to a tendency in Wach when he reports "that Wach's principal activity concerned formal, philosophical questions."[13] In the discussion of a religious phenomenon, Wach placed it within a typological scheme, discussed the supporting philosophical and sociological justifications for doing so along with objections, and once this methodological procedure was accomplished, he moved on.

Eliade's discussion stayed much closer to the phenomenon. After Wach, it was a rather strange style. In describing a ritual or symbol he hardly ever used the term, "and they believe that." His statements were more like, ". . . and at that moment the deity appeared." We were thus introduced to another kind of rhetoric, a rhetoric that attempted to present the imaginary religious world to us. Methodological discussion apart from data tended to bore him. After some time, those transitional students were asking *à la* Wach, "What is his method?"

There was a method, but it was presented in a very different manner. As one of his early expressions on this issue after coming to Chicago, Eliade published in *The History of Religions: Essays in Methodology* an essay entitled "Methodological Remarks on the Study of Religious Symbolism."[14] Here, as in most of his strictly methodological studies, he gives us a language derived from the religious phenomena to undertake the study of religion. In this case it is the religious symbol; in his other works we acquire hierophany, *axis mundi, in illo tempore,* the center, etcetera. Not since Rudolf Otto has the historian of religion had such a rich language for encompassing the religious life. This language was predicated upon religious expression, whereas Otto's language was directed toward the phenomenology of experiencing as a subjective mode of human consciousness. In contrast to Wach, whose major works, *Das Verstehen, Types of Religious Experience, Comparative Religion, Understanding and Believing,* express a general philosophical orientation, Eliade's major works, *Patterns in Comparative Religion, Yoga, Shamanism, Initiation,* and *Australian Religion,* among others, are indicative of a refocusing of attention on the data of religion. This is also true of his students, whose dissertations were focused in the same manner.

This orientation does not mean a change in the fundamental goal. If anything, Eliade has been as intensely devoted to the hermeneutical task of understanding the nature of religion as Wach.

In an article reminiscent of Haydon's articles of 1922 and 1926, "The History of Religions in Retrospect 1912–1962," Eliade undertakes an assessment of the field.[15] And, again in a manner that reminds us of Haydon, he signals the year 1912 as an important date in the history of religion with the publication of Durkheim's *Formes élémentaires . . .,* Schmidt's *Ursprung . . .,* Raffaele Pettazzoni's *La Religion primitive Sardegna,* Jung's *Wandlungen,* and Freud's *Totem und Tabu.*

> Four different approaches to the study of religion—none really new—were illustrated by these works: the sociological, the ethnological, the psychological, and the historical. The only new approach potentially, that of the phenomenology of religion, was not to be attempted for ten years. But Freud, Jung, Durkheim, and Wilhelm Schmidt did apply new methods and claimed to have obtained more enduring results than their predecessors.[16]

In the course of this article he discusses the major trends that have taken place within these four approaches and adds the approach of the phenomenology of religion.

Toward the end of the article he raises the issue of tension between the historicists and the phenomenologists. The alternative of a religious phenomenology or history of religion needs, he remarks, to be transcended so that we might reach a broader perspective in which these two intellectual operations are equally valuable for a more adequate knowledge of *homo religiosus.* "For if the 'phenomenologists' are interested in the *meanings* of religious data, the 'historians' on their side attempt to show how these meanings have been *experienced* and *lived* in the various cultures and historical moments, how they have been enriched, or improvised in the course of history."[17] This discussion centers on the internal problems of method in the discipline. As a hermeneut Eliade has always been concerned with the cultural situation of the interpreter and the impact of the discipline within the broader milieu. On three occasions he addressed this issue, and these remarks echo Haydon's complaint regarding "the relationship of religion to life." In "Crisis and Renewal in the History of Religions," he chided historians of religions, accusing them of a lack of courage.

> Let us recognize it frankly. History of religions, or comparative religion, plays a rather modest role in modern culture. . . . Certainly one could respond that in our day there is no Max Müller, Andrew Lang, or Frazer, which is perhaps true, not because today's historians of religion are inferior to them, but simply because they are more modest, more withdrawn, indeed more timid.[18]

This timidity among historians of religion occurs precisely at a time and in an epoch in which knowledge concerning man increased considerably due to psychoanalysis, phenomenology, and revolutionary artistic experiments, and, above all, at the moment when the confrontation with Asia and the "primitive" began. This fact is paradoxical and tragic.

According to Eliade,

> a creative hermeneutics does not always guide the work of historians of religions because, perhaps, of the inhibitions provoked by the triumph of "scientism" in certain humanist disciplines. . . . Neither the History of Religions nor any other humanist discipline ought to conform—as they have already done too long—to models borrowed from the natural sciences, still more as these models are out of date (especially those borrowed from physics).[19]

In his article, "Cultural Fashions and the History of Religions," published in the collected essays of the last of these conferences in 1966, Mircea Eliade pointed out the vogue of certain popular cultural styles as indicative of the desire and thirst on the popular levels of our society for a deeper, less mundane, more primordial, ahistorical meaning in life.

Allow me at this point to summarize this history by pointing out the cluster of problems revealed in this discussion. Most of these issues are endemic to the study of the history of religions wherever the discipline is practiced. There is first of all a recognition of the quantitative mass of religious data from the entire history of humankind that confronts the interpreter, and these data represent several methodological orientations. Second, there is a general agreement that no theology and, in the case of Haydon, no thetic principle could form the basis or be the principle for the organization of this mass of materials.

But if not theology, neither should any one of the methodological approaches within the discipline serve as the principle of organization. This is the issue of reductionism. Religion was not to be interpreted simply from the point of view of historical method, anthropology, sociology, psychology, and so on. The science of religion was thus to be an autonomous discipline that integrated not only the data but also the various methodological approaches. This kind of integration represented the autonomy of the discipline.

Now corollary to this kind of integration and autonomy of the discipline was the notion of hermeneutics. Hermeneutics was not only a procedure of interpretation, it was equally the vision and *telos* of autonomy and unity. It implied the notion of a "pre-understanding" that allowed for the initial perception of the form and modality of the phenomena of religion as "religious"; at this point it was related to phenomenology. Hermeneutics then described the connection that these phenomena had to life. In this sense it served a reintegrative function; understanding should change the cultural life and situation of the interpreter. The play and problematic of the discipline has centered on these issues in their positive exemplary expressions and in the critiques that have been made of this tradition.

Critical attention by historians of religion has tended to question not only the solutions to these problems but the authenticity of this kind of portrayal of the discipline itself.[20] I refer here to Hans Penner's work, which has not only questioned the validity of the notion of functionalism but has also raised issues regarding the use of phenomenology as a valid method within the discipline. The critical essays of Jonathan Smith and Charles Long have raised questions regarding the meaning of the center as related to the data on the one hand and as epistemological structure on the other. Joseph Kitagawa's critical appraisal of Wach's legacy has illumined and thus clarified the structural elements of his hermeneutic of understanding and salvation.[21]

Within the tradition we are discussing, two tendencies have been expressed. Wach's heritage, represented by his *Sociology of Religion,* was historical and sociological; Eliade's, morphological and ahistorical. I have elsewhere suggested a manner in which these two approaches could be combined.[22] I put forth a form of Charles Sanders Peirce's logic as a model for this conjunction. I am still persuaded that such a joining of approaches is a good idea, but I do not think that this can be done without a critical evaluation of the intentions of the two positions.

Let me suggest that the discipline has been concerned with two kinds of religious manifestations, religion as an extraordinary expression and religion as a modality of the ordinariness of life. The emphasis in the first understanding of religion employed phenomenological and morphological methods to express the extraordinariness of the religious appearance. It is the world of Rudolf Otto's *mysterium tremendum et fascinosum* and of Eliade's *hierophanies* and *kratophanies.* Religion as ordinary made use of the disciplines of history, sociology, and anthropology. It emphasized the integrative nature of religion in the life of society, the generality, normality, and regularity of the expression of the religious life. These two modes are not antithetical. Rudolf Otto in his schematization shows how the extraordinary is the basis for the ordinary and how Durkheim's *cultural effervescence* is as necessary to his theory as are the totems. These are not only two different aspects of the religious life but also two hermeneutical and premethodological meanings of the nature and meaning of religion in the modern Western world.

However, as desirable as the combination of the ordinary and extraordinary or phenomenology and history or the relationship of religion to life might be, can we accomplish this from the perspectives of this history? Can the "story of the methodological drifts," in the words of Haydon, provide unity or express the relationship of religion to life? Wach's resolution of this problem of the relationship to life veered toward a theology, and Eliade's discussion of this issue is never as precise as his interpretation of the religious data itself. But this problem should not be relegated to the final stage of interpretation. As the hermeneutical problem, it constitutes the vision as well as an internal principle of the discipline. Issues related to the future of the discipline might best be discussed in relationship to this issue.

Models and Methods

Problems of interpretation emerge in a context of distance and relationship. The distancing is the veil of difference, dissimilarity, and the mysterious quality of the datum. The relationship is in degrees of vague similarity and likeness, the necessity to create an intelligible order for the datum that has appeared as the locus for the interpretive act.

Religious phenomena constitute such data for the science of religion, and the goal of a science of religion as a total hermeneutic is to give a systematic and total interpretation of these phenomena. Such a task is procedural and visionary; it takes on both logical and aesthetic dimensions. The two exemplars of this work have been Joachim Wach and Mircea Eliade.

Wach's work in its philosophical and formal dimensions involved the stylistics of Kantianism and a hermeneutics derived from romanticism. In each case there was a rejection of classical formulations of the datum either from the point of view of a formal Christian theology and its tradition (false/true religion) or from the point of view of conventional Western culture. Romanticism was a rejection of reification; the religious phenomena of all cultures were included as living realities, even ultimate realities of human existence. The systematization of these realities into a science tended to create an architectonic structure as the aesthetic and visionary order of organization and thus an inner tension within the structure of the system. In the case of Mircea Eliade, the morphological order as the pattern for the range of religious phenomena replaced the evolutionary progressivistic and linear bourgeois history as the basis for placement and deployment of *homo religiosus*. When I read his works, I am reminded of a phrase from Marcel Griaule's wonderful *Dieu d'Eau,* "Et le corps de ballet . . . est l'image du monde entier"[23] (And the corps of the ballet . . . is the image of the entire world). The logical order is morphological: the aesthetic, the theater, the drama.

In both cases, a new world inhabited by *homines religiosi* appears on the scene. These works considered positively are a critique of those worlds created by modern materialists and rationalists. The language of experiencing in Rudolf Otto, the orders and structures of this religious world in the forms of centers, symbols, and time are explicated in Eliade's work. The types of communities, the forms of therapies and the ranges of communication, exploration, and imagination are given precise treatment in Eliade's *oeuvre.*

It is this world of *homo religiosus* that has attracted students and researchers to this discipline; it has at least attracted me, for I had tired of the rather banal sociological and historical studies of the "unofficial groups" in Western society put forth by the conventional "classical" disciplines devoted to their interpretation. There was an other world, a *heterocosm* whose echoed resonances reminded me of a world I had known but which was now distant from me. However, in making the strange familiar, it had paradoxically become more intensely *Other.*

In my opinion most critiques of this orientation, the good ones and the misinformed, touch upon this same issue; the timidity of the historian of religion might well be related to this same issue. The logical and aesthetic dimensions of system as scientificity prevent the critique implicit in the knowledge of the Others from flowing back into the normality of one's cultural life.

Jonathan Smith put it this way:

> Is the material Eliade describes best organized under the categories, "archaic" and "modern"? If one accepts the basic dualism just described between those cultures which affirm the structures of the cosmos and seek to repeat them; which affirm the necessity of dwelling within a limited world in which each being has a given place and role to fulfill, a centrifugal view of the world which emphasizes the importance of the "Centre" as opposed to those cultures which express a more "open" view in which categories of rebellion and freedom are to the fore; in which beings are called upon to challenge their limits, break them, or create new possibilities, a centripetal world which emphasizes the importance of periphery and transcendence; in which, in Eliade's terms one has chosen not installation in the world but absolute freedom . . . the annihilation of every conditioned world—ought one to suggest the periodization implied by the terms "archaic" and "modern"?[24]

In my own discussion of 1966, I had questioned the locus of the archaic in relationship to the interpreter as an epistemological issue. The same kind of question might be posed in the works of Wach. In his *Sociology of Religion,* he makes a distinction between religion and natural groups and specifically religious organization of society. The identification of religion and natural groups takes place in less complex societies, whereas specifically religious groups occur in more complex societies. I do not wish to argue the proposition, though it is arguable, but I do wish to question what the statement obscures. Why does the specifically religious occur apart from the totalization of religion within a society? Why is the specifically religious present only as a case of differentiation? In his discussion of a specifically religious community, the master and the disciple, he points to a distinct form of relationship and the dynamics and dialectical meaning of this form of bonding. Given his genius and knowledge, we would have all profited by an extension of this discussion into the religious or quasi-religious implications of Hegel's master/slave dialectic.

The study of the Other as a science is a modern preoccupation of the West. The origins of these disciplines are in the Western Enlightenment. This orientation correlates the notion of reason to the idea of the human. Although all human beings and societies do not express the same quality or modality of reason, reason is still the norm as capacity and potentiality. This orientation is the background for the human sciences—a science in which the human constitutes both the object and the interpreter of the science. It is obvious that the human as interpreter and the human as object of interpretation are not quite the same. The context for both is posited as some form of Enlightenment rationality on the one hand, or, as in the case of Giambattista Vico, the capacity of all humans to create and understand cultural forms. The status of the interpreter, the position created by the act of interpretation, sets forth other heuristic norms as models of the interpretative acts. In the history of religions, at least from its origins, two heuristic norms, one emphasizing the similarity and the other the dissimilarity, dominate. Philology and written languages, an expression common to interpreter and object of interpretation, constitute one side; the other from the side of that which is dissimilar is that of the primitives—they are not like us, being without written languages and noncivilized. The science of religion proposes to encompass both these modes within a common order of intelligibility through recourse to a deeper and more primordial order: the sacred, religious experience, and so forth. But however this deeper order is articulated, the objects of interpretation are still constituted as *Others.*

But this constitution of the Others as objects of interpretation is more than simply a procedure of investigation, for it represents the constitution of the interpreter—the desire to make sense of the meaning of the Others in one's personal and cultural life. From this point of view there is confusion or conflation of what is Other in the culture and history of the interpreter with the reality of the Others who are the object of interpretation. This is a central problem in the study of religion as a *science of religion.* The pretensions of the Enlightenment heritage explain the reason that this science has not been accomplished but is nevertheless always anticipated.

From Science to Discourse

Advances in our field at the level of method will occur if we place the Enlightenment model of science and its derivates in an *epoché* for a while. Several reasons dictate this restraint. In the first instance, we confront a very different historical situation. Many of the cultures that provided the data for the orientalists and primitivists are no longer passive or dominated by the West. Self-identification on their part poses theoretical and practical problems regarding the meaning of knowledge different from the nuances of the Enlightenment, theoretically, or colonialism, practically. This does not mean that these cultures cannot or should not be studied, but it requires a different relationship to the problem of knowledge. Even if these cultures accept the project of the sciences of the human, what might be involved for them is a different meaning of both human constitution and the constitution of a human science.

Second, historians of religion should undertake more studies of religion in their own cultural traditions. Such studies are needed to reveal in a precise manner the ambiguity and valences of the sacred in a culture that forms the tradition of the interpreter. Studies of this kind might also cause a shift in the meaning of otherness; the constitution of the other is not simply formed by geographies. Some studies of this kind are already appearing from the pens of social historians.

Fernand Braudel's *Mediterranean* is an example of a form of this work. A work of this scope devoted to religious matters could very well change methodological parameters. I have in mind another work, that of Lionel Rothkrug. Rothkrug's study, *Religious Practices and Collective Perceptions: Hidden Homologies in the Renaissance and Reformation* is devoted to the cult of relics in the late medieval period. In this work he establishes the relationship between power and place as these relate to the veneration of relics. From this discussion, we draw inferences regarding the relationship of religion to society in Lutheran and imperial traditions. His study, which began as an analysis of relics, draws a direct relation between this primordium of the West and some of its major philosophical presuppositions.

> Consider, for example, Kant's concept of the moral life. The Kantian actor recognizes no moral law outside his own judgment, for, in every moral decision he must act always as if he were a cosmic legislator about to promulgate a universal law. Conceiving moral life to originate in sources outside the sphere of social or cultural fact, Kant describes an autonomous moral will—it determines itself entirely within itself—that imposes upon the individual an absolute duty to transcend his own social environment in pursuit of the goals of the universality, completeness and totality. . . . But the point to emphasize is that German intellectuals in the eighteenth century were receptive to Kantian or to some other radically cognitive type of moral philosophy because neither they nor their predecessors in previous centuries had ever thought themselves to be members of a civil society.[25]

Rothkrug's study has the merit of showing how certain philosophical principles that are part and parcel of the discussion of objectivity are rooted in specific religious orientations. Marshall Hodgson's *The Venture of Islam* is one of the few studies of another religion that carefully lays out cultural presuppositions and thus undertakes a critical examination of the signifying nature of the context of the study, in his case Islam. These signifying tendencies have to do with the precommitment of the interpreter, the range of cultural biases, not simply about Islam, but about civilization, maps, history, etc. What would otherwise appear as sheer pedantry in his work is transformed into an essay on the role of signification in a disciplinary approach to another culture.

This leads to another kind of study. I call this "the history of the study" type of study. Some studies of this genre have already appeared, such as Eric J. Sharpe's *Comparative Religion: A History*. Sharpe's work is a good and readable text covering the entire range of approaches to the study of religion. More precise studies come to mind: Steiner, *Taboo;* Lévi-Strauss, *Totemism;* Guy Welbon's *Nirvana;* and Benjamin Keen's *The Image of the Aztecs.* These studies enable us to see the history of the changing meanings and fluctuations of what on one level was supposed to be an objective datum. They show the interrelationship of interpreter and the object of interpretation. More studies of this kind dealing with various religions and various forms of data should be undertaken. The development of a "historical phenomenology" from studies of this kind is a possibility.[26]

Now that several disciplines of the human sciences find themselves in the same situation, if not impasse, as our discipline, discourse with them could be fruitful. In my own case, I am thinking of social historians, anthropologists, philosophical psychoanalysts. Our understanding and methods, especially as related to a theory of praxis, might enable us to supplement our understanding of the theoretical and doctrinal meaning of religion.

I should finally like to see us develop a body of studies devoted to the religious situation of contact. I am not here referring to what is called syncretism. I would include that kind of meaning in my definition, but I intend the situation of contact itself as a religious mode. First of all, a study of the contact situation of the West with other cultures should be undertaken. The beginnings of studies of this sort devoted to Euro-American and Euro-African contacts are already in the making. On the American scene, Frances Jennings's *The Invasion of America* and Michael Taussig's *The Devil and Commodity Fetishism* represent this type of study. For Africa, there is Sheila Walker's study of the Harrist Church and Karen E. Field's *Revival and Rebellion in Colonial Central Africa.*[27]

Second, situations of contact between the several other religious traditions in various parts of the world would afford a range of meaning for these religious modes. These types of studies obviously provide us with more materials, but the poverty of materials has never been our basic problem. I have suggested studies of this kind so that we might begin a new kind of discourse in the study of religion.

The anticipations for a science of religion, a *Religionswissenschaft,* have not been fulfilled; these expectations have been simply postponed from one generation to the next. One might ask whether such expectations are legitimate. I am beginning to have my doubts. We all stand in appreciation and awe of the work that has been accomplished through making use of what we have learned from this history of our discipline. But is a "science" in the Enlightenment sense the proper receptacle of these meanings? I am suggesting that the human science that would be the proper receptacle will develop when the shadows surrounding the interpreter and his culture as "otherness" are made a part of the total hermeneutical task. Our goal would then not be a science, but a serious human discourse.

Notes

1. Ralph Barton Perry, *The Thought and Character of William James,* vol. 2 (London: Oxford University Press, Humphrey Milford, 1935), p. 501.
2. *The Journal of Religion* 2, no. 6 (November 1922), pp. 577–587; and *The Journal of Religion* 6, no. 1 (January 1926), pp. 17–40.
3. *The Journal of Religion* 2, no. 6, pp. 578–579.
4. Ibid., pp. 582–583.
5. Ibid., p. 587.
6. *The Journal of Religion* 6, no. 1, p. 18.
7. Ibid., p. 33, italics added.
8. *The Journal of Religion* 5, no. 4 (July 1925), p. 439.
9. *The Journal of Religion* 3, no. 1 (January 1923), pp. 89ff.
10. *The Journal of Religion* 25, no. 2 (April 1945), p. 140, italics added.
11. See especially his *Sociology of Religion* (Chicago: University of Chicago Press, 1944). One of the epigraphs to this volume is that of William

James from his *The Varieties of Religious Experience*. The statement is as follows, "The divine can mean no single quality, it must mean a group of qualities, by being champion of which in alternation, different men may all find worthy missions." This orientation might seem to be antithetical in Wach's program for a "science of religion" and the *sui generis* nature of the religious experience. In my opinion Wach interpreted James's statement more in terms of expression than of experience, and it was at the level of experience that he sought the unitary nature of religion. Cf. Ernst Troeltsch's review of James's *Varieties*... in "Empiricism and Platonism in the Philosophy of Religion," *Harvard Theological Review* 5 (1912): 401–422. In addition, see Wach's *Types of Religious Experience* (Chicago: University of Chicago Press, 1951); *The Comparative Study of Religions*, ed. J. M. Kitagawa (New York: Columbia University Press, 1958). Also Joseph M. Kitagawa's commentaries on the work of Wach in "Joachim Wach et la sociologie de la religion," *Archives de Sociologie des Religions* 1 (January–June 1956): 25–40; *Joachim Wach—Vorlesungen* (Leiden: E. J. Brill, 1963). For an insightful critical review of Wach's method and pedagogy, see Kees Bolle's review article of Wach's posthumous *Understanding and Believing*, "Wach's Legacy: Reflexions on a New Book," *History of Religions* 10, no. 1 (August 1970): 80–90. Bolle points to a fundamental ambiguity in Wach. On the one hand he is eager to defend the validity of non-Christian religions against real or supposed attacks and thus he speaks of general revelation; on the other hand, he as often speaks of the uniqueness of Jesus Christ and special or final revelation. This ambiguity matches his admiration for works such as James's *Varieties* while still espousing a systematic and *sui generis* understanding of the nature of religion.

12. Joachim Wach, *The Comparative Study of Religions*, ed. Joseph M. Kitagawa (New York: Columbia University Press, 1958), p. 2.
13. Kees Bolle, "Wach's Legacy: Reflexions on a New Book," *History of Religions* 10, no. 1 (August 1970): 81.
14. Mircea Eliade and Joseph Kitagawa, eds., *The History of Religions: Essays in Methodology* (Chicago: University of Chicago Press, 1959), pp. 86–107.
15. Mircea Eliade, *Journal of Bible and Religion* 31, no. 2 (April 1963); republished in *The Quest* (Chicago: University of Chicago Press, 1964), pp. 12–36.
16. Ibid., p. 98; *The Quest*, p. 12.
17. Ibid., p. 107.
18. Mircea Eliade,"Crisis and Renewal in the History of Religions," *History of Religions* 5 (1965): 1–17; reprinted in *The Quest*, pp. 55–71. Quote is from *The Quest*, pp. 60–61.
19. Ibid., p. 7 and pp. 60–61, respectively.
20. See the issue of the *Journal of Religion* devoted to the history of religions, vol. 52, no. 2 (April 1972). This issue contains the following articles: "Is a Science of Religion Possible?" pp. 107–133, by Hans H. Penner and Edward A. Yonan; Jonathan Z. Smith's "The Wobbling Pivot," pp. 134–149; Jay J. Kim, "Belief or Anamnesis: Is a Rapprochement between History of Religions and Theology Possible?" pp. 150–169; Douglas Allen, "Mircea Eliade's Phenomenological Analysis of Religious Experience," pp. 170–186. See also Hans H. Penner's "The Poverty of Functionalism," *History of Religions* 11, no. 1 (August 1971), pp. 91–97; Jonathan Z. Smith's collected essays in *Map Is Not Territory* (Leiden,

1978), and *Imagining Religion* (Chicago, 1982); Charles H. Long, "Prolegomenon to a Religious Hermeneutic," *History of Religions* 6, no. 3 (February 1967); "Human Centers," *Soundings* 61, no. 3 (Fall 1978), pp. 400–414; "The Study of Religion: Its Nature and Its Discourse," Inaugural Lecture of the Department of Religious Studies, University of Colorado, Boulder, Colorado, October 7, 1980. All of these studies express a tension between the science of religion and hermeneutics as an interpretive mode within this science. These discussions range from the problem of logical and definitional meanings within religious studies to those of contingencies within the study of religion. The issue of contingencies stems from what one may call a premature consistency regarding the universality of the nature of religion as this is understood on the level of a science of religion and the empirical historical meaning of religion.

21. See note 10, above.
22. "Prolegomenon."
23. Marcel Griaule, *Dieu d'eau* (Paris: Fayard, 1966), p. 225.
24. Jonathan Z. Smith, "Wobbling Pivot," p. 146.
25. Lionel Rothkrug, *Religious Practices and Collective Perceptions: Hidden Homologies in the Renaissance and Reformation,* Historical Reflections, Vol. 7, no. 1, Spring 1980, University of Waterloo, Ontario, Canada, p. 187.
26. Cf. Marshall Hodgson, *The Venture of Islam,* 3 vol. (Chicago: University of Chicago Press, 1974); Eric J. Sharpe, *Comparative Religion* (London, 1975); Franz Steiner, *Taboo* (London, 1956); Claude Lévi-Strauss, *Totemism,* trans. by R. Needham (Boston, 1963); Guy Welbon, *The Buddhist Nirvana and Its Western Interpreters* (Chicago, 1968); Benjamin Keen, *The Aztec Image in Western Thought* (New Brunswick, 1971).
27. See Francis Jennings, *The Invasion of America* (Chapel Hill, 1975); Michael Taussig, *The Devil and Commodity Fetishism in South America* (Chapel Hill, 1980); Sheila Walker, *The Religious Revolution in the Ivory Coast* (Chapel Hill, 1982); Karen Field, *Revival and Rebellion in Colonial Central Africa* (in press).

The Foundations of the History of Religions and Its Future Task

Kurt Rudolph

The following numbered paragraphs outline concisely my understanding of the meaning, task, and object of the history of religions (*Religionswissenschaft*):

1. Because the history of religions arose in the Enlightenment, it is today still bound by the Enlightenment's demand for tolerance, objectivity, critical judgment, and humanitarianism. To these demands the nineteenth century added a legacy of history, philology, and comparison. In the twentieth century, the history of religions has been broadened by the addition of sociology and psychology.[1]

2. The philological-historical orientation of the history of religions established in the nineteenth century orients the discipline toward a universal "science of culture" (*Kulturwissenschaft*). This orientation may be seen especially in the works of H. Usener and A. Dieterich.[2] The special character of the history of religions, however, lies in its combination of philology, history, and comparison. Being synchronic, the comparative or systematic method supplements the diachronic (historical) method. In their "dialectical" interdependence, both methods determine the relative autonomy and integrity of the history of religions and make their specific contribution to its hermeneutics.

3. The traditional concept of religion is not appropriate as the object of the history of religions. That concept cannot be justified on historical, comparative-systematic, or hermeneutical grounds. Historically speaking, for example, there are only religions, not religion. In the foreground stand *Sachverhalte* (facts), which can be considered "re-

ligious" according to a threefold frame of reference, that is, through the independence and interdependence of the scholar's tradition (his prior understanding or *Vorverständnis*), the object of scholarly investigation (foreign traditions), and the framework of scientific methodology underlying our inquiry.[3] One may also add the factor of time, which, together with factors of culture and geography, the historian of religions must take into account. The critical task of the history of religions is to master the problems in each procedural step and thus conceive of "religion" as a function and integral part of society and culture.

4. Knowledge of subject matter and knowledge of methodology belong together; they depend on one another. There is no specifically religio-scientific methodology, but the close ties between the philological-historical and comparative-systematic procedures mentioned in the preceding paragraph, and also between these two and the sociological and psychological methods, are central to the history of religions.[4] The discipline can accept neither a special intuitive, "phenomonological" method (in the sense of G. van der Leeuw) nor the exclusive claim of a method of "understanding" (*Verstehen*). "Understanding" (*Verstehen*) the meaning and intention of a *Sachverhalt* (fact) and "explaining" its causal nexus according to scientific rules belong together. Neither can be divided from nor opposed to the other. The "self-understanding of the believer" cannot be a criterion for truth or correctness in the history of religions. Here, ultimately, the rules of scientific method apply, rules that demand from the scholar a critical distance. Likewise, the scholar must suspend religious judgments and prejudgments. The history of religions is a relatively value-free and objective pursuit. Its duty is to know; it cannot succumb to passivity, nor can it lack critical acumen.[5]

5. The practical dimension of the history of religions is indirect but nonetheless real.[6] The discipline functions to emancipate and critique the ideologies of traditionally ossified and naïve religious self-understandings.[7] Thus it is significant—albeit indirectly—for the Third World. In that setting, the history of religions reflects critically on the Third World's own traditions, and as a result it leads to tolerance and to the removal of religious prejudices.[8] The history of religions also expands one's own self-understanding and thus helps to remove dangerous ethnocentrisms and to overcome outdated modes of thought (see below).

These five paragraphs summarize—almost too briefly—my view of the history of religions. One might well ask, What should the future tasks of this discipline be? What is its relevance to the problems of the present time? To answer these questions, I begin with several comments on philology.

To my mind, philology is very instructive for the hermeneutical problems of the history of religions.[9] The primary hermeneutical question asks how a discipline or science obtains a perception of its object, in the case of the history of religions, how this discipline obtains a perception of the so-called religious facts. In the history of religions, literate traditions, and consequently texts, stand in the foreground. Thus, the discipline's hermeneutical situation is related to that of philology and literary studies, and to a considerable extent, the history of religions engages in both these pursuits. The foundations of the history of religions lie in the understanding of religious texts.

Peter Szondi has written,

> Philology is dynamic, not only because, like all other sciences, it is constantly changing through new points of view and through the accumulation of new knowledge. It is also dynamic because it consists only of a continuous confrontation with the text, only of the uninterrupted correction of knowledge on the basis of what one encounters, on the basis of the understanding of the poetic world.[10]

Philological knowledge arises in the continuous interplay between perception and understanding. Without a doubt, the reciprocal relation between "facticity" and interpretation decisively influences research and the attainment of knowledge. Thus, it is *not* true that "philology" as a discipline is unaware that, in the explanation of individual facts, the scope of an interpretation influences the results of research.

> Any argument which intends to work only with facts shatters on the insufficient thought it has given to presuppositions in the theory of perception. It will never be sufficiently thought out so long as it trusts blindly in the facts. Interpretation may not set aside the facts which the text and its history provide, but likewise the appeal to the facts may not ignore the conditions under which the facts are perceived.[11]

There is a sort of dialectical relation here, which lays bare the state of the hermeneutical problem in religio-historical work: "On the one hand, the demonstrable character of the factual is disclosed only by interpretation. On the other, the factual shows interpretation the way it must proceed. This symbiosis of evidence and perception manifests the so-called hermeneutical circle."[12]

This insight is important for the philological research which is fundamental to the history of religions. The "symbiosis of evidence and perception," which is essential to both comparative and historical investigation, resides in the insight that

> evidence is the adequate criterion to which philological perception must subject itself. In evidence the conditioned nature of the language of the facts

> (*Tatsachen*) is neither ignored nor misunderstood; rather, that language is understood to be subjectively conditioned and mediated in subjective perception. Therefore it is understood first and foremost in its true objectivity.[13]

From these brief remarks on philological perception, it is clear that the history of religions is well-advised to avail itself of philology as the point of departure for its own work. Philology does not reduce to naked "facts" and their simple, direct interpretation. Rather, through careful reflection it relates facts to the researcher's strategies of interpretation, his experience, his knowledge and his place in time (his "life-world"). This insight also contributes to the way in which future work in the history of religions can profit from looking toward its neighboring disciplines and their methodological knowledge.[14]

But methodological discussion will not be the primary factor determining the present and future position of the history of religions, even if such discussion ponders fundamental problems and adopts significant positions. The discipline's present and future situation will be defined by a series of other points which I will summarize below. On the one hand, I will be concerned with formulating a strong profile for the discipline (which implies a firm place in academia, although I will not be able to discuss the institutional setting here). On the other hand, I will advocate a new collaboration with neighboring disciplines, especially the humanities. Both sides, naturally, are bound closely together.

1. After the history of religions had gained and defended its autonomy and integrity, especially in opposition to theology—or at least after it had done so in large measure and had achieved a clear profile—the discipline needed close contact with the other humanistic studies. In the early days, its relations with these areas were very close. To some extent, they continue even today. History, philology (the scientific study of regions), ethnology (anthropology), and sociology have been and still are highly relevant to religio-historical investigations. They help free the history of religions from theological or philosophical ambitions, a legacy from the days when the history of religions was the "handmaiden" of theology which still partly governs the discipline's work.

The study of history has developed methods and procedures of great significance for the history of religions and its work[15]: the comparison of regional and transregional processes; the application of sociological methods, especially in relation to the mutual dependence of historical (political-economic) and ideological events (first noticed by Karl Marx, then reformulated by Max Weber)[16]; quantitative methods and ethnological investigations.

Philologists have broadened their field considerably by including new views in literary studies such as structuralist and text-linguistic approaches; and ethnology, one of our discipline's oldest "sisters," has made great progress. Not only has it refined its field methods and evaluated its underlying ethnocentrisms self-critically. It has made strides also in the utilization of assembled material. I think here above all of the ground-breaking work of Victor Turner on the ritual process and its social symbolism and of Mary Douglas, especially on concepts of purity. Both of these anthropologists have used new methods from social psychology. The interpretations of C. Lévi-Strauss are just as significant, even if we should not overlook that in the end his ahistorical approach produces empty binary oppositions. Together with Lévi-Strauss I should mention the work of Edmund Leach.[17]

On sociology I need to say little. Sociology has dominated religio-historical investigation for some time. It has in fact almost annexed the history of religions to itself (consider the "scientific study of religion"). This annexation goes too far. Still, *homo religiosus* is and always has been at the same time *homo sociologus*. The history of religions can never abandon this insight. Religion as an object of religio-historical research is primarily a social phenomenon, even if it does not merely evaporate into the social.[18] When the history of religions replaced its traditional, religio-theological premises with premises that were historical and sociological in character, it gained a great deal. The adoption of these premises ultimately furthered the discipline's emancipation from theology. They should not be abandoned in the course of its future development.

Despite the strongly "unphilosophical" character of the history of religions, the discipline can and must cultivate relations with a particular philosophical train of thought, linguistic philosophy, and the "logical propaedeutic" which it has developed. Because this philosophical orientation can contribute to clarifying terminology and fundamental theoretical propositions, historians of religions should take more account of it than they have in the past. The "areas" of Wittgenstein's "language games" are relevant to the history of religions. They can be understood as analogous to what in history are cultural and religious worlds. Relevant, too, is the inference Wittgenstein drew in his lucid comments on J. G. Frazer's *The Golden Bough:* "A whole mythology is deposited in our language."[19] We must evaluate both our colloquial and our scientific language self-critically if we are to obtain a better, more refined terminology. Such reflection is one of our discipline's future tasks. It will also directly affect the construction of theories. As Wittgenstein showed with reference to Frazer, our language is dependent upon unconscious religious and cultural presuppositions. The history of theories in the history of religions requires a new treatment in this light, a treatment that considers more than the changing sets of factual materials from ethnology and history which the history of religions has drawn upon. "Logical propaedeutics" should serve the discipline as a preparatory course in rational discourse; it should supply a terminology that is clear and concise.[20]

2. Thus, in the future, the history of religions must collaborate with the humanities more closely. Borrowing, adapting, and discussing newly developed methods and research strategies should prove especially helpful in establishing this new relationship. Several methods and strategies, some of which I have already mentioned, may be singled out for comment:

a. ethology, or the investigation of behavior. Since man obviously seems to be a ritual being,[21] ethology is significant above all in the study of rites and rituals.[22] The study of history, too, has already applied ethology to problems of historical change.[23]

b. ethnological research into structures and symbols, as carried out by Victor Turner and Mary Douglas, whose works are also important for ritual and myth.

c. psychological role theory, which can treat tradition's power to shape character better than can the traditional, individualistic psychology of religion, oriented to the "concept of the soul" and to "experience."[24]

d. research into sociological structures, as in the analysis of *Homo hierarchicus* made by Louis Dumont, a successor of Durkheim and Mauss.[25]

e. literary theories, especially textual linguistics and semantics.[26]

f. the historical study of society, important for connections between religious elements, society, and politics, and also applicable to the study of the motivating power of religious ideologies.[27]

3. It would be a mistake if the close collaboration of the history of religions with other disciplines led to a renewed attempt to reduce the history of religions to these disciplines instead of to its integration with them. The future of the history of religions cannot lie in such a reduction. More than it has in the past, the history of religions must successfully formulate and, through the results of its research, successfully demonstrate the unique contribution it can make to the other humanities at the same time that it remains open to being stimulated by them. To my mind, this is one of the most difficult, but one of the

most necessary, tasks facing future work in the history of religions. Only by accomplishing this task can the discipline firmly assume its place within the humanities. I will not recur here to the object of religio-historical research (religions, in the sense of religious traditions, belief-systems, and forms). Such an argument has been tried repeatedly, but the specific object of inquiry does not guarantee the unique contribution which religio-historical work as such will make; at most, it guarantees the discipline's claim to be the *ex officio* trustee for this object.[28]

The difficulty in specifying the discipline's unique contribution lies in the fact that in the history of religions this problem is traditionally bound up with the question of religious truth. Thus it leads very quickly to the dangerous waters of theology or philosophy. To resort to an inborn human predisposition to religion—a residuum of the "natural religion" of the Enlightenment—or to resort to the notion of a divine, immortal kernel in humanity would provide precise deductions or presuppositions with which to answer this question. Such deductions or presuppositions have been seen—and on occasion are still seen—as the ultimately inalienable and unique contribution which the history of religions can make. Little opposition can be mustered against such a view, once the claim is advanced that the history of religions is a component—or a "handmaiden"—of theology, whether a new form of the old *theologia naturalis* (as with Søderblom) or, more recently, the "theology of religion." This claim, however, simply reduces the discipline and destroys its independence. Such a reduction has also been attempted from the other side by the humanities, although in an undogmatic manner (consider the approach of the sociology of religion). When the discipline's atheological (but not antitheological), historical, and philological foundations are preserved, historians of religions may adduce several points as comprising, at least in part, their discipline's particular contribution:

a. comparison, in a regional as well as a universal sense. The purpose of comparison is to place the individual religious element in a larger context, whether as parallel, homologue, or contrast.[29]

b. the inductive rather than the deductive search for "universals" in the sense of religious elements that are found globally. Only such universals can provide a basis from which to answer far-reaching questions about religious constants in history.

c. the question of meaning, that is, the question of the meaning and the purpose of religious assertions (for example, worldviews) in history, including both that which motivates these assertions and that which they in turn effect.[30]

d. the question of the change and the predominance of religious assertions, for example, of images and symbols (M. Eliade).

e. the question of the contribution of religious elements, worldviews, mythologems, symbols, and rituals, to human anthropology, especially from a historical point of view; that is, the contribution of "religion" to the origin of *Homo sapiens*, his place in the world and in history.[31] Clearly, this problem or area of investigation departs from direct religio-historical work. It is, however, a speculative consequence of that work which should not merely be left to theology, anthropology or sociology, and philosophy. Here, too, the history of religions has something to contribute to other disciplines. It can often speak a word of correction.

These five issues circumscribe, it seems to me, the primary difficulties that future work in the history of religions will have to address, for the discipline must establish its right to a special place in the realm of the humanities. In establishing that place, the history of religions of today and tomorrow will do well to shape its work with an eye to a number of points:

a. *The valence of the cultic.* The preponderate orientation of the history of religions toward "ideology"—whether mythology, cosmology, or theology—should recede in favor of a greater emphasis on the practical field of the cultus. At least from a historical point of view, cultus stands at the center of any religion. Religious communities are chiefly cultic communities, not associations of individual myth-makers or cosmologists. To my mind, only that which contributes to the veneration of the gods (powers) and God in praxis, or rather, that which is related to this praxis, is relevant to religion. It is from practice that mythology derives its religious significance; otherwise, it is only literature. This conception carries *ad absurdum* the prevalent view that seeks religious facts only in ideologies and worldviews and that understands "religion" only in those terms. That historian of religions is mistaken who believes that mythology as such, including symbolics, provides access to the "heart of religion."

b. *Self-critical reflection on and updating of traditional theories in the history of religions,* from fetishism to the structuralist interpretation of myth. This is one of the central problems of religio-historical hermeneutics. The traditional theories are attempts and hypotheses that seek to understand *and* explain the predominant religious forms. Without them, history of religions is not possible. Beginnings in this direction have been made repeatedly.[32] The updating and critical sifting of traditional hermeneutical schemas, which belong to the realm of religio-historical terminology, testify to the dynamic character of the discipline. New methods and research strategies cannot be taken over successfully without first investigating their origin and the scope of their reference. That is, new methods and strategies must be adapted, not merely adopted.

c. *The ideological-critical side of religio-historical work,* which I have discussed elsewhere.[33] Religio-historical methods bracket the religious claim to truth and profanely "explain" religious traditions and assertions scientifically by recourse to both philological-historical and comparative procedures. They acknowledge neither revelation nor religious intuition, and as a result they are implicitly ideological-critical. To be sure, the religious self-understanding of the faithful is also subjected to critical reason, otherwise the history of religions would not be possible. But to accept the self-understanding of the faithful as a criterion for truth and falsity in the history of religions surrenders the foundations of science to the object of investigation. The history of religions would itself become a religious subject. Despite protests to the contrary, individual practitioners of the discipline have already made this surrender. But the history of religions is the *history* of religious faith; it is not such faith itself. This distinction, decisive for the future of the discipline, should always be maintained.

4. Today every branch of learning is asked what it can contribute to solving the problems of the modern world. The history of religions cannot remain sequestered from such questions. As a component of history and philology, the history of religions contributes to our present awareness of history. It adds to the accumulation of knowledge which improves our self-understanding, our image of past and present humanity, and the orientation of our life-activities through historical consciousness. But the history of religions also has specific tasks which may not flow directly and immediately from its work, but which it must still ponder and take into account. History and the investigation of history are able to alter human consciousness on a most profound level. This ability can be seen above all by comparing cultures possessing a developed historical consciousness with cultures that are still not infused—or not completely infused—with such a consciousness. The process of developing a historical consciousness and its consequences cannot be reversed or avoided. Only totally useless romantic and pious desires dream that it can. Such dreams divert the process from its current course without steering or guiding it into paths that would be useful for the present or the future. "An awareness of history is not something which humans can either have or not have; it is universally human"; it is grounded in the inner historicity of human life itself.[34] Because human activity is itself historical, humans have in the end a historical consciousness. What is new about

the modern awareness of history is that it is critical. It relates critically to traditions that have been passed down and it reflects the historical dimensions of time—past, present, and future—as distinct but also as mediated through processes. In the modern sense, history as the content of consciousness is knowledge of the temporal changes which human beings and their world have undergone.

Without a doubt, the growing world-consciousness of our time is significant for the history of religions. Not only does our consciousness require "global thought" in synchronic terms. It requires global thought in diachronic terms, too. In both the synchronic and diachronic aspects, the world of religions—their traditions and their convictions—possesses an important and traceable dimension which cannot be overlooked, a dimension which, as we see over and over again, produces effects that may even be directly political (as in Iran). To my mind, the history of religions must take an interest in this dimension, which was, is, and always will be one of its concerns. As a result, it must conceive of religions and their traditions as contributing to human growth and to the formation of an image of humanity. Through its work—and thus, with a thoroughly critical spirit—the history of religions should demonstrate that human beings as such are incomplete without religious dimensions.

To be sure, man is not *homo religiosus* from birth, but he is still *homo religiosus,* just as he is *homo sociologus* or *Homo sapiens.* The "wisdom" that marks off humanity has, above all, religious roots. Apart from these roots man cannot be understood. To say this is not to regress to the religious a priori of former times. It is an insight into the process by which humanity has become the present *homo historicus* and *homo technicus.* Understanding past and present reality—and in "reality" I include also that which Karl Jaspers has very wisely designated the "encompassing," the *Umgreifende*—is not possible apart from a consideration of religious history. With the help of "religion," human beings have made their world intelligible in practice (cultus) and idea (myth), and they will continue to do so.[35] There is no other way to convey meaning, even if, as we know and experience, "religion" will be transformed into the expression of the transcendent in that which "encompasses" our being [*Dasein*], an expression that will have nothing more to do with the mythological world of gods and spirits (including the biblical worldview).[36] The history of religions can make known this always encountered but ultimately inexplicable "residue" of human being, even if it cannot directly express it.

Thus, it remains for the history of religions, today and in the future, to investigate religions as essential parts of human history and thereby in its own way to keep this dimension alive. Since the history of religions is a science, its business is critical and historical reflection, not the propagation of religious claims or messages. Consequently, as I see it, the discipline's contribution, above all its contribution to the unavoidable and irreversible process of forming historical consciousness, is precisely the depiction of the world of religions. As I have already said, in doing this the discipline gains significance for the Third World. It opens a new avenue from which to approach tradition, a new avenue which is desirable in the wake of the modern destruction or undermining of tradition. This approach is not immediate and direct but is mediated by the history of religions.

But the history of religions has also attained new importance for the Euro-American world, which is still broadly characterized by Christianity. Its significance derives from the movement for dialogue between various religions and confessions and, related to this movement, from the already mentioned elimination, or better, the curtailment, of ethnocentrism. In the end, ethnocentrism cannot be rooted out completely, unless one surrenders all humanity; but both sides can become aware of ethnocentrism and can thereby keep it within bounds.

Naturally, the history of religions cannot lead directly to dialogue, but it is not uninterested in dialogue. Through dialogue the history of religions receives an increased amount of public attention, especially in theological circles. On this topic, I would like to cite Hans Küng[37]:

> 1. Only if we seek to understand others'—our neighbors'—beliefs and values, rites and symbols, can we truly understand people.
> 2. Only if we seek to understand others' faith can we really understand our *own*: its strengths and weaknesses, its constants and variables.
> 3. Only if we seek to understand others' faith can we discover that common ground which, despite all differences, can become the basis for a peaceful life in this world together.

These unusual remarks by a leading ecumenical theologian are not new to the history of religions. The discipline's founders—for instance, F. Max Müller—were already aware of such ideas. In fact, at the beginning, they formed the discipline's credo in opposition to the orthodox theological tradition. If today they are expressed on the theological and church-historical side—unfortunately still too infrequently—the history of religions should not ignore that development. Rather, it should see its work as contributing to it. As much as ever, knowledge is power, and a knowledge of history, above all of religious errors and animosities, is not without influence on changing consciousnesses within the various religions themselves. Thus, the history of religions is challenged more strongly than ever before to transmit to the public correct knowledge about its field of study.[38]

One aspect of ethnocentrism as it pertains to the history of religions is the relation of human beings to their environment. This issue has rapidly become one of the most pressing questions concerning human survival, next to the direct threat which our weapons of destruction pose to human life on earth. The attitude of the biblical, that is, the Judaeo-Christian, tradition to nature and the environment has been raised for discussion. Leading personages—theologians among them—have reflected critically on this tradition's role, which has not been without effect on the development of technology. We now experience the consequences of technological development, to which the profanization or secularization of the relation between man and nature has contributed decisively.[39]

The history of religions knows other attitudes to nature or the environment, such as the attitudes of Hinduism and Buddhism. These attitudes give historians of religions something to say to environmental issues. I do not mean to summon us to flee to lands that are temporally and spatially distant, but to contribute to the universal image of humanity, which our Western conceptions advocate only in a particular form. Here, too, it should be apparent that the history of religions is a universal discipline. To be sure, it often disintegrates into particular research and specialties. Specialization is unavoidable. But by virtue of its object and its claim, the history of religions holds the entire globe before its eyes.

My thoughts on the situation of the world today with reference to its relevance for the history of religions make clear that the history of religions is not and does not need to be antiquarian. It arose from curiosity about that which was foreign. It was—and still is—sustained by the tolerance promoted by the Enlightenment and by advocates of religious harmony. It was shaped by the scientific ethos, the unconditioned pursuit of truth and self-criticism. With this heritage, the history of religions is just as young and dynamic as it was in its beginnings, when it understood its tasks and its claims for the present and the future not merely as those of a particular human science but as the tasks and claims of a science of universal humanity.

Notes

1. Cf. my "Basic Positions of *Religionswissenschaft*," *Religion* 11 (1981): 97–107; originally presented at the Fourteenth International Congress of the International Association for the History of Religions in Winnepeg, Canada, August 17–22, 1980.
2. Ibid., pp. 98–99.
3. Ibid., p. 101.
4. Cf. my "Das Problem der Autonomie und Integrität der Religionswissenschaft," *Nederlands Theologisch Tijdschrift* 27 (1973): 105–131.

5. See "Basic Positions," p. 104. I am quite aware that in recent times the European-American ideal or image of "science" has been criticized as ethnocentric, especially by non-Europeans. To be sure, this ideal displays a specific, ethnic heritage, but it is a heritage that has been, or will be, received worldwide and cannot be surrendered unless one wishes to slip back into a precritical, prescientific view of the world, a slippage that in practice is possible only in individual cases. Properly understood, "science" is a human concern or dimension, even if it does not establish itself as an absolute which we cannot renounce. It is directly responsible for the destruction of ethnocentric, in our case, of religious, prejudices, which have led in the past not to an understanding of "others" but to conflict with them. The European ideal of science is rooted in humanism. To that degree, it is founded on universality and renounces the false ethnocentrisms, or better, "egoisms," and the subjectivism that dominated earlier times.
6. Ibid., pp. 106–107; see also now U. Berner in *Zeitschrift für Religions- und Geistesgeschichte* 35 (1983): 113ff. Berner is correct in saying that a critique of ideologies does not grow without a break (*bruchlos*) from religio-historical work but is rather a consequence of it.
7. Cf. my article, "Die 'ideologiekritische' Funktion der Religionswissenschaft," *Numen* 25 (1978): 17–39. Here I have used the notion of a critique of ideologies (*Ideologiekritik*) in a more neutral sense as given directly with the scientific attitude toward the worlds of traditional religions. As I have said above (cf. n. 5), this sense is part of the humanistic ideal of science in the fields of historical, philological, and comparative investigation. Perhaps the expression has been too strongly stamped by sociology and political science to be at home in the history of religions. In that case, we should find another term for the undeniable state of affairs resulting from the attitude and the practice of religio-historical (*wissenschaftliche*, "scientific") work vis-à-vis religious traditions and faiths: "religion" becomes an object, as in an anatomist's dissection (cf. my remarks in L. Honko, ed., *Science of Religion: Studies in Methodology* [The Hague, 1979]). To do otherwise is not possible, unless one impugns completely a scientific investigation of this aspect of human becoming and being. That one must be aware that such a procedure occurs reflexively is just as much of a platitude as the assertion that science neither can nor wishes to replace "religion" (as has been observed in many quarters where a "scientific Weltanschauung" common to the nineteenth century is propagated and where as a result science is given quasi-religious characteristics, characteristics which are not innate to it since at heart science is a method, not a belief). R. R. Cavanaugh and T. William Hall also stress the emancipatory effect of the study of religions; see their *Introduction to the Study of Religion* (New York: Harper & Row, 1978), pp. 27–28.
8. "Die 'ideologiekritische' Funktion," p. 37; "Basic Positions," p. 105.
9. With reference to what follows, see Peter Szondi, "Über philologische Erkenntnis," *Hölderlinstudien*, 3d edition (Frankfurt am Main: Suhrkamp, 1977), pp. 9–35 (originally published in *Die neue Rundschau* 73 [1962]: 146–165).
10. Ibid., p. 10.
11. Ibid., p. 25.
12. Ibid., pp. 26–27.

13. Ibid., pp. 27–28.
14. Cf. also the new "historik" of Jörn Rüsen, *Historische Vernunft* (Göttingen, 1983), who follows Droysen and Dilthey.
15. See my "Das Problem," esp. pp. 116ff.
16. Cf. R. von Dülmen, "Religionsgeschichte in der historischen Sozialforschung," *Geschichte und Gesellschaft* 6 (1980): 36–59.
17. See now the summary statement of Leach's views in his *Social Anthropology* (New York: Oxford University Press, 1982). Although the book does not contain much about religion, it is not without profit for historians of religions.
18. Cf. one of the last relevant collections of articles, edited by A. W. Eister, entitled *Changing Perspectives in the Scientific Study of Religions* (New York, 1974).
19. Ludwig Wittgenstein, *Bemerkungen über Frazers "Golden Bough,"* ed. Rush Rhees (Atlantic Highlands, N.J.: Humanities Press, 1979), p. 10 (English, p. 10e). The significance of Wittgenstein's language philosophy for the hermeneutics of the history of religions is pointed out by C. W. Wood, *Theory and Understanding: A Critique of the Hermeneutics of J. Wach* (Missoula, Mont.: American Academy of Religion, 1975), pp. 84ff., 133ff.
20. Cf. W. Kamlah and P. Lorenzen, *Logische Propaedeutik: Vorschule des vernünftigen Reden,* 2d ed. (Mannheim, 1973). Such methods have been applied to terminology in the history of religions in C. Colpe, *Theologie, Ideologie, Religionswissenschaft: Demonstrationen ihrer Unterscheidung* (Munich, 1980); G. Neuf, "Religionswissenschaft aus der Sicht der analytischen Philosophie," in G. Stephenson, ed., *Der Religionswandel unserer Zeit im Spiegel der Religionswissenschaft* (Darmstadt, 1976), pp. 339–354; H. Seiwert, "Möglichkeiten und Grenzen einer Anwendung der Prinzipien des kritischen Rationalismus im Rahmen der Religionswissenschaft," unpublished *Magisterarbeit,* Bonn, 1977, and "Religiöse Bedeutung als wissenschaftliche Kategorie," *Annual Review for the Social Sciences of Religion* 5 (1981): 57–99; and K. Rudolph, "Der Beitrag der Religionswissenschaft zum Problem der sog. Entmythologisierung," *Kairos* 12 (1970): 183–207; "Religionswissenschaft als alten und neuen Wegen," *Theologische Literaturzeitung* 104 (1979): 11–34, "Synkretismus: Vom theologischen Scheltwort zum religionswissenschaftlichen Begriff," in *Humanitas religiosa: Festschrift für Haralds Biezais* (Stockholm, 1979), pp. 194–212; and "Wesen und Struktur der Sekte," *Kairos* 21 (1979):241–254. Suggestive for the narrative side of the history of religions is A. Demandt, *Metaphern für Geschichte: Sprachbilder und Gleichnisse im historisch-politischen Denken* (Munich, 1978).
21. Cf. also L. Wittgenstein, p. 7 (7e): "We could almost say, man is a ceremonious animal."
22. Cf. Robert A. Hinde's survey, *Ethology: Its Nature and Relation with Other Sciences* (New York, 1982), with bibliography. Unfortunately, the author does not refer to the history of religions. For applications of ethology to the history of religions, see W. Burkert, *Structure and History of Greek Mythology and Ritual* (Berkeley: University of California Press, 1979), and *Homo necans: The Anthropology of Ancient Greek Sacrificial Ritual and Myth* (Berkeley: University of California Press, 1983); and the symposium "Ritual in Human Adaptation," *Zygon* 18, no. 8 (September 1983), esp. E. G. d'Aquili, "The Myth-Ritual Complex: A Biogenetic Structural Analysis," pp. 247–269.

23. Cf. A. Nitschke, *Historische Verhaltensforschung* (Stuttgart, 1981).
24. Essential reading on this topic is H. Sundén, *Die Religionen und die Rollen* (Berlin, 1966); "Die Religion und die Rollen. Ein Selbstanzeigen," *Archiv für Religionspsychologie* 7 (1962): 277–281; and "Die Rollenpsychologie als heutige Aufgabe der Religionspsychologie," *Archiv für Religionspsychologie* 8 (1964): 70–81, with discussion, pp. 81–84.
25. Louis Dumont, *Homo Hierarchicus: An Essay on the Caste System* (Chicago: University of Chicago Press, 1970).
26. Cf. H. Penner, "The Problem of Semantics in the Study of Religion," in R. D. Baird, ed., *Methodological Issues in Religious Studies* (New Horizons Press, 1975), pp. 79–94, with a discussion among Penner, J. Neusner, and W. C. Smith. For a concise summary, see T. Eagleton, *Literary Theory: An Introduction* (Minneapolis, 1983); in greater depth, F. Kermode, *The Genesis of Secrecy: On Interpretation of Narrative* (Cambridge, 1979). Biblical text-linguistic study is now going on, among other places, in Uppsala, with L. Hartman, D. Hellholm, and B. Olssen.
27. Cf. Eister, and R. von Dülmen. For a concise statement, see A. Burger, *Religionszugehörigkeit und soziales Verhalten* (Göttingen, 1964), pp. 11–100.
28. Cf. my "Autonomie und Integrität," pp. 116ff.
29. Ibid., pp. 118ff.
30. Consider especially the work of Max Weber. See also G. Dux, *Die Logik der Weltbilder* (Frankfurt am Main: Suhrkamp, 1982).
31. Consider ibid., p. 149: "Religion must make the world intelligible as a whole. On this depends human self-understanding, the sensibility of a human mode of living." N. Luhmann tries to describe with precision the function of religion in terms of systematic, theoretical sociology; see his *Funktion der Religion*, 2d ed. (Frankfurt am Main, 1982) and the critical remarks by Dux, pp. 117ff.
32. See J. Z. Smith, *Map is Not Territory: Studies in the History of Religions* (Leiden, 1978), and *Imagining Religion: From Babylon to Jonestown* (Chicago: University of Chicago Press, 1982); and my introduction to the history of religions (in preparation).
33. See n. 7 above.
34. J. Rüsen, pp. 69–70.
35. Cf. Dux, p. 151: "Religion is bound to the human, existential task of thematizing the fundamental structure of reality and of inquiring into its consequences for human existence in the world (*Dasein*). Thus, there is no religion which has not constructed a cosmology. In making reality intelligible (cosmology), humans have at the same time made themselves intelligible." On the possibility of the continuation of religion in its function of formulating a meaningful worldview under the task of the subjective interpretation of a mythological past, see Dux, pp. 304ff., and n. 36 below.
36. Dux, p. 306, says correctly: "Throughout history, god and gods have found their basis in the conception of reality. Today every basis, including every rational basis, has been lost. It is not possible to escape the suspicion that every thought about the divine is only an hypothesis of human subjectivity." It is one of M. Eliade's desires (a desire not necessarily to be avoided) to show how the religious dimension has been a constant in human history. Compare my critical remarks, "Eliade und die Religionsgeschichte," in Hans Peter Duerr, ed., *Die Mitte der Welt: Festschrift Eliade* (Frankfurt am Main: Suhrkamp, 1983), pp. 49–78.

37. See W. G. Oxtoby, *The Meaning of Other Faiths* (Philadelphia: Westminster, 1983), preface, p. ix; and J. Neusner's remarks in the preface to the volume he edited under the title, *Take Judaism, for Example* (Chicago: University of Chicago Press, 1983), p. xvii, beginning with: "When we describe, analyze, and interpret religions, . . ."
38. On the lack of such a public undertaking on the part of the history of religions in West Germany and on the misinformation that commonly circulates there, see the remarks of U. Tworuschka, "Religionsgeschichte in der Öffentlichkeit," *Zeitschrift für Religions- und Geistesgeschichte* 35 (1983): 117–131. Similar investigations are also available for other countries.
39. See, for example, J. B. Cobb, *Is It Too Late?* (New York, 1972). (I owe this reference to Mrs. Christel Betz of Chicago.) Already in the nineteenth century, George Perkins Marsh had noted the destruction of nature by human beings and its devastating consequences.

The History of Religions (*Religionswissenschaft*) Then and Now

JOSEPH M. KITAGAWA

In *Elements of the Science of Religion* (1897–1899), the eminent Dutch historian of religions Cornelis P. Tiele (1830–1902) noted that more than twenty-five years had passed since Friedrich Max Müller's (1823–1900) lectures at the Royal Institute of London (later published under the title, *Introduction to the Science of Religion*). In Tiele's view, Müller's lectures were more an apologetics for the young discipline of *Religionswissenschaft* than an introduction to the discipline itself. Tiele wrote: "We are now farther advanced. The last twenty-five years have been specially fruitful for the scientific study of religion. That study has now secured a permanent place among the various sciences of the human mind."[1]

In 1924, twenty-five years after the publication of Tiele's *Elements,* Joachim Wach observed that in view of the considerable progress made in the new discipline, Tiele's book was no longer adequate. Many questions not known in Tiele's time had been raised. "There are above all a number of presuppositions for the work of Religionswissenschaft, which must be resolved before we can begin to present the basics of our discipline as an introduction. . . . My present 'Prolegomena' intends to treat a number of such questions and problems."[2] In contrast to Tiele's optimistic statement in 1899 that "[the science of religion] has now secured a permanent place among the various sciences of the human mind," Wach's observations in 1924 were much more cautious and sobering. Wach recognized that *Religionswissenschaft* still suffered from confusion concerning its methodological foundations. He sensed, therefore, the great need to articulate a clear understanding of the questions and delimitations regarding the theory and logic of the discipline.[3]

Almost forty years after the publication of Wach's *Religionswissenschaft,* Mircea Eliade addressed himself to the state of the discipline. He, too, was keenly aware that changes in the twentieth-century *Zeitgeist* had a great bearing on the development of the discipline. For example, he noted the publication in 1912 of such important works as Emile Durkheim's *Formes élémentaires de la vie religieuse (The Elementary Forms of the Religious Life),* the first volume of Wilhelm Schmidt's *Ursprung der Gottesidee (The Origin of the Idea of God),* Raffaele Pettazzoni's *La religione primitiva in Sardegna,* and C. G. Jung's *Wandlungen und Symbole der Libido,* followed by Sigmund Freud's *Totem und Tabu* the next year.[4] The various approaches to the study of religion represented by these works—sociological, ethnological, psychological, and historical—together with the phenomenological study of religion which developed a decade later "contributed highly to the *Zeitgeist* of the last generation, and their interpretations of religion still enjoy a certain prestige among nonspecialists."[5] Eliade seems to be alarmed, however, by the current state of *Religionswissenschaft:*

> Despite the manuals, periodicals, and bibliographies today available to scholars, it is progressively more difficult to keep up with the advances being made in all areas of the history of religions. Hence it is progressively more difficult to become a historian of religions. A scholar regretfully finds himself becoming a specialist in *one* religion or even in a particular period or a single aspect of that religion.[6]

In another article he states his position more explicitly:

> Let us recognize it frankly. History of religions, or comparative religion, plays a rather modest role in modern culture. When one recalls the passionate interest with which the informed public in the second half of the nineteenth century followed the speculations of Max Müller on the origin of myths and the evolution of religions and followed his polemics with Andrew Lang; when one recalls the considerable success of *The Golden Bough* . . ., one cannot contemplate the present situation without melancholy.
>
> Certainly, one could respond that in our day there is no Max Müller, Andrew Lang, or Frazer, which is perhaps true, not because today's historians or religions are inferior to them, but simply because they are more modest, more withdrawn, indeed more timid. . . . Why have the historians of religions allowed themselves to become what they are today?[7]

Whether or not we agree with Eliade's observation, those of us who are engaged in the history of religions, as well as those who have more than a casual interest in this academic enterprise, are compelled to reflect on the nature of the discipline and the various issues that confront it in our time.

Maps of Reality

One of the nagging questions haunting someone who has come from the non-Western world, as I have, is why such a discipline as the history of religions developed in Europe rather than elsewhere. Religions have been known to exist everywhere from time immemorial. Sages and thinkers in India and China have asked searching questions about the nature of religion. But the kinds of questions they raised did not lead to the development of a *Religionswissenschaft.* It is taken for granted that in every corner of the earth, each thinker, each religion, and each culture has had a "map of reality,"[8] or a schema for understanding and dealing with reality. These maps, to be sure, have undergone constant revision. And yet the kinds of questions that have been raised in the history of religions did not surface on the "maps of reality" of Orientals or Africans, nor did they become important questions on the mental horizon of Europeans until the nineteenth century.

I have long been impressed by C. P. Tiele's observation that *Religionswissenschaft* was not "founded" in the sense implied by this term, but that in the mid-nineteenth century it was "called into being *by a generally felt want* in different countries [in Europe] at the same time and as a matter of course."[9] If his observation is correct, it is important for us to try to understand (1) the "map of reality" of the mid-nineteenth-century European intellectual world which sensed a "generally felt want" for something like *Religionswissenschaft;* and (2) the map of reality that characterized the new discipline of *Religionswissenschaft.*

The Nineteenth-Century European Map of Reality

Undoubtedly the map of reality possessed by an intellectual in mid-nineteenth-century Europe was quite complex. To understand its complexity, we might consider briefly some basic characteristics of the historical developments that led up to the Enlightenment.

William S. Haas, in *The Destiny of the Mind—East and West,* suggests that in contrast to Asia, where historically a number of civilizations have stood "side by side each in juxtaposition to the others,"[10] European civilizations, by absorbing and assimilating foreign elements, followed a course toward unity from the time of the birth of Greek culture. According to Haas, Greek culture

> was a matrix of Western civilization. Then the Greek spark sprang over to cognate Rome. Henceforth, this classic culture shaped the body of medieval civilization, Rome giving to the Church its visible organization and Greek philosophical thought permeating the structure of its dogma. Europe, thus integrated by westernized Christianity, at last proceeded to the scientific and technical age, which was based on the secularization of the medieval world conception and conditioned by the interest of the Greeks in science, biology, and medicine.[11]

Running through the process of the unification of Western civilization was the notion of "evolutionary time." This Western concept of time differs markedly from that of the Orient, where time is perceived as a "formal and extraneous condition to the unfolding of civilization."[12] It is to be noted that the notion of evolution, which in itself is neutral and implies no value judgment, is not a unique Western product. What is uniquely Western is the perception of time in evolutionary terms, which in turn provides a perspective to view history as an organic whole.[13] The Western view of history was greatly influenced by the various "revealed religions"—Zoroastrianism, Judaism, Christianity, and Islam—which affirmed, in their respective ways, the notions of the history of salvation, the unity of humankind, and the *eschaton*. Inevitably, many Western religious thinkers had to wrestle with the problem of the relation between salvation history and empirical history. This was particularly the case with Christian thinkers, because they were convinced that their God had become incarnate in history. For the most part, Christian thinkers divided salvation history into two phases, the phase before Christ as *praeparatio evangelica* and the new phase starting with the Christ event. They then proceeded to use this formula to develop their philosophies of history (for example, Augustine and Joachim of Fiore). Later, Joachim's view of history was appropriated by Giambattista Vico (1668–1744) and was further secularized by Auguste Comte (1798–1857).

Meanwhile, the triumph of the Christian tradition in Europe overshadowed the Greek legacy. Greek thinkers had developed the three main themes of religious inquiry: world (cosmos), divinity, and humankind. In addition, the Sophists affirmed the autonomy of human beings over against the world (cosmos) and the gods. But under the impact of Christianity, Europe accepted for centuries the sovereignty of God over humankind and the world of nature, and the supremacy of theology over anthropology and cosmology.

While Christian Europe's map of reality acknowledged the Greek legacy only tacitly and nearly ignored the Jewish contribution, after the seventh century it had to confront the rise of Islam. Actually, as Hendrik Kraemer astutely observed, medieval Latin Christendom was greatly indebted to the world of Islam for many things, from the introduction of Greek philosophy, astronomy, and mathematics to commerical and maritime techniques and such mundane items as foods and drinks, drugs and medicaments.[14] But due to Christian Europe's notion of salvation history, it could not accept Islam's self-claimed status as the culmination of all previous revelations. It could only interpret Islam as the fulfillment of the Johannine apocalypse concerning the coming of the false prophet. This perception provided religious justification for the bloody Crusades. Subsequent religious developments in Europe (for example, the Reformation, the Counter-Reformation, and the rise of Pietism) intensified further the prejudice not only against Islam but also against other non-Christian and non-Western religions and cultures. As Norman Daniel observes, once a normal channel of communication breaks down

> under the pressure of their sense of danger, whether real or imagined, a deformed image of their enemy's beliefs takes shape in men's minds. By misapprehension and misrepresentation an idea of the beliefs and practices of one society can pass into the accepted myths of another society in a form so distorted that its relation to the original facts is sometimes barely discernible.[15]

Significantly, several factors—the establishment of the universities, the Renaissance and the Enlightenment, Western colonial expansion, the Christian missionary movement, and the increase in world trade—combined to alter slowly and to correct the monolithic map of reality held by the European intelligentsia. We learn from Hastings Rashdall that medieval Europe took pride in three great institutions, *Sacerdotum, Imperium,* and *Studium* or the Church, the Empire, and the University—which represented respectively the spiritual, the temporal, and the intellectual domains of life.[16] Unlike the academies of ancient Greece, Rome, India, and China, the European university aspired to the lofty ideal of establishing an autonomous community of scholars concerned with common subject-matters pursued either in their different aspects or by different methods. It was hoped that in such a community the limitations of the individual could be overcome. (A *universitas* concerned with one subject, for example, law, theology, or medicine, was called a *studium,* while one concerned with relating several subjects was called a *studium generale.*) Although the university was in a sense a child of the Church and the State, it enjoyed unusual autonomy because it pursued rational principles in the study of things divine and human. The development of universities gave great impetus to the Renaissance and the Enlightenment. The universities also educated leaders of the Reformation, the Counter-Reformation, and the missionary movement. It was the university, not the Church, that fostered the new understanding of *theologia* as *scientia,* a scholarly "discipline" that demonstrated its conclusions. Thus, as Edward Farley states:

> Theology along with law and liberal arts could occupy a legitimate place, in fact, the reigning place, in . . . the university. Thus it would have a method of its own, hence method itself could be thematized and become the occasion of controversy. *Sacra doctrina* is a discipline, sufficiently parallel to physics and metaphysics to be a science. As such it had founding principles and it proceeded to connect the principles with conclusions.[17]

The Renaissance, initiated by Italian humanists in the fourteenth century, was, among other things, a reaction against the scholasticism that had dominated the medieval universities. Initially deprived of university posts, humanists developed their own academies and societies and promoted the rediscovery of antiquity as a legitimate part of the European cultural heritage. It was Collingwood, I believe, who characterized the Renaissance man as being more Christian than classical. Nevertheless, humanists shifted the center of gravity from heaven to earth. During the fifteenth and sixteenth centuries, Christian Europe's mental horizon was further expanded both by the Reformation, which stimulated a new interest in the interpretation of the scriptures and in the history of the Church, and by the Counter-Reformation. In addition, the colonial expansion of the Iberian kingdoms, whose missionaries, explorers, and traders brought home information about non-Western peoples' mores, cultures, and religions; and the rediscovery of Greek science and the popularization of printing and illustration also contributed to the expansion of the European worldview. Already during this period, men of unusual talents, such as Nicholas of Cusa, Copernicus, and Leonardo da Vinci, prepared the ground for the giants of the seventeenth century (Galileo, Kepler, Harvey, etcetera).

Little needs to be said about the Enlightenment of the seventeenth and eighteenth centuries, which was close to the memory of nineteenth-century Europeans. It has often been noted that the cornerstone of the Enlightenment was not new knowledge but new methods of inquiry. "The great geniuses of the seventeenth century," says David Harris, "confirmed and amplified the concept of a world of calculable regularity, but, more important, they seemingly proved that rigorous mathematical reasoning offered the means, independent of God's revelation, of establishing truth."[18] With the new methods of inquiry, Europeans began to ask such questions as whether human nature could be fitted into a chain of causal development, that is, whether the method of studying nature could be applied to history. In England, the homeland of deism, Lord Herbert of Cherbury advocated the notion of *religio nat-*

uralis, acknowledging, however, the existence of a supreme *Numen* or first cause—the source of all things, eternal, good, just, wise, infinite, omnipotent, and free.[19] In Holland, the jurist Hugo Grotius (1583–1645) defended the Dutch East India Company's seizure of a rival Portuguese ship by invoking the law of nature as the law of humankind. To him, the law of nature could be discerned by right reason independent of theology. Grotius was called the "jurist of the human race" by Giambattista Vico (1668–1744), who himself attempted to combine historical and social scientific methods, coupled with philological and philosophical inquiries, in formulating his "new science of humanity." Holding history as the story of "our" past, Vico stressed the importance of mythologies, sagas, and legends for the rediscovery of the origins of civilization and the articulation of the laws of historical development.[20] Vico's search for the principles of universal history foreshadowed one aspect of the twin concerns of *Religionswissenschaft.*

The eighteenth century marked the second great period of European universities, marked by a new spirit of critical inquiry, even in philosophy and theology. The growth of knowledge in various disciplines resulted in the publication of many dictionaries and lexicons, as well as multi-volume encyclopaedias in philosophy, law, medicine, and theology. These works exerted a great influence on European intellectuals. Farley calls our attention to the far-reaching implications of the German Enlightenment "with its commitment to the general principle of 'reason' in matters of religion and its strong focus on historical consciousness and method,"[21] which contributed to the separation of theology from religion. "Religion may contain insights, disclosures, realities which have to do with faith, salvation, and the sacred, but theology is a matter of useful concepts pertaining to the ever historically changing doctrines of Christendom."[22] Once this division was accepted, in spite of some later theological attempts to reverse it, the ground was prepared for the eventual development of scholarly studies of religion(s) independent of the theological disciplines.

The eighteenth century also witnessed the emergence of Protestant Christianity's overseas missionary activities, spearheaded by Continental Pietists and British Evangelicals. The Roman Catholic church, which earlier had been active in Asia and the Americas, renewed its missionary activities. In contrast to European and American rationalists and romanticists, who were fascinated by non-Christian, non-Western religions and philosophies as evidence of *religio naturalis,* most missionaries sought to convert the adherents of other religions. Nevertheless, many of them took a keen interest in the religious beliefs and practices of Asia and Africa and made important contributions to the Western understanding of non-Western religions. Indeed, some of them became pioneers in Indology, Buddhology, Islamics, Sinology, Japanology, and African studies.

Given the intellectual, cultural, scientific, technological, and economic vitality at home, coupled with enormous colonial expansion and the global missionary enterprise, many Europeans of the nineteenth century and their American cousins came to believe that they were the agents of the "progress" of history.[23] According to their map of reality, they could "dispose the destiny of the world, because the absorption of the [non-Western] by the Western world appeared to come inevitably."[24] Even in the study of religion(s) it was taken for granted that non-Western religions were studied simply to provide data for Western methodologies and conceptualizations. Thus, *Religionswissenschaft* emerged as both the embodiment of and corrective to the map of reality held by nineteenth-century Europeans.

RELIGIONSWISSENSCHAFT'S MAP OF REALITY

As we have seen already, Tiele observed that *Religionswissenschaft* was "called into being by a generally felt want" in the mid-nineteenth century as "one of the sciences of the human mind." Like other *Geisteswissenschaften,*[25] it was a child of the Enlightenment. Gustav Mensching, in discussing the influence of Enlightenment thought on the new disciplines, points out two of its enduring influences on *Religionswissenschaft*: (1) the emphasis on individual reason which led to the formulation of subjective theories of religion; and (2) the interest in the objective world that led to the phenomenological study of religion(s).[26] To these, we might add a third, namely, the historical emphasis in the sense of the study of both the origin and the historical development of religions, which is the legacy of German Romanticism.

Henry Benjamin Constant (1767–1830) is usually credited with having produced the first "scientific" study of religions, *De la religion, considérée dans sa source, ses formes, et ses dévéloppements,* 5 vols. (Paris, 1824–1831). In it he utilized the theory of development to differentiate the essence and forms of religion. According to Tiele, two sources provided the impulse for the development of the study of religion(s) as a scholarly discipline. One was philosophy, which held that "the great religious problem cannot be solved without the aid of history; that, in order to define the nature and origin of religion, one must first of all know its development."[27] Material for this study, however, came from another source. "Philological and historical science, cultivated after strict methods, archaeology, anthropology, ethnology, no longer a prey to superficial theories and fashionable dilettanti only, but also subjected to the laws of critical research began to yield a rich harvest."[28] From these two sources developed a general, though vague, consensus concerning the need for a scholarly discipline to study religion(s).

In spite of this generally felt want, there was no unanimity in the nineteenth century about the nomenclature for the scholarly study of religion(s).[29] A completely satisfactory name has yet to be found. The designation "Hierology," or a "treatise on sacred (*hieros*) things," was favored by some of the discipline's pioneers. Others preferred 'Pistology,"[30] or the study of "faith" or "belief" systems. Other designations proposed and used in some quarters were "Comparative Religion," "Science of Comparative Religion," "The Comparative History of Religion," "The Comparative History of Religions," "The Comparative Science of Religion," "Comparative Theology," and "Science of Religion."[31] (In recent years, the designation "Comparative Religion" has been used generally in Great Britain, where history of religions and philosophy of religion are not sharply differentiated. "History of Religions" has been adopted officially by the International Association for the History of Religions (IAHR) as the English counterpart to *Allgemeine Religionswissenschaft*.)

The variety of proposed designations for the emerging study of religions was due in part to the different disciplinary backgrounds of the scholars involved in the new enterprise. Nevertheless, the majority shared similar philosophical and epistemological assumptions inherited from the Enlightenment, such as the notions of phenomena as the data of experience, or the dissolving and restructuring functions of reason. In addition, they accepted both the negative and the positive attitudes of the Enlightenment toward religion. They abhorred transcendental justification, ecclesiastical authority, and the dogmas of particular religions, but they recognized at the same time humanity's natural inclination and deeply rooted need for religion. Religion, these scholars felt, had become obscured by historical accretion. Thus, consciously and unconsciously, they were committed to the reformation and education of humanity by rediscovering the original—that is, the natural and universal—nature of religion and by correcting irrational and perverted knowledge concerning religion. As one might expect, their idea of universal religion was not derived from notions of salvation history propounded by any particular religious tradition. Rather, it was grounded in a new conception of history inherited from the Enlightenment, a conception that affirmed that "the eternal and immutable norms of reason" were unfolded and "realized in the course of empirical historical development."[32] Thus, the problem history posed to the philosophy of the Enlightenment arose, according to Cassirer, "in the field of religious phenomena, and it is here that this problem first became urgent."[33] It was the problem of history that encouraged nineteenth-century scholars—philosophers, historians, ethnologists, archeologists, biblical scholars—to pursue the historical study and classification of a wide variety of religious phenomena, for which the data were becoming increasingly more available, and to formulate theories about the origin and nature of religion, usually along the "evolutionary" model.

Initially, there was no consensus as to assumptions and methods for interpreting religious data, because various scholars brought into the study of religion their respective disciplinary premises and methods of inquiry. It was Friedrich Schleiermacher (1768–1834) who raised the issue of "understanding" as a serious scholarly problem and who inaugurated a system of hermeneutics. Schleiermacher's work, together with that of August Boeckh (1785–1867) and Wilhelm Dilthey (1833–1911), have provided methodological guideposts for *Religionswissenschaft*'s map of reality.[34] Schleiermacher was particularly sensitive to the perennial problem of *Religionswissenschaft,* that is, the relation of the parts to the whole—"we always know the whole only in the part and the part only through the whole."[35] With his characteristic transcendental perspective, Schleiermacher interpreted the whole–part relation as an architectonic connection in which the whole depends on its parts. According to Makkreel, Schleiermacher's notion of "divination" (that is, "divining" the whole from its parts) is similar to Kant's symbolic knowledge. "It has affinities with reflective judgment because it locates order from within, but is more specific in focusing on some crucial and indispensable part for intuiting the nature of the whole."[36] To Schleiermacher, religion was a matter of our immediate "divining" self-consciousness (feeling) of dependence, not a matter of metaphysics or morality.

Boeckh, a classicist and the master of another system of hermeneutics, tried to reconstruct the mental world of antiquity from written and other sources. In his view, the subject matters of cognition were the two "manifestations of life," nature and mind, together with history, the evolution of mind. Consequently, Boeckh defined the task of *Wissenschaft* as bringing into view the whole of all particulars of everything knowable. He advocated an important hermeneutical principle of recognition, by which the scholar "re-cognizes" that which has been previously cognized, presents it in its pristine character, and "reconstruct[s] in its totality that which does not appear as a whole."[37] Boeckh presented two hermeneutical canons which have had great impact on *Religionswissenschaft:* (1) that which is foreign must be assimilated by the researcher as his/her own; and (2) when that is done, the researcher must be able to observe that which has become his/her own as an objective something to be appraised.[38]

Although Dilthey admired Schleiermacher's hermeneutical system, he rejected the latter's Romantic premise of the unity of spirit and matter. He also disagreed with Schleiermacher's architectonic approach and appealed to history for the basis of his theory of knowledge. According to H. A. Hodges, Dilthey wanted to write a "Critique of Historical Reason" which might do for the *Geisteswissenschaften* "something like what Kant had done for the natural sciences." In the course of his work, he broke new philosophical ground by studying "the relations between lived experience, expression, and understanding (*Erlebnis, Ausdruck,* and *Verstehen*); the interdependence of self-knowledge and knowledge of other persons; and . . . the understanding of social groups and historical processes."[39] While Dilthey accepted Schleiermacher's notion of "divination," he "stressed the need for a comparative method, not just to confirm what has been intuited, but also to correct and deepen it."[40] To him, the subject-matter of the *Geisteswissenschaften* was the understanding of the human mind as it objectified itself in various social and cultural spheres. Hermeneutics, therefore, was "an essential component in the foundation of the human studies themselves."[41] In the 1920s, Joachim Wach wondered why Dilthey, in spite of his deep religio-scientific comprehension, had not exerted more influence on *Religionswissenschaft.*[42] In more recent decades, however, there has been a greater appreciation of Dilthey. His agenda—for example, historical research, the comparative method, and the concern for the relations between experience, expression, and understanding—have been widely accepted as the main tasks of *Religionswissenschaft.*

In the preface to his *Chips from a German Workshop* (1867), Friedrich Max Müller predicted the development of the "Science of Religion," noting that it "may be the last of the sciences which man is destined to elaborate."[43] He did not claim to be its founder, nor was he the first person to use the designation, "Science of Religion." The French expression, *la science des religions,* and the German term, *Religionswissenschaft,* had been used earlier.[44] It is not clear whether Müller, a German-English scholar, had in mind the German sense of "Wissenschaft" or the English usage, according to which "science" refers more often to a model of "natural science" characterized by prediction. Certainly in both German and French, the notion of "science" is used to designate any rigorous scholarly study or methodology, so that what we call humanities and social sciences in English may be referred to in German as *Geisteswissenschaften,* and history can rightly be called a *Wissenschaft.* At any rate, Max Müller used this ambiguous English designation, and, because he was an influential scholar and an effective popularizer of the study of religion, it has continued in use until our own time. The term has caused unnecessary confusion, as illustrated by recent controversies as to whether a "science of religion" is possible or not.[45] It reminds me of Evans-Pritchard's comment on the designation "primitive" in anthropology: ". . . the word was perhaps an unfortunate choice, but it has now been too widely accepted as a technical term to be avoided."[46] However, another widely used designation, "comparative religion," has its own set of problems and ambiguities.

Under these circumstances, we might as well use the designation, "History of Religions," stating explicitly that it refers to *Allgemeine,* or general, *Religionswissenschaft,* and distinguishing it from some of the connotations of the English expressions, "Science of Reilgion" or "Scientific Study of Religion," until such time as a more universally acceptable designation can be found. I readily admit that our current use of "History of Religions" may be easily misconstrued by some as referring to (1) history, an important aspect of *Religionswissenschaft,* but not the whole; (2) the residue of the earlier *Religionsgeschichtliche Schule;* or (3) the history of any particular religious tradition without consideration of the common assumptions and methodological principles of *Religionswissenschaft,* as is too often the case today. To judge from the articles submitted to the journal, *History of Religions,* many potential contributors have no conception of what the discipline of the history of religions is. Evidently, there is a widespread misconception that any study of non-Western and "primitive" religions—but, significantly, *not* Christianity—that relies on any methodological principles and concepts—sociological, psychological, anthropological, or what have you—constitutes history of religions. The same misconception dictates the policy of hiring "historians of religions" in various colleges and universities, and this in turn nurtures a misconception about the nature of the discipline among students.

The confused map of reality which *Religionswissenschaft* possesses in our time reflects the checkered history of its "emancipation" (to use Wach's phrase) during this century. We might recall Tiele's observation that the initial impulse to develop a new discipline to study religion came from philosophy as well as from other branches of learning, such as philology, ethnology, anthropology, sociology, psychology, and archeology. Some envisaged the new discipline as "unified and autonomous"; others thought of it as an "interdisciplinary or cooperative" venture, composed of a number of "sciences" dealing with religion(s). Accordingly, pioneers in the history of religions held a number of different organizing principles, whether implicitly or explicitly. The lack of internal cohesiveness during the discipline's initial phase did indicate, however, a sense of anticipation and excitement. For example, the fact that the first Congress of the History of Religions, held in connection with the Paris exhibition in 1900, attracted such notable scholars as Alfred Bertholet *(Religionsgeschichte),* Gaston Maspero (Egyptian archeology and mythology), Alfred Foucher (Buddhist art), Emile Durkheim (sociology), Hermann Oldenberg (Buddhology), Nathan Søderblom (history of religions), Edward B. Tylor (anthropology), and Arnold van Gennep (ethnography) indicates the level of quality and the variety of disciplines involved in the new scholarly enterprise. Thanks to these tutelary disciplines, *Religionswissenschaft* acquired a broad foundation upon which to build its disciplinary framework.[47] In this sense, *Religionswissenschaft* is the recipient and the embodiment of the rich heritage of the Enlightenment tradition, transmitted through the various disciplines of the *Geisteswissenschaften.*

Yet *Religionswissenschaft* also presented a critique of the negative aspects of Enlightenment thought about religion, that is, its overly rationalistic view of the nature of religious phenomena and its blindness to the transcendental referent of religion. On the other hand, *Religionswissenschaft* has accepted uncritically the insights and methods of other *Geisteswissenschaften* and has been slow to develop its own self-identity as a discipline. As Wach so poignantly observed, *Religionswissenschaft,* unlike other branches of the *Geisteswissenschaften,* continued to allow other disciplines to interfere with its own self-definition.[48] In this regard, Eliade insists that a religious phenomenon can be understood only if it is studied as something *religious.* "To try to grasp the essence of such a phenomenon by means of physiology, psychology, sociology, economics, linguistics, art, or any other study, is false; it misses the one unique and irreducible element in it—the element of the sacred."[49] Wach was sensitive to the all-pervasive influence of philosophy, theology, and psychology. To his *Religionswissenschaft,* he added an appendix on the deleterious effects of "*Psychologismus*" on the discipline.[50] More recently, other disciplines, such as cultural anthropology, cultural area studies, and comparative ethics, have become influential "conversation partners." The history of religions urgently needs to articulate its own identity and to define its own mode of relating to other fields of inquiry, instead of allowing other disciplines to define the relationship from their perspectives.

Although the emergence of *Religionswissenschaft* aroused great excitement among European intellectuals, the discipline had grave difficulties in establishing itself in academic institutions. This occurred despite the fact that endowed lectureships were established, congresses for the history of religions continued to attract able scholars, and Hasting's *Encyclopaedia of Religion and Ethics,* as well as the monumental series of the *Sacred Books of the East,* edited by Max Müller,[51] were in the process of being published.[52]

When certain subsections of *Religionswissenschaft,* such as the historical study of religion (*Religionsgeschichte*) or comparative religion, were accepted by European universities, they were usually placed in theological faculties. Only in France was this not the case.[53] It should be noted that while theology had been a prominent part of medieval universities, in the modern universities it had to justify its place as a legitimate "science." Thus, Schleiermacher asserted that theology, "an enterprise whose methods yield cognitions, knowledge, and [which] gathers the . . . particulars of its area into a systematic whole," is a "science." He also defined theology as a *positive* science: "because positivity names a culturally determinate form of experience, it has to do with a specific religious community," and "the knowledge which theology accumulates is the knowledge (theory) needed by the leadership operative in religious community."[54] With such an understanding of theology, many theological faculties in European universities around the turn of the century either wanted to appropriate some aspects of *Religionswissenschaft* for theological and apologetic purposes, or took a hostile or indifferent attitude toward the new discipline because of its evolutionary orientation. By contrast, the antitheological and anticlerical atmosphere of the French academic world, where "the study of religion could only be carried out under conditions of the strictest scientific stringency,"[55] was very conducive to the steady growth of *Religionswissenschaft*.

The process by which *Religionswissenschaft* was "emancipated" in the early twentieth century was frustrated by misunderstanding of the nature of the discipline and its relation to theology. Many Christian theologians claimed an exclusive privilege in studying the Christian religion and denied to *Religionswissenschaft* a right to deal with Christian religious data. Others declared theology itself to be *Religionswissenschaft* and sought to interpret all religious phenomena from a theological perspective. On its side, *Religionswissenschaft* acknowledged theology's right to study Christian data but insisted on its own right to deal with these data religio-scientifically. Further, *Religionswissenschaft* acknowledged the possibility of justifying something like a "theological history of religion(s)," but as a theological study, not *Religionswissenschaft*.[56] Because it is not a normative discipline like theology or the philosophy of religion, *Religionswissenschaft* may construct a relative norm in its hermeneutical procedure, but it is not concerned with normativeness in reference to religious truth. Unfortunately, this point was not understood by the *Religionsgeschichtliche Schule*. It is more unfortunate that even today some will not acknowledge that theology and *Religionswissenschaft* are equally legitimate enterprises and that Christianity, for example, is a proper subject matter for both Christian theology and *Religionswissenschaft*, each approaching the data with different motives, objectives, and methodologies.[57]

Unlike the other *Geisteswissenschaften*, *Religionswissenschaft* gained its independence from philosophy rather slowly. The delay occurred in large part because the pioneers of *Religionswissenschaft* lacked a proper understanding of the nature of the discipline itself. According to Wach, the relationship between *Religionswissenschaft* and the philosophy of religion was somewhat analogous to the relationship between the history of art and the philosophy of art, or between jurisprudence and the philosophy of law. The positivistic mood of these *Wissenschaften* in the nineteenth century rejected the speculative interests of professional philosophies (*Fachphilosophie*). Max Müller, for example, reacting to speculative philosophy, depended on philology as the framework for *Religionswissenschaft*. In this respect, Müller and his colleagues were Romantic philologists. Although they opposed Romanticism in substituting precise study of the sources for unfettered speculation, they remained Romantic in their desire "to comprehend religion as the expression of a universal mode of human thinking."[58] Other pioneers acknowledged the basic philosophical character of *Religionswissenschaft* but rejected speculative philosophy in favor of folklore, archeology, and ethnology as the methodological frameworks for the new discipline. Tiele, for example, who rejected a metaphysically or religiously grounded philosophy, still considered *Religionswissenschaft* as a "philosophic" part of the inquiry into religious phenomena. Thus, in differentiating *Religionswissenschaft* from a general historic knowledge of religion (*Religionskunde*), he characterized *Religionswissenschaft* as an "empirical science" that nevertheless was philosophical because of its dependence on the deductive method.[59] That is to say, Tiele's work remained essentially a philosophical inquiry into the universal reality called "religion" which he thought to underlie all empirical religions.[60] This understanding of *Religionswissenschaft* has persisted in various forms. It appears in van der Leeuw's phenomenology of religion, although his system does not claim to encompass *Religionswissenschaft* in its entirety. In addition, van der Leeuw's system, which owed much to the phenomenology of religion of P. D. Chantepie de la Saussaye (1848–1920), was understood as a part of a theological encyclopaedia and not as a philosophical inquiry. Rudolf Otto's (1869–1937) *Das Heilige*, too, was a part of Otto's larger agenda in the philosophy of religion.

In the early twentieth century, many scholars of *Religionswissenschaft* were strongly influenced by evolutionary thought and positivism. "Description was to take the place of evaluation. Norms and values were to be 'explained' historically, psychologically, and sociologically. . . . Specialization was highly developed and 'objectivity' was the supreme demand. Great interest prevailed in the study of origins."[61] In the midst of this situation, Ernst Troeltsch (1865–1923) held simultaneously the notion of a religious a priori and the concept of history as individuality and unique development. For Troeltsch, *Religionswissenschaft* was a normative discipline, a synthesis of psychology, epistemology, philosophy of history, and metaphysics of religion.[62] It was Max Scheler (1874–1928) who, according to Wach, located the proper place for the religio-scientific discipline—the "concrete phenomenology of religious objects and acts"—between the "positive science of religion," on the one hand, and the "essential phenomenology of religion," on the other. The task of this discipline, according to Scheler, is not to view religious phenomena philosophically or scientifically but "religio-scientifically," aiming both at the fullest possible understanding of the intellectual content of one or more religions forms and at the understanding of the consummate acts in which these intellectual contents are given.[63]

Regarding the development of *Religionswissenschaft* in America, I wish to add very little to what I have already written.[64] Briefly stated, the American world has produced many disciplines that historically have been closely related to *Religionswissenschaft*. However, scholarly interests in religion(s) were confined to (1) a narrow sense of "history of religion"—objective, descriptive, and often oriented toward evolution (not to be confused with the "history of religions" as *Allgemeine Religionswissenschaft*); and (2) "comparative religion" and "philosophy of religion." Many North American scholars agreed with Jordan's pyramidical three-layered schema for the study of religion. At the bottom he placed the history of religions, which supplies reliable, raw religious data; in the middle, comparative religion, which classifies historical data by means of the comparative method; and at the apex, the philosophy of religion, which connects and interprets the classified religious data. What Jordan called the "science of religion" was nothing but a general descriptive term for the totality of these three layers of religious inquiry.[65] On the other hand, Morris Jastrow, the spiritual father of what is now called "Religious Studies" in America, advocated the centrality of historical method in the general study of religion, which embraced studies of "religion and ethics," "religion and philosophy," "religion and mythology," "religion and psychology," "religion and history," and "religion and culture." In his opinion, while courses on the philosophy and psychology of religions "fall within the range of a university curriculum, . . . the real study of them must be postponed until one has secured a safe historical basis. The university and seminary will fulfill their function if they succeed in training students in a historical method. The Philosophy and Psychology will then take care of themselves."[66]

Historical studies of particular religious traditions were also promoted by "The American Lectures on the History of Religions," established in 1892 jointly by Columbia, Cornell, Johns Hopkins, Pennsylvania, Yale, and other institutions, "for the purpose of encouraging the intelligent study of religions."[67] The establishment of this lectureship was followed by the World Parliament of Religions, held in Chicago in 1893. Many Americans felt that the Parliament, a nonscholarly interfaith gathering, was closely related to the cause of history of religions or comparative religion. Subsequently, courses on history of religions and comparative religions became popular subjects in American colleges, universities, and seminaries. Jacob Neusner suggests that the historic openness of American universities to the study of various religions, historically or comparatively, was due to the ethos of what he terms "cultural Protestantism," which permeated institutions of higher learning:

> The truth is that the university has been basically *Protestant*—though nonsectarian, liberal, and of a kindly disposition toward Jewish, Catholic, as well as Hindu, Buddhist, and Moslem students and their religions. It was the Protestant vision which shaped American university perspectives until the most recent past. That vision is, one must add, broader or more mature than the Jewish or Roman Catholic equivalents. . . . I think one may fairly add that the history of all forms of the study of religion in secular American universities can be written in terms of the history of cultural, if not religious, Protestantism.[68]

For the most part, American universities, which have been interested in the historical or comparative study of various religions, were not concerned with inquiring into the historical, comparative, and phenomenological study of religion(s) until after World War II.

I must admit candidly, however, that even now the term "history of religions" connotes many different perspectives, procedures of inquiry, and objectives, from simplistic comparisons of religious forms and doctrines, disguised evolutionary histories of religion(s), dialogues of religions, rationalistic and positivistic "scientific" studies of religion, to more sophisticated philosophical, theological, ethical, psychological, anthropological, and sociological inquiries into various religious data, or a series of specialized studies of particular religious traditions. Fortunately, thanks to the efforts of scholars like Joachim Wach and Mircea Eliade, the perspectives and methodologies of the history of religions *(Allgemeine Religionswissenschaft)* are beginning to make serious impressions on the map of reality of our discipline.

Conclusion: Romance, Precision, and Generalization in *Religionswissenschaft*

The study of any discipline, according to A. N. Whitehead, involves three stages: romance, precision, and generalization. The stage of romance is marked by the vividness of novelty: "Romantic emotion is essentially the excitement consequent on the transition from the bare facts to the first realizations of the import of their unexplored relationships [with] possibilities half-disclosed by glimpses and half-concealed by the wealth of material."

The stage of precision requires discipline in method, without which exactness of formulation is impossible; yet during this stage, the romance of learning may easily be lost due to the burdens and pressures of work. The stage of generalization is a "return to romanticism with the added advantage of classified ideas and relevant technique."[69] The learned generalizations thus achieved will lead one, not to any final resolution of intellectual quests, but to another higher level of the threefold cycle, which is repeated again and again. This type of understanding of the stages of intellectual growth is very relevant to *Religionswissenschaft.*

Two things should be kept in mind in this regard. First, as in any other serious intellectual endeavor, dividing lines between the stages of romance and precision, or between precision and generalization, are usually blurred. Second, as in many other areas of study, perception of the nature of the discipline is usually influenced by the *Zeitgeist* and cultural milieu. For example, the interest that motivates various persons to study the history of religions and the kinds of questions they bring to the study are not the same everywhere, and they may vary greatly at different times. Nevertheless, those who have caught glimpses of any aspect of *Religionswissenschaft* may be excited by the novelty and the possibilities of what they expect to find in the discipline. In the stage of romance, *Religionswissenschaft* often appears to be more glamorous than other areas of studies in religion, due to the vastness and the exotic nature of the material for those who are intellectually curious or those who are rebelling against their own religious and/or cultural backgrounds. Already at this stage, the tension between intellectual and religious commitment is felt. Often those who cannot revise their maps of reality drop out or approach history of religions as simply a technical knowledge, *à la* mathematics, without letting the study disturb the equilibrium of their mental maps. A few are looking for religious alternatives. They approach history of religions as a new religion or concoct their own synthetic religion based on a smattering of religious data, some exotic and some familiar. Similarly, novices in *Religionswissenschaft* are awed by the infinite variety of religious forms, myths, symbols, cults, and the languages involved in studying them. In this regard, Joachim Wach insisted on teaching two introductory courses, one a historical approach to the religious history of humankind from archaic times to the present, and the second, a history of the study of religion(s) from the classical period to the present. It was his conviction that these two courses were essential for orienting students to the discipline. Eliade likewise devoted years to producing *From Primitives to Zen: A Thematic Sourcebook of the History of Religions* (1967), as well as other works to orient students to *Religionswissenschaft.* I am increasingly convinced that the future of the history of religions depends largely on the quality of introductory courses.

In regard to the second stage, precision, Whitehead noted that, in the case of mathematics, one should be thoroughly familiar with the elements of algebra before moving into differential calculus. Similarly, the student in the second stage of *Religionswissenschaft* should become familiar with both the methods and the contents of the discipline. The transition from the stage of romance to the stage of precision, which implies one's entry into *Religionswissenschaft*'s map of reality, involves something analogous to *metanoia.* Students now must learn to view all particular religious data from the perspective of the whole, so that their interests in particular religious traditions are redirected toward a new understanding of the part–whole relationship, following Schleiermacher's principle of the priority of the whole. In this stage, as Eliade laments, some students who cannot make the mental shift come to pursue specialized studies of primitive religions, Islam, Hinduism, Buddhism, Chinese, or Japanese religions. While these are legitimate enterprises, they are not *Religionswissenschaft.* Some students at this stage choose to "compare" two or three religious traditions rather than learning to deal with them from the perspective of the whole. Equally disturbing to many students is *Religionswissenschaft*'s priority of method over content. Many have little patience for the historical study of the discipline's methodological principles and procedures, *Religionswissenschaft*'s counterpart to the study of algebra within the discipline of mathematics. They would rather adopt one scholar's approach—van der Leeuw, Wach, Eliade, Turner, Geertz, et al.—and then try to use it for analyzing particular religious data. Those who are willing to undergo a disciplined study of the methodological heritage of *Religionswissenschaft* will learn how to climb on the shoulders of the giants of the discipline and so broaden their interpretive horizon. Then, they will learn how to "test" the methodological approaches of those giants in terms of the particular religious data they are studying. That is to say, in the second stage students must acquire "precise" knowledge about the contents of a limited number of religious traditions in order to "test," "verify," and "refine" previous scholars' methodological approaches. Ironically, the methodological emphasis of *Religionswissenschaft* is often misconstrued, and students think that they can jump into the study and formulation of methods without gaining familiarity with the general history of religions or with religious data on a limited number of religious traditions. As Wach repeatedly insisted, the hermeneutics of *Religionswissenschaft* must be grounded in the study of empirical religious data, and the methodological principles thus formulated must be constantly revised in terms of the further study of religious data.

Without firm commitment to the task of constantly refining its methodological principles, *Religionswissenschaft* will not be able to relate its knowledge to that of other disciplines.

The third stage, generalization, is usually marked in *Religionswissenschaft* by the student's writing of the dissertation. As in other disciplines, this exercise involves raising an important intellectual problem, appraising various methods that have been used by previous scholars in dealing with similar or related questions, formulating methodological principles, delimiting the area of data that might be illuminated by such a method, and testing the adequacy of the method used. These are procedures familiar to any university discipline. What distinguishes *Religionswissenschaft* from other disciplines concerned with the study of religion(s) is the special contribution to knowledge that it can make by providing "generalized statements" concerning the nature and history of religion and religions, derived neither from speculative perspectives nor from the perspective of the study of one or several religious traditions with which the investigator is familiar. Here the historical and systematic dimensions of *Religionswissenschaft* must be correlated. In following the threefold cycle of romance, precision, and generalization, students should become aware of the interrelations between religious experience—not simply the experience of individuals nor the experience of isolated religious communities but the historic experience of the human race—and the enormous variety of its expressions. Only then can they proceed to make generalized statements, however tentative, regarding "religion." In the case of *Religionswissenschaft,* "religion" does not refer to any ontological reality but to a reality once removed from religions, somewhat like making generalized statements about "language," which is a reality once removed from language.

In retrospect, *Religionswissenschaft* emerged both as the embodiment and the critique of the intellectual heritage of the Enlightenment. In its development, it has been indebted to many other disciplines, although it has continuously endeavored to become an autonomous discipline with its own "integrated understanding" (Wach) and "total hermeneutics" (Eliade). The sole objective of *Religionswissenschaft* is the "understanding"—not the explanation, apologia, or promotion—of the nature of "religion" and the concrete religious configurations that have unfolded in human history.

Notes

1. Cornelis P. Tiele, *Elements of the Science of Religion,* Part I. *Morphological* (New York: Charles Scribner's Sons, 1897), p. 2.

2. Joachim Wach, *Religionswissenschaft: Prolegomena zu ihrer wissenschaftstheoretischen Grundlegung* (Leipzig: J. C. Hinrich'sche Buchhandlung, 1924), "Vorwort," p. iii.
3. Ibid.
4. See M. Eliade, "The History of Religions in Retrospect: 1912 and After" (originally published in *The Journal of Bible and Religion*), in his *The Quest: History and Meaning in Religion* (Chicago: University of Chicago Press, 1969), p. 12.
5. Ibid., p. 13.
6. M. Eliade, "History of Religions and a New Humanism" (originally published in *History of Religions*), reprinted as "A New Humanism," in his *The Quest,* p. 1.
7. M. Eliade, "Crisis and Renewal in History of Religions," reprinted in *The Quest,* pp. 54–55.
8. This phrase is taken from M. Scott Peck, *The Road Less Travelled* (New York: Simon & Schuster, 1979).
9. C. P. Tiele, "On the Study of Comparative Theology," in John Henry Barrows, ed., *The World's Parliament of Religions* (Chicago: Parliament Publishing Co., 1893), Vol. I, p. 568.
10. William S. Haas, *The Destiny of the Mind—East and West* (London: Faber & Faber, 1956), p. 37.
11. Ibid., p. 14.
12. Ibid., pp. 15–16. "In the Occident . . . time is one of civilization's great determining elements. It penetrates to the very heart of Western civilization, and it is a constituent part of that civilization, conferring on its development the distinct shape of evolution."
13. Ibid., p. 16.
14. Hendrik Kraemer, *World Cultures and World Religions: The Coming Dialogue* (Philadelphia: Westminster Press, 1961), pp. 30–55.
15. Norman Daniel, *Islam and the West: The Making of an Image* (Edinburgh, 1960), p. 2.
16. Hastings Rashdall, *The University of Europe in the Middle Ages,* 2nd ed. (Oxford: Oxford University Press, 1936, reissued 1958), Vol. I, pp. 2ff.
17. Edward Farley, *Theologia: The Fragmentation and Unity of Theological Education* (Philadelphia: Fortress Press, 1983), p. 38. He goes on to say: "It may be argued that this is not 'science' in a very full sense. Thomas's calling sacred doctrine a subalternate science acknowledges this. The very thing that qualifies its scientific character, the supernatural origin of its principles, is, however, also what makes it the reigning queen and provides it with a superior knowledge."
18. David Harris, "Enlightenment," *Encyclopaedia Britannica* (1971 ed.), vol. 8, p. 599.
19. A. C. Bouquet, *Comparative Religion* (London: Penguin Books, 5th ed., revised, 1956), pp. 21–22.
20. Cassirer argues that Vico exerted no influence on the philosophy of the Enlightenment because he had removed rationalism from historiography. Thus, Cassirer states that Vico's work on a philosophy of history, *Principles of a New Science of the Common Nature of Nations,* for example, "remained in obscurity until Herder late in the century brought it to light again." Ernst Cassirer, *The Philosophy of the Enlightenment,* trans. F. C. A. Koelln and J. P. Pettegrove (Princeton, N.J.: Princeton University Press, 1951), p. 209.

21. Farley, *op. cit.*, p. 64.
22. Ibid., p. 65.
23. On the idea of "progress," see Paul Tillich, "The Decline and the Validity of the Idea of Progress," in *The Future of Religions*, ed. J. C. Brauer (New York: Harper & Row, 1966), pp. 64–79.
24. Hendrik Kraemer, *The Christian Message in a Non-Christian World* (London: Edinburgh House Press, 1938), p. 36.
25. Not to be confused with the Hegelian notion of the *Geistwissenschaft* (philosophy of the spirit).
26. Gustav Mensching, *Geschichte der Religionswissenschaft* (Bonn: Universität-Verlag, 1948), pp. 42–43.
27. Tiele, "On the Study of Comparative Theology," p. 584.
28. Ibid., p. 585.
29. See, for example, Louis Henry Jordan, *Comparative Religion: Its Genesis and Growth* (New York: Scribner's, 1905), pp. 24–28.
30. See Tiele's *Outlines of the History of Religion* (London, 1877; 6th ed., 1896), p. vii.
31. Tiele, "On the Study of Comparative Theology," p. 583: "Theology is not the same as religion; and, to me, Comparative Theology signifies nothing but a comparative study of religious dogmas, Comparative Religion is nothing but a comparative study of the various religions in all their branches. I suppose, however, . . . 'Comparative Theology' is to be understood to mean what is now generally called the Science of Religion, the word 'science' not being taken in the limited sense it commonly has in English, but in the general signification of the Dutch Wetenschap (H. G. Wissenschaft) which it has assumed more and more even in the Romance languages."
32. Cassirer, op. cit., p. 183.
33. Ibid., pp. 195–196.
34. On Schleiermacher's forerunners, Friedrich Ast and Friedrich A. Wolf, as well as the hermeneutical theories of Schleiermacher, Boeckh, and Wilhelm von Humboldt, see Joachim Wach, *Das Verstehen: Grundzüge einer Geschichte der hermeneutischen Theorie im 19. Jahrhundert*, I. *Die Grossen Systeme* (Tübingen: J. C. B. Mohr, 1926; Hildesheim: Georg Olms, 1966).
35. A statement by Dilthey, quoted in Rudolf A. Makkreel, *Dilthey: Philosopher of the Human Sciences* (Princeton, N.J.: Princeton University Press, 1975), p. 264.
36. Ibid., p. 265.
37. Wach, *Das Verstehen*, I, p. 178.
38. J. M. Kitagawa, "*Verstehen* and *Erlösung:* Some Remarks on Joachim Wach's Work," *History of Religions*, 11, no. 1 (August 1971): 37–38.
39. H. A. Hodges, "Dilthey, Wilheim," *Encyclopaedia Britannica* (1971 ed.), Vol. 7, p. 439.
40. Makkreel, *op. cit.*, pp. 270–271.
41. Ibid., p. 272.
42. Wach, *Religionswissenschaft*, p. 195.
43. F. Max Müller, *Chips from a German Workshop* (London, 1867).
44. See H. Pinard de la Boullaye, *L'Etude comparée des religions*, 4th ed. (Paris, 1929), Vol. 1, p. 548, and Eric J. Sharpe, *Comparative Religion: A History* (London: Duckworth, 1975), p. 31.

45. See references cited in Donald Wiebe, "Is a Science of Religions Possible?" *Sciences Religieuses/Studies in Religion* 7, no. 1 (1978): 5–17.
46. E. E. Evans-Pritchard, *Social Anthropology* (New York: Free Press, 1952), p. 7.
47. See Fred Louis Parrish, *The Classification of Religions: Its Relation to the History of Religions* (Scottdale, Penn.: Herald Press, 1941), Chaps. I–VII.
48. Wach, *Religionswissenschaft,* p. 20.
49. M. Eliade, *Patterns in Comparative Religion,* trans. R. Sheed (New York: Sheed & Ward, 1958), p. xi.
50. Wach, *Religionswissenschaft,* "Anhang: Über den Psychologismus in der Religionswissenschaft," pp. 193–205.
51. On Max Müller's thought and academic career, see J. M. Kitagawa and John Strong, "Friedrich Max Müller," in the forthcoming volume on *Religious Thought in the Nineteenth Century,* eds. N. Smart, J. Clayton, S. Katz, and P. Sherry (Cambridge University Press).
52. Sharpe, *op. cit.,* Chap. VI, "The Quest for Academic Recognition," pp. 119–143.
53. Ibid., pp. 122–123.
54. Farley, *op. cit.,* Chap. 4, pp. 30–31.
55. Sharpe, *op. cit.,* p. 123.
56. Wach, *Religionswissenschaft,* pp. 60–63.
57. Ibid., p. 66.
58. G. van der Leeuw, *Religion in Essence and Manifestation,* trans. J. E. Turner (London: George Allen & Unwin, Ltd., 1938), p. 693.
59. In Tiele's view, the deductive inference in *Religionswissenschaft* must proceed from that which is constituted through induction, through the empirical, historical, and comparative method. This principle was followed and articulated in America by Morris J. Jastrow, Jr., *The Study of Religion* (New York: Scribner's, 1902).
60. Wach, *Religionswissenschaft,* p. 119.
61. Joachim Wach, *The Comparative Study of Religions* (New York: Columbia University Press, 1958), p. 4.
62. Wach, *Religionswissenschaft,* pp. 122–123.
63. Ibid., pp. 126–128.
64. See my articles: "The History of Religions in America," in M. Eliade and J. M. Kitagawa, eds., *The History of Religions: Essays in Methodology* (University of Chicago Press, 1959), "The Making of a Historian of Religions," *Journal of the American Academy of Religion,* 36, no. 3 (September 1968): 191–202, and "Humanistic and Theological History of Religions with Special Reference to the North American Scene," *NUMEN* 27, fasc. 2 (December 1980): 198–221.
65. Jordan, *op. cit.,* p. 10.
66. Jastrow, *op. cit.,* "Preface," pp. ix–x.
67. Jordan, *op. cit.,* pp. 571–572.
68. Jacob Neusner, "Judaism in the History of Religions," in *History and Theory: Studies in the Philosophy of History,* Supplement 8: *On Method in the History of Religions,* ed. James S. Helfer (1968), p. 37.
69. A. N. Whitehead, *Aims of Education* (New York: Macmillan, 1929), pp. 29ff.

Afterword

The Dialectic of the Parts and the Whole: Reflections on the Past, Present, and Future of the History of Religions

GREGORY D. ALLES AND JOSEPH M. KITAGAWA

Change and Persistence

To look at the history of religions is to look at a constantly changing kaleidoscope. Light from ever-shifting methods and tools plays upon different selections of material from the seemingly inexhaustible store of human religious experience to produce patterns and configurations—thoughts and interpretations—that are ever new. Temporal flux threatens to frustrate even the most astute observer of the discipline. Once forms have been defined, they are already past, while the present, conditioned by what preceded, continuously becomes what has not yet been. On the fast-moving interface between retrospect and prospect, the object of observation may seem to be more a blur than a single, if complex, image. When one looks at the second Chicago conference on the history of religions, the topic for discussion—"the history of religions, past, present, and future"—only makes the question impossible to ignore: how can a mere mortal keep hold of this Proteus who seems capable of an infinity of transformations?

But as the history of religions changes, certain elements persist. One of these is the concern to incorporate all religious phenomena within its grasp. Historians of religions use several criteria to judge their methods and theories. Among them, the capacity to apply to all religious data without distorting any assumes a major place. Obviously, no method or theory satisfies this criterion completely. Goal and failure commingle to engender what we will later call the dialectic of the parts and the whole.

Because it persists in the midst of change, the concern for the whole can serve as a fixed point from which to view the discipline as it is situated in the flux of time. Our immediate goal is to survey a moment in what has now become the discipline's recent past, the Chicago conference on the history of religions held in May 1983. Taking the conference proceedings as representative of the (relative) present, and reflecting on that present with the help of the concern for the whole as we will formulate it, we will venture several observations on the discipline's possible future. But present and future are inescapably conditioned by the past. As a result, we must first look briefly at previous thought about parts and wholes, both in the history of religions and, before that, in the Western intellectual tradition.[1]

PARTS AND WHOLES IN WESTERN THOUGHT

Western reflection on parts and wholes began in Greece. Plato spoke of various wholes, for example, the state (*Republic, Laws*), the human being (*Charmides, Phaedrus*), arts such as poetry (*Ion*), and the object of love (*Republic*). He also questioned whether the whole was identical with notions such as the all (*Theaetetus*) and the one (*Parmenides*). Aristotle, too, spoke of wholes, but most important for our theme was his division of a speech into its constituent parts. Because ancient education was largely rhetorical, the notion of parts and wholes was put to interpretive use. For example, St. Augustine lays down the principle that more obscure passages of Scripture should be interpreted in harmony with the meaning of Scripture as a whole. Later, the Reformation, in its concern to revive that in Christianity which, to its eyes, had been made alien through the interposition of the medieval, scholastic tradition, once again invoked the parts/whole distinction. Luther interpreted Old Testament figures, for example, as types of the Christ who was to come, because to him all Scripture spoke to a single purpose, the fostering of Christ (*Christum treiben*). But according to Dilthey, it was the Gnesio-Lutheran M. Illyricus Flacius who, in his *Clavis,* first used the principle of the parts and the whole (in the guise of *caput* and *membra*) to develop a hermeneutical system.

The next and perhaps the major step in the course of the parts/whole dialectic through Western thought was the formulation of the so-called hermeneutical circle by Friedrich Ast and especially by Friedrich Schleiermacher in the early nineteenth century. Ast grounded his conception of the hermeneutical circle in the unity of *Geist*. The *Geist des Ganzes* (the "spirit" of the whole), the source of all development, imprints itself on individual parts which, as a result, are understood from the whole. The whole, in turn, is understood from the inner harmony of its parts. In developing his psychologistic theory of hermeneutics, Schleiermacher gave classical expression to the hermeneutical circle—the whole must be understood in terms of its parts; understanding the parts presupposes an understanding of the whole—in both objective and subjective senses. On the one hand, the words of a sentence are understood in the context of the meaning of the sentence as a whole and vice versa, the sentence in context of the work as a whole and vice versa, the work in context of the genre to which it belongs and vice versa. On the other hand, a single creative moment in an author's life must be understood in context of his life as a whole and vice versa. Toward the end of the nineteenth century, Wilhelm Dilthey expanded the scope of this circle from Schleiermacher's textual hermeneutics by assigning it a major role in his general conception of the *Geisteswissenschaften*. In Dilthey's view, the circular relation between the parts and the whole was particularly well-suited to understanding the peculiar dynamism of historical life. Consequently, he repudiated the notion of a presuppositionless science of humanity based on the equivalent of mathematical axioms, and he called into question any constructionist approach to human studies.

In the twentieth century, a significant branch of hermeneutical thought, introduced by Martin Heidegger and developed most fully by Hans-Georg Gadamer, has shifted concern with the hermeneutical circle from the attempt to provide an epistemological foundation for human studies to an ontological analysis of the process of understanding itself. Here the relation of parts to whole does not occur so much on the level of object (for instance, words and sentence) or of subject (creative moment and entire life) as in the encounter between "subject" and "object." It is seen to be a fundamental condition of existence in the world (*Dasein*). In the area of interpretation, understanding of something at hand is seen to be grounded in a totality of involvements, that is, in one's fore-having, fore-sight, and fore-conception. But as Gadamer points out, this fore-understanding does not simply dictate meaning to a text. When it projects a meaning incompatible with a text, the text pulls the interpreter "up short." Because in Gadamer's eyes neither interpreter nor interpreted is closed but are both open to the new (horizons are not absolutely limited but dynamic, self-transcending, open to transformation in the interpretive encounter), their relation is more dialectical than circular.

Of course, this brief overview cannot give a very complete picture of any one view. It does, however, introduce two areas in which thought in terms of parts and wholes pertains to the history of religions in general and to the Chicago conference in particular: (1) parts and wholes as characterizing relations within the object of study (most broadly in the history of religions, the relations of religion and its constituents) together with an appropriate subjective reflex; and (2) parts and wholes as characterizing the encounter between the interpreter and that which is to be interpreted. We believe that both parts/whole relations are dialectical rather than circular. That is, in addition to the dialectic formulated by Gadamer, parts and wholes conceived as relations within the object of study, too, never exactly coincide. Rather, in their interaction they are open to and driven to the new. But their dialectical character manifests itself only when, to echo Gadamer, one becomes aware that parts and wholes, as currently understood, are incongruous. This dialectical character, as well as the fact that awareness of the incongruity underlying it is always only partial, both result from human finitude, that is, from the "part-icular" nature of that which tries to conceive the whole.

A Dichotomy in the Discipline

Reflecting on the dialectic's final if only approximable goal (full understanding), hermeneutical thought has generally favored a circular relation between parts and wholes. By contrast, historians of religions have confronted in practice the incongruity from which the dialectic takes rise, and they have tended to relate parts and wholes in terms of dichotomy. The first edition of Pierre Daniel Chantepie de la Saussaye's *Lehrbuch der Religionsgeschichte,* published in 1887, was a portent of things to come. Chantepie conceived his work as preparing for a philosophical study of the issues posed by religion. He included in the *Lehrbuch* a section—deleted from later editions—intended to bridge historical study and philosophical reflection. To the discussion which this section contained he assigned an ominous name, "phenomenology."

Chantepie's phenomenology was nothing subtle, simply the grouping of religious phenomena as they appeared worldwide into various classes: sacred trees, sacred stones, myths, and so on. Later phenomenologists, such as Gerardus van der Leeuw, would flirt with various aspects of philosophical phenomenology, but in general, historians of religions have understood the task of "phenomenology of religion" to be essentially classificatory or "systematic." What was portentous about Chantepie's publication was the form it assumed. Chantepie's work divided into two crudely juxtaposed major sections, the ethnological-historical and the phenomenological. By the mid-twentieth century his rhetorical stumbling had become the fundamental methodological problem facing the discipline. A full eighty years later, in the late 1960s and early 1970s, scholars would still be trying to overcome the apparent and undesirable dichotomy between two fundamental methods, history and phenomenology. In fact, the announcement of the second Chicago conference, ninety-six years after the appearance of Chantepie's first edition, invited scholars to a joint enterprise that might attempt in part to overcome the pernicious division which Chantepie had unwittingly fathered.

It should go without saying that the dichotomy between history and phenomenology involves several fundamental issues, such as the distinction between synchrony and diachrony frequently mentioned in discussions of structuralism. Among other issues, the presumed dichotomous relation between parts and wholes figures significantly. On the one side stand those who seek to comprehend the whole of religion as such. In this camp we may include not only phenomenologists so-called, such as van der Leeuw, but also other great synthesizers such as Joachim Wach and, later, Mircea Eliade. To be sure, these three formulated their methods differently—systematic (comparative and typological) studies (Wach) or morphology (Eliade) as opposed to phenomenology—but they all sought to express directly a vision of religion in its entirety or, as in the case of Friedrich Heiler's well-known study of prayer, to grasp in its entirety one central religious element. They drew their material widely, organized it logically, and attempted to understand the very heart of religion, the irreducible characteristics which set it apart as a distinct object of study.

The attempt to comprehend the whole drew sharp criticism from defenders of the parts, that is, from the historically minded, most notably perhaps from Raffaele Pettazzoni, but from many others as well. According to the historical critique, phenomenologists and their academic cousins had only described pseudo-wholes which could not do justice to any of the parts. They ignored the individual characteristics of the particulars and their contexts which alone made correct interpretation possible. They employed methods that could not endure critical scrutiny, for example, the well-known "sympathetic understanding." And although they admitted that the parts—the individual religions and religious elements—appeared only through time (historically), their constructions destroyed, the critics said, virtually every last intimation of historical movement. Van der Leeuw's extravagant statement —"Phenomenology knows nothing of any historical 'development' of religion"—evoked much response, and even Mircea Eliade was dubbed the "anti-historian of religions."

The dichotomy between history and phenomenology satisfied no one, but once firmly formulated, it set the central methodological question for the discipline. Of course, not all tried to find a solution. Historians of religions turned increasingly to specialized, historical studies. Often they found inspiration in tools still on the methodological horizon, especially tools of structuralism and semiotic anthropology. But of those who still reflected on the methodology of the history of religions as such, the majority focused on the threatened methodological dualism and the inability of either history or "phenomenology" to stand on its own. Later in his career, Pettazzoni began the attempt to bridge the gap. Others soon followed, some erecting spans from one side, some from the other: Ugo Bianchi in Italy, Geo Widengren and Åke Hultkrantz in Scandinavia, C. J. Bleeker and Th. P. van Baaren in the Netherlands, and Kurt Rudolph in Germany, to name those who have become well known. Each developed a personal variation, more or less complete, on the common theme: the history of religions *(Religionswissenschaft)* conceived in terms of historical study on the one hand, "phenomenology" or systematic study of some sort on the other, with sociology and psychology as codas in the public domain. None of the variations won widespread acceptance, and none fully resolved the issues that had evoked them all.

The Conference Proceedings

From time to time scholars in any discipline find it necessary to gather together. They compare notes, share information, stimulate and at times confront one another, then leave to pursue their research changed, if the gathering was successful, by their mutual encounter. In this spirit, historians of religions from North America, with selected European representatives, assembled at the University of Chicago in May 1983. The prehistory of this conference has already been told (see Introduction). Here we present its course. In the interests of being fair, we have included comments from various participants that may not pertain directly to our unifying theme (the dialetic of parts and wholes) but that we still deem worthy of notice.[2] In the next section we will examine the issues raised at the conference and their possible implications for the discipline's future. It is there that the dialectic of parts and wholes will again emerge as the focus of attention.

At each session, participants in the conference discussed one aspect of the discipline's situation in time. Major papers were presented on the discipline's past, present, present relations with other disciplines, and future. Authors of these papers represented major European and American traditions: Michel Meslin (the Sorbonne), Ugo Bianchi (Rome), Ninian Smart (Lancaster, England, and Santa Barbara, California), and Charles Long (Chapel Hill, North Carolina, and Duke). Three North American scholars responded to each. One speaker on the future of the discipline, Kurt Rudolph, then of Karl Marx University, Leipzig, did not receive his government's permission to travel and so could attend only in spirit. After the conference, he drafted a paper on his original topic. Because Rudolph represents a distinctive view of the history of religions, we will include his paper in our discussion here.

Taking Account of the Past

As readers of his essay know, Michel Meslin wrote on the discipline's past as it impinges upon the present. He chose to emphasize past issues rather than past personages, and he found in these issues a key to how, in his opinion, the discipline should develop in the future. He began by noting the early distinction between two conceptions of religio-historical work, history of religions in the narrow sense as the study of the existence of religions, and *Religionswissenschaft* (literally, the "science" of religion) proper as the study of the essence of religion. Coming from the French tradition, with a heavy inclination toward positive and critical history, Meslin sees the earliest form of the discipline as essentially historical investigation of various sorts, philological, palaeographical, archeological, ethnographical, and so on. But, he continues, indisputable cross-cultural patterns (which may with justice be divorced from cultural contexts) and the encounter with the various human sciences beginning at the end of the nineteenth century demonstrate the insufficiency of relying solely on a narrowly historical approach. Such an approach stumbles on the fundamental fact of religious meaning. As a way of getting at religious meaning, Meslin suggests that historians of religions move from a narrowly conceived notion of *histoire* to an interdisciplinary, multileveled *anthropologie religieuse* whose concerns are, roughly, symbolic. He takes the late Victor Turner as his guide for what one phase of such an *anthropologie religieuse* might be.

The first respondent, Lawrence E. Sullivan (University of Missouri-Columbia), reiterated what he considered the main points of Meslin's presentation. Then he asked several questions about Meslin's procedures and results, focusing on "(1) the sociology of our discipline and its ideas, (2) the career of methods, and (3) the trajectory of religious language."

Sullivan pointed out that in discussing issues apart from persons, Meslin may have painted a smooth picture of methodological development deceptive for its lack of significant elements. Meslin, he said,

> presents the development of our discipline and other human sciences as initiatives, inventions, or strategies able to foresee the consequences of their

> choices. . . . The impression his analysis provides is one of inevitable progress. . . .
>
> It may at least be open to question whether the direction which methods have taken has been prompted less by the sure guiding hand of a knowledgeable navigator than by the appearance of strange cultural sails on the horizon. History of religions may be more a reaction to the obscurities of its time than a beacon of guiding light. By tracing the inexorable march of hermeneutics one avoids poking through the rubble of conflicts which may illuminate the nature and role of method.

Sullivan wondered why certain methods had been abandoned. Did they display their inadequacies in the very process of being used successfully? Did scientific fashions change? He suggested that historians of religions might look beyond intellectual history.

> Aren't methodological schools more often than not a function of residence patterns, "founded" by leaders whose "methods" were retrospective justifications for the way in which their subjectivity was bound up with their data? . . . This does not necessarily call into question the need for method. It does ask that we examine the conditions of methodological creativity.

Among such conditions Sullivan noted the sociology of academic institutions and the shifting audiences which historians of religions address.

Although Sullivan did not question the need for method, he certainly went on to raise questions about its place.

> Professor Meslin has amply demonstrated the role of method in establishing the criteria of cognitive validity. . . . But how has method come to occupy the enormous role it does, especially in light of its successive failures? . . . We ought to ask what *kind* of thing [method] must be. What is its epistemological status? How has method come to make an almost metaphysical claim on us?

Sullivan suggested one possible answer, "the inestimable *social function* of method, its ability to consititute an enterprise and a *corporate sense* among scholars in diverse specialties if only by feud."

Sullivan's comments betray a "deeper" view which sees method not on the objective surface but embedded in the hidden subjectivity of the practicing scholar. In reacting to Meslin's comments on religious meaning and religious language, he raised a similar issue.

> What is the status of the order underlying the multidisciplinary approach Professor Meslin suggests? We ask this question because the new disciplines which grew up with history of religions have employed methods

> which declare that essential aspects of human nature lie *hidden* by the very act of self-understanding. "Shared, surface meanings" are deceptive and alienating; i.e., through the very symbolic language one uses to ground oneself, individually and collectively, one alienates oneself from the true ground of one's being. In these circumstances, method is endowed with the status of a technique of reintegration with one's true meaning and ground, one' reality. . . .
>
> Professor Meslin hesitates to see religious language in this way. In fact, in his view the symbolism of religious language explains the human and his/her place in the world. Nonetheless, since religious meanings and acts are culture-bound, and since people do not worship abstract concepts or hidden archetypes, Meslin holds that method in history of religions ought not search for a universal hard-core, common to religions. Rather, he contends, our comparative language is reductive to terms compatible with meaning. The goal of method in history of religions is not to find common forms but to discover uniquely different and creative ones. These are "enrichments," as Meslin calls them which point toward a totality. Is this an acceptable historical enterprise? We would like to hear more.

The second respondent, Diana Eck (Harvard University), did not criticize Meslin's failure to deal with the effects of hidden subjectivity but noted with approval the humanness and hiddenness (that is, mysteriousness) that characterize Meslin's view of the object (religion). Still, in contrast to Meslin's transhistorical anthropology, she saw a "*history* of religion in the singular" as the only way to discover the essence of religion. Such a view, she said, clearly distinguishes history of religions from area studies, especially from area studies limited to non-Jewish and non-Christian traditions, and requires more sophistication than a "presuppositionless" notion of history. In addition, Eck called for a refined terminology that could account for differences between Western and non-Western terms, such as "sacrifice" and "*yajña*."

The third respondent, Kees Bolle (University of California, Los Angles), expressed fundamental agreement with Meslin. Meslin proposes, said Bolle, "not an anthropology in the specialized, departmental sense—not another anthropology next to cultural, social, and physical anthropology. It is anthropology in the proper, philosophical sense, coherent, defensible, articulate thought on man's reality. Who would not agree to this noble purpose?"

Beginning with the role played by Meslin's specialty (early Christianity) in promoting and determining his general reflections, Bolle highlighted particularly the relations between specificity and generality in Meslin's project. In Bolle's view, these two constitute the discipline's inheritance.

> Professor Meslin is right in noting the original tension in the history of religions between the multitudes of histories (facts) and the eager search for

> the essence of religion. The history of religions has a double parentage: the multifariousness of new, nineteenth century historical and philological interests, and the moderization of the Christian theological establishment. This double origin reveals itself at every turn. This, I think, is the realization with which Professor Meslin's account is concerned from the outset.

The double inheritance sets up a problem, but it is "not only, and not even principally, a problem of various methods. . . . The problem is what bothers us when we get close to someone's specific view of the relation between the variety and unity in our specific field." For example, Bolle notes his own discomfort when his teacher, Wach, is called "an old-fashioned generalizer." He realizes that views of the relation between variety and unity inevitably change, and with them comes a change in valuation.

> Factuality and completeness become the key-words when generalizations are dismissed as no longer relevant. It is a mere change of fashions. We are probably ready for a change of fashion once more. We may need one. We may need a new attempt to generalize. But are the new general statements like those of a generation ago? Here, I think, our attentiveness to what Professor Meslin has to say should zero in. He is right in returning to *general* reflections. Yet the details count.

And of course, Meslin is not unaware of the details.

> Much in his paper turns around the multiplication of methods, of interpretations, of hermeneutics. And for the discipline of our study, for its scientific soundness, it is essential to see that the *multi-leveledness* Professor Meslin sees is not merely the result of the many humane sciences our world has created, but is the scientific, empirically necessary response to the nature of our data.

But while endorsing Meslin's suggestions, Bolle also suggests modifications. At times, he feels, Meslin is too bold semantically; at others he is too timid rhetorically. Meslin's description of theology's task ("describing to its devotees the object of their faith") is understandable but, in Bolle's view, inaccurate.

> No specific theology in any tradition describes itself in the terms Professor Meslin uses. Neither Thomas Aquinas, nor Avicenna or al Ghazali, nor Rāmānuja would have spoken quite the way Professor Meslin does. This is not a negligible point, for the history of religions—no matter how and why or even whether one begins to speak of the *essence* of religion—must face the evidence of the traditions it is responsible to. I do not think a theological

tradition will ever easily define itself as an endeavor to describe God to its devotees.

Caution, too, is needed in the terms historians of religions use.

> This [caution] should be the result of the greater reflection Professor Meslin urges. In discussing *religious experience*—a subject we can hardly avoid—we easily use the term "transcendent." This term too is hard to avoid. Yet, as a qualification of the object of religious experience it is often questionable. The Sanskrit *para-* is not necessarily 'transcendent.' Neither seems the experience of the Algonkin Indians who listen to what the thunder has to say, and can carry on conversations with rocks.

Bolle insists on more semantic timidity "not to detract from Professor Meslin's argument, but to reinforce it," that is, to preserve the multileveledness on which Meslin rightly insists.

From a desire to reinforce, Bolle also urges Meslin, and all other historians of religions as well, not to more timidity but to greater boldness when it comes to rhetoric.

> The historian of religions is not uninterested in biology, or market systems, or anything else. They are all of importance, but the object of our study is one because of the scientific decision to study man as a *homo religiosus.* We do not have to motivate the biologist to study man as a biological being. That is his good right. A conclusion almost too simple to voice must be made quite audibly: *there is no need for apology.* Why be so defensive? This is my principal, very serious question. If one insists on a truly worthwhile religious anthropology, why does one have to make a case for it in such a humble manner?

Bolle closed his response to Meslin's reflections on the past with an exhortation directed toward future practice and phrased in terms of an analysis of the present.

> It is not necessary to become so militant as to make the history of religions into the fount of all history: political, legal, cultural, intellectual, social, economic. This is not the time for a new imperialism. But it may be in order—to reinforce once more Professor Meslin's argument—to recall Charles Péguy. He said somewhere that *philosophy* was the most important subject to study. And why? Because, he said, carrying on the conversation in his essay, it was *his* discipline. One must always see one's own discipline in the center of the intellectual arena. . . . The other disciplines are there, too. We are constantly struggling with other methods. But above all: we deal with the multifarious documents of many traditions—and each of them has al-

ways rightly maintained its claim to universal validity. Here is our struggle, in the center, without apology, and without timidity.

A DIVIDED DISCIPLINE

The task before Ugo Bianchi at the next session was to survey the current state of discussion in the history of religions. His ultimate aim was to indicate where the discipline is heading and where it needs to head. In a densely written essay, Bianchi develops his views deliberately in the context of the Italian tradition of history of religions, a tradition leaning strongly toward historical-comparative and culture-historical work. Seeing the history of religions as ideally characterized by two forms of holism, cultural and cross-cultural, Bianchi contrasts two religio-historical modes, history and phenomenology, or preferably idiographic and synoptic work, which need to be not merely juxtaposed but linked and harmonized. In this situation, Bianchi sees two issues in particular as standing out, the problem of definition and the problem of historical comparison. Through inductive examination, definitions should be formed and comparisons made on the basis not of an identity but of an analogy between different religio-historical objects. Analogy is respected by the dialectical process of formulation, a dialectic of what the scholar has previously learned (through acceptable scholarly methods) and what he or she now experiences. But in Bianchi's view, it is not only the investigative process (dialectic) that is dynamic. The object of study is thoroughly dynamic, too. Thus, he insists that synoptic as well as idiographic work be not taxonomic but historical, and that the goal of historical comparison is to develop what Bianchi calls a historical typology.

With the first respondent, William Scott Green (University of Rochester), Bianchi's Italian, historicist tradition encountered a different mode of thought, an Anglo-American tradition heavily influenced by linguistic analysis and constructionist goals. Green began by outlining the distinctive traits of Bianchi's history of religions.

> On the basis of reading Professor Bianchi and the people with whom he has regular scholarly exchange, I take it that the history of religions is to be differentiated from other methods by claims for its unique possession of four distinct and integrated cognitive capacities. In the view of its practitioners, only the history of religions is capable of studying religion fundamentally, irreducibly, comprehensively, and scientifically. The history of religions treats religion fundamentally both by making religion in itself, religion *as such,* the sole object of investigation and by asserting that religion is primary, central, and utterly basic in all of human existence. It treats religion irreducibly by attempting to devise categories of description and analysis

> that are religiously referential, categories that preserve, reflect, and convey the integrity, the autonomy, the dynamics, and experiences of religion and religious life. It treats religion comprehensively by examining it culturally, diachronically, and synchronically, that is, by attending to its origination in specific social and linguistic contexts, its development through time, and its indelible, universal forms. Finally, the history of religions treats religion scientifically by grounding all analysis in the palpable data of various religions, and by basing its interpretations not on the special knowledge of initiates, on metaphysical speculation, or on theological or confessional assertion, but on the examination and comparison of the observable manifestations and empirical facts of discrete religions. By claiming to be scientific, as opposed to theological, we might suppose the observations about religion ought in principle to be susceptible of verification or disconfirmation by appeal to the empirical facts—although the list of historians of religions who subject themselves or their work to such scrutiny probably is not long.

It would appear, Green continued, that the force of the history of religions comes from its capacity to formulate "accurate, encompassing, and durable generalizations about religion." However, "the question of how to generalize about religion, or, more precisely, how to produce generalizations of sufficient rigor and precision to be analytically useful, has divided opinion among historians of religions for nearly a century and a half. The issue apparently remains unresolved, for it is one of the main preoccupations in Professor Bianchi's paper."

Green found three advantages to Bianchi's dialectical, analogical procedure:

> First, it produces generalizations that properly take into account cultural, social, and historical vagary. Second, it preserves the cultural embeddedness of discrete religions. Third, it generates research that is authentically historical by focusing attention not on static, formalized structures, but on what he calls "the process of religious novelty," through which religions undergo dramatic and sometimes decisive transformations.

And Green sees positive value in Bianchi's "insistence on the importance of the particular, the local, and the contextual over and against the general, the universal, and the abstract." But he also find in Bianchi's presentation "some difficult questions that require answers and clarification."

> First, despite claims for their theoretical distinction, at the level of practical research the inductive and deductive methods tend to become indistinguishable. Historians and philosophers of science have made it quite clear that facts do not speak to us, rather, they are constructed by us out of some theory; we select, order, and interpret them on the basis of what we want to know and of what we expect to see. On this basis, it is preferable from a

practical standpoint and for the sake of communication to be explicit about our theories at the outset of research. For if we cannot say what we think, how can we know how to correct ourselves?

We may legitimately inquire, then, what in Professor Bianchi's inductive-analogical method prevents the historian of religions from discovering herself absolutely everywhere, or from reading herself into the plot of every religious text she studies? Where in Professor Bianchi's method are the hermeneutical roadblocks to prevent, for example, the historian of Japan from inventing the incongruity known in the scholarly literature as "the Buddhist church"? And, more important, how, on the basis of the inductive-analogical method Professor Bianchi proposes, could we persuade such a historian that she is mistaken?

Second, if the study of religious change is a desideratum of the history of religions, how does the historian perceive it in the absence of some explicit analytical definition, some articulated theory of how a given religion is structured and how it works? Without such a notion, it would seem impossible to know if, never mind how or when, what superficially appear to be varieties of a single religion have become two different religions that divergently refract common symbols and texts to solve quite distinct problems.

Third, on what account are sociological and anthropological theories of religion incomplete? What do they leave out that is evident in the observable data that allegedly constitute the basis for all *religionsgeschichtliche* generalizations? Following Professor Bianchi's method, what are the inductive demonstrations (or, how do we know?) that, for instance, a Durkheimian or Marxist theory or explanation of a particular religion, a theory that uses the same data we use, is less comprehensive than one derived from the history of religions? To be sure, the charge of reduction or incompleteness will ring hollow if it depends on the invocation of the category of the sacred.

To get at the important problems raised by Professor Bianchi's paper, I suspect, will require a fuller version of method than he has offered.

By contrast, the next respondent, Alf Hiltebeitel (George Washington University) belongs by training and practice to a tradition close to Bianchi's. He expressed a great deal of "general and even particular agreement" with Bianchi's views. He singled out for approbation Bianchi's openness to both continuity and novelty, his insistence that religion is a part of culture, the importance he assigns to historical problematics in methodological struggles, and Bianchi's notion of analogy, which Hiltebeitel found preferable to insisting upon univocity or equivocity in terminology, to constructing "'ideal-types' or mere generalizations . . . and . . . certainly preferable to seeking new and supposedly neutral terms, which is probably impossible."

Hiltebeitel devoted the greater portion of his response to further reflections on the split between the historical and systematic dimensions of work in the history of religions. He aligned himself quite clearly with Bianchi's position: "Put simply, I place myself among those . . . who attempt to ['define and refine our methods (not) in terms of systematics' but] through arguments that emerge, to quote Bianchi, from 'sound comparative, cultural-historical research.'"

In addition to agreeing with critiques of phenomenology advanced by Bianchi (and others), Hiltebeitel pointed out that the problematic nature of phenomenological thought is not strictly limited to cross-cultural comparison. It pertains also to research on specific religions. For example, "certain studies of the Goddess in Hinduism . . . have been written from the phenomenological perspective. Their authors' assumptions about the *independent* history, theology, and 'power' of this phenomenon—the Goddess—are largely imaginary, and do not take into account the contextual, historical, and relational-structural dimensions of her 'part' in the 'holism' and 'dynamic' of Hinduism."

But what Hiltebeitel regards "as [the] most crucial [point] that arises out of many if not all . . . attempts at systematic study of religion" is "the primacy given to religion over religions." He shares Bianchi's conviction that the former is a mirage, but he finds the arguments used to advance the more radical position—that religions themselves are not valid objects of inquiry (W. C. Smith)—"one sided and often naive." Rather, in Hiltebeitel's view, "an amazing amount of work [needs] to be done" in studying the various dimensions of these religions, including the fascinating issue of their own negative self-definitions.

The third respondent, David Carrasco (University of Colorado, Boulder), neither analyzed and critiqued Bianchi's thought nor agreed with and elaborated on it. Rather, he gave a single, extended account of the significance of the Templo Mayor recently unearthed at the site of the ancient Aztec capital, Tenochtitlan, and asked for Bianchi's comments on his method. In further questioning, he noted that Bianchi had proposed a similar methodological program in Rome in 1969 and he wondered what specific advances had been made in applying the method since then. Citing difficulties in using Old World models in the study of New World cities, he asked Bianchi from what centers historians of religions should extend their comparisons. Finally, he pleaded that historians of religions take non-Hindu religious material, especially American material, seriously.

A Balance of Trade?

Apart from a few glances to the side, Bianchi and the three who responded to him limited their gaze to the history of religions in and of itself. They did so intentionally. But the history of religions does not exist in isolation. Any survey of its current state must consider not only internal affairs but relations with areas outside the discipline as well.

Ninian Smart set the stage for the third discussion with his paper on the partners with whom historians of religions converse.

Smart's background is considerably different from that of either Meslin or Bianchi. In Britain, philosophy of religion and history of religions were never sharply separated. The common designation, "comparative religion," unites elements of both. And of course, the British temper has always tended toward empiricism and nominalism, except in unusual periods, such as the turn of the century, when British idealism flourished. In keeping with this tradition, Smart begins from the premise that all distinctions between disciplines are more a matter of convenience than of reality. He thus prefers to think in terms of "religious studies" rather than in terms of "history of religions." The former is a collection of all approaches that study religion. It includes both the history of religions and its conversation partners under the same head. It is no surprise, then, when Smart sees the relations between these various conversation partners as congenial. In consonance with the analytical tradition's widespread separation of descriptive and prescriptive utterances, he formulates a fundamental distinction between the descriptive and the normative and posits theory as an intermediate, generalizing level between the two. In his view, the history of religions resides on the descriptive side, with a necessary theoretical overlay. The bulk of his paper is given to detailing some significant imports and exports between the history of religions and other participants in religious studies—anthropology, sociology, psychology, area studies, but also philosophy and theology—at the level of description and theory.

In reply, Bruce Lincoln (University of Minnesota) contrasted Smart's statements with what Lincoln had himself experienced. He pointed to the lack of serious attention that history of religions receives in North America and questioned what, in his eyes, was Smart's overly optimistic portrayal:

> I have not noticed the great wealth of valuable conversations which [Professor Smart] describes actually transpiring. But I do note that he often makes use of subjunctive or quasi-subjunctive phrases to describe these conversations, stating that they "should," or "could," or "might," or "ought to" take place, so perhaps there is not so much a difference between our experiences as there is between our attitudes, he being considerably more optimistic than I. In truth, if I may adopt Smart's metaphor of "imports" and "exports," I fear that historians of religions have suffered quite an unfavorable balance of trade.

Lincoln identified three factors "militat[ing] against the success of historians of religions in the academic marketplace."

> First, there is the sociology of our field. Not only does history of religions have few active practitioners in this country, but they are also a curious lot, a large proportion being former clergy and clergy *manqué,* often former missionaries and missionaries' children, which is to say, those who were first active advocates of one religion and later moved to study religion within a comparative framework. This background . . . has left a residue in the work of many: a covert confessionalism or nostalgic romanticism about religion which interferes with their "degree of descriptive success" (as Smart puts it). This covert confessionalism has rightly aroused the suspicion of scholars in disciplines outside the narrow confines of a Divinity School.
>
> Second, historians of religions have tended to be preoccupied with questions of method and general theory, conversely neglecting the collection, organization, and analysis of specific data. In large measure, this is the product of the linguistic limitations of most American historians of religions. Americans in general are lamentably ignorant of languages, and in some disciplines—molecular biology and English literature, I suppose—one can get away with this. But in a field where almost all primary data and much of the most important secondary literature is not in English, this is impossible. Unable to pursue real primary research—which, thankfully, our European colleagues do with such ardor—many Americans attempt an end run around it all, becoming "methodologists" and preaching to others how they ought to go about their work. The result, predictably, is not a happy one.
>
> The obsession with "method" has another source, however, in the general tendency to value mental labor above physical. For if one who thinks is better than one who shovels, then one who thinks about thinking must be best of all. To be sure, no healthy field is without its methodologists and theoreticians, but a small field can afford only so many. When a large proportion devote themselves to "thinking about thinking," it becomes disastrously clear that all real wealth comes from labor, and not from some rarefied species of meta-labor.
>
> Finally, historians of religions have managed to cut themselves off from other disciplines and from certain major intellectual issues by their stubborn insistence on the "irreducibility" of religion. While they understand their stance against "reductionism" as a proper resistance to vulgar materialism that would ignore the intrinsic interest and importance of religious phenomena, such scholars themselves construct an idealism which is no less vulgar—and considerably less justifiable in our age—when they forget that the body must eat before the mind can dream.

Yet in his own way, Lincoln, too, leaves room for hope. If historians of religions overcome "their covert confessionalism, their preoccupation with method, and their dread of 'reductionism,'" they can speak significantly to a problem important to "all scholars today": the need for "a more sophisticated and more precise understanding of how material and social realities both affect and are affected by ideological systems and other constructs of the imagination."

If Smart's essay evoked from Lincoln reflections on the alleged superiority of the mental to the physical in the practice of the history of religions, it moved the second respondent, Joanne Punzo Waghorne (University of Massachusetts, Boston), to address the same alleged superiority, now applied to the object historians of religions study. At one point in his essay, Smart suggests that "worldview" might be a more encompassing and more useful term to use than "religion" in denoting the object of our comparative study. Waghorne acknowledged Smart's intent to encompass secularized phenomena within the purview of the history of religions, but she took exception to his specific formulation: "The major question of definition becomes the starting point for discussion. Can the conversation between the history of religions and the formal academic disciplines within the present university structure begin solely by speaking the language of worldview?"

Smart's concern, of course, is to include Marxism within the scope of the history of religions. But, Waghorne maintains, "worldview" "does not exhaust the realm of secular forms of unnamed religion: there are other modes of religion in the modern world." Citing examples of formerly supraphysical interests which have become transformed into physical and psychological concerns, she observes:

> The secularization of religion in the modern world has moved "religion" in two directions: (1) toward the mind as ideology: here religion remains defined as a state-of-mind but (2) also toward (or, rather, beyond) the physical into a discussion of the full nature of Being: religion defined as a state-of-body. The second mode of the religious has its own conversation partners—a set of potential protagonists in the modern world which the history of religions cannot afford to ignore.

The old conversation partners still remain—theology, philosophy, the social sciences (anthropology, psychology). A history of religions conscious of "religion as a state of body" contributes to them and acquires from them new insights and different emphases. Discussions with theology now include such topics as "the nature of matter and spirit, the meaning of bodily resurrection, the nature of mystic unity with God, and the interrelationship of divine and human being"; discussions with philosophy include "the old matter of metaphysics"; with cultural anthropology, "transactional analysis"; and with psychology, external religiousness, on which behavioral psychologists might make significant observations. More intriguingly, though, Waghorne maintained that a consciousness of religion as a state of body bestows high value on conversation with new partners possessed of keen insight into the "religious" nature of the physical: artists and aestheticians, physicists, biologists, and physicians—people whose religious interests and insights historians of religions have all too often failed to take seriously.

Thus, like Smart and Lincoln, Waghorne holds out hope for the discipline and its extradisciplinary discussions, but she proffers at the same time a major qualification: "The history of religions, to become the truly global enterprise that Professor Smart envisions, must be willing to emerge from the matrix of worldview."

The third respondent, Richard C. Martin (Arizona State University), stated that he, like Smart, is "a convert to history of religions, he from philosophy and I from Middle Eastern studies." Moreover, Martin, too, is oriented in many ways toward recent Anglo-American philosophy. Perhaps for this reason he did not object to Smart's focus on worldviews.

In any case, like Lincoln, Martin pointed out that Smart's paper had raised expectations that were not fulfilled in experience, particularly in encounters with "scholars who engage in historical-critical and textual-critical studies." Such scholars, Martin found, seem to have little use for a general history of religions. In addition, he expressed perturbation at the number of scholars in other fields who usurp for their work the title of "religious studies" or "comparative religions." He suggested that historians of religions "suffer from inadequate exposure and involvement in the liberal arts, where they appear to be searching for a proper identity." In this situation, Martin felt, Smart's suggested inventory of imports and exports misses the point. It "may produce an interesting list of history of religions contributions and interrelationships to the academic study of religion, but it does not establish a whole product on which to stamp our history of religions brand label."

Thus, from reflecting on the poor condition of conversations between historians of religions and others in academia, Martin came to reflect on the poor health of the history of religions itself. Acknowledging the influence of recent writings by Stephen Toulmin and Richard Rorty, he suggested his solution to the problem of identity. The history of religions, he said, could be considered an academic discipline in the sense that a sufficient number of people have adopted and are persuaded by a common discourse. But conceiving the discipline in this way does not immediately cure all its ills. Martin raised three further questions. First, what evidence is there that the history of religions is as fecund as Smart seems to claim? Second, claims to fecundity aside, the discipline seems to be stagnating under the influence of past giants such as Otto, van der Leeuw, Wach, and Eliade. How can historians of religions preserve a sense of the persisting significance of these figures and their work without being condemned to uncreative mimesis? Third (essentially a sociological and geographical version of the second question), how can historians of religions in North America nurture a distinctive tradition of religio-historical work from shoots that still bear clear marks of their European ancestry?

LOOKING TOWARD THE FUTURE

In essence, Martin's questions ask what can be done to make the future of the history of religions lively. In Kurt Rudolph's absence, Charles Long had the honor of being sole conference seer. He began his look into the future by surveying the past. From the Chicago tradition of the history of religions he deduced several characteristics which typify the discipline as a whole: the universal range of the object of study and the massive amount of resulting material, the rejection of theology as a *modus operandi,* an integrative rather than a reductionistic approach, and the fundamental role of hermeneutics as more than a technique of interpretation. Long then turned to consider the interpretive situation or, in his terms, the interaction of distance and relation, of self and other. Because of its roots in the Enlightenment, the history of religions has always identified the interpreter with the self and the interpreted with the other. But in Long's view, such an identification leads to confusion, obscuring the other in the interpreter and the self in the object of interpretation. It represents the theoretical correlate to the practice of colonialism. For the future, he sees an approach that acknowledges the self in the object of study (anticolonialism) and does not refrain from studying the other of the interpreter (the religious traditions of the West). Such an approach, together with the other practical suggestions Long makes, would, he suggests, transform the Enlightenment's notion of science into something very different, the activity of serious human discourse.

After responding briefly to several points which Long and other participants had raised, Willard Oxtoby (University of Toronto) surveyed at some length his own program for the history of religions. He developed it not from a historical context (compare Long's reflections on the Chicago tradition) but by systematically outlining its elements. First, he distinguished three "clusters of approaches" to the study of religion on the basis of the type of appeal used to substantiate claims: historical approaches (documentation through sources), philosophical approaches (systems or structures of argument), and social scientific approaches (generation of new data). He deliberately left aside the question of whether there might not be some distinct study of religion as a phenomenon *sui generis.* Then he briefly identified several tensions within the discipline on which future reflection might focus: autonomy versus division into several distinct disciplines; particular versus general; scientific (humanistic) orientation versus theological, reflective participation in a religious heritage; observation versus participation and the need for a viable principle of analogy; and secularism (work done by outsiders) versus pluralism (ratification of statements by insiders). In closing, he endorsed the studies of contact which Long had advocated, and he urged his collaborators to include Christianity within the scope of the history of religions.

Instead of providing an alternative program for the history of religions, Judith Berling (Indiana University) reflected extensively on a major issue raised by Long, distance and otherness. She noted an instance in her own work where the issue received a new twist, what she called "double otherness" or "double alienation": the compounding of her own distance with the antagonism of native sources toward the movement she was studying (the religious reformation in twelfth-century China). Her experience in overcoming this difficulty led her to advocate a comparative history of religions oriented not toward similar themes but toward similar religious contexts. She found such an approach preferable to several other solutions to the problem of distance —conversion, simple acceptance of what the other says, empathy, and shallow universalizing. She also felt that such an approach might be a potentially profitable way of organizing Long's study of religious contact.

The third respondent, Benjamin Ray (University of Virginia) took seriously Long's admonition to include the shadows of the interpreter and his culture as otherness within the hermeneutical task. He began not by analyzing Long's presentation but by presenting the shadows of his own past at the University of Chicago, at Oxford, and in Uganda. To assess several points in the last section of Long's essay, he took his own work with the Ganda story of Kintu as a model. In contrast to those who questioned applying Western terms to non-Western cultures, he noted that using the Western term "myth" heuristically and self-critically allowed him to ask very relevant questions of the story. Analysis led to an appreciation of the role of the ordinary (social relationships) in making the enigmatic and extraordinary (death) ordinary. Thus, he agreed with Long that a focus upon the ordinary (the construction of a hermeneutical context) is the place where history of religions must begin. Citing his experience with the baGanda, he also agreed that the others whom historians of religions study are no longer willing to remain passive objects. But he found Long's terminological shift from science to discourse too sloppy. In the end, said Ray, historians of religions control the discourse for their own purposes. Through their questions, they seek to construct their own meanings, not simply to listen to the meanings of others.

Ray's endorsement of the scientific endeavor found its echo in the major paper that could not be presented. Like Long, Kurt Rudolph looks toward the future of the discipline, but he does so from a very different context. Long's interest in African and other "archaic" religious traditions has confronted him squarely with the issue of the self and the other and with European colonialism. Rudolph has seen the Enlightenment's ideal of objective science perform valuable service in opposition to pressures from both Nazi Fascists and Marxist ideologues. Thus, when Rudolph looks for the future of the history of religions, he sees science, not discourse, playing the major role. He begins by outlining schematically what he considers to be the salient characteristics of the discipline. Then, after expanding on the hermeneutical situation of the interpreter—a dialectic between proof and perception as found in a sophisticated notion of philology—he turns to consider those points that determine the present condition and will determine the future state of the discipline, the strength of its identity and its relations with its neighbors. In his view, the history of religions needs to coordinate its activities more closely with the other humanities, both in terms of adapting certain methods and consciously contributing its own insights to them. But Rudolph also emphasizes the importance of addressing an audience outside academia, the public at large. In an earlier article, he had pointed out that through a critique of ideologies, the history of religions could contribute to processes of liberation in the Third World. Here he points to its possible contributions on the European and American scenes, taking popular concern for the quality of the environment as exemplifying an issue to which the history of religions can speak.

The Discipline in Prospect

Diversity is undeniable: the Chicago conference touched upon a wide variety of methodological problems from a wide variety of perspectives. Still, it is interesting to note how many topics discussed at the conference can be seen as aspects of an underlying if unrecognized dialectic of parts and wholes. In fact, almost every aspect of the dialectic inherited from the past found its place in conference discussions. The disjunction between the place of the parts/whole dialetic in explicit methodological reflection and in actual methodological discussions will lead us to venture several observations on its possible future in the discipline. The temporal range of our view will then be complete: from the dialectic's past career, through the present conditioned by the past, to the future as present possibilities and failings might allow it to be. First, however, we must give some indication of the extent to which the dialectic is implicated in the present by taking the proceedings of the Chicago conference as our guide.

Parts and Wholes at the Chicago Conference

As we have seen, the parts/whole dialectic has been inherited from the past in two primary senses, one a dialectic occurring in the object of study (with a subjective reflex), the other a dialectic describing the interpretive situation (the relation between interpreter and interpreted). Between them, the two conveniently encompass the various parts/whole issues raised at the Chicago conference.

The Objective Dialectic. The first, the "objective" dialectic, comprises a large number of issues. In their continual concern with definition, scholars seek to identify one pole (the whole, religion) so that it can participate in dialectical mediation. On the one hand, Green recognized that some sort of working definition is necessary to locate the parameters of the object of study. On the other, Bianchi pointed out that a definition of the whole can never be complete. It is always in the process of formation by a dialetic of past (scholarly) experience with present and future (scholarly) encounters. These abstract concerns were realized concretely in two proposals to modify the received definition of religion, that of Smart (religion as worldview) and that of Waghorne (religion as state of mind but also as state of body).

Dialectical mediation also requires that the integrity of the parts be preserved; otherwise, no true dialectic exists. Bianchi openly placed himself within a tradition concerned with the integrity of particulars. It was precisely this concern on his part that received the most positive response: approval from Green, ascription from Hiltebeitel, and practical exemplification from Carrasco. By contrast, Meslin moved away from a tradition similarly based in "particularistic" history. He argued that transcending the particular and culture-bound was legitimate and necessary. In doing so, he evoked from Bolle both words of support and an admonition to greater timidity in regard to the universality of the terms historians of religions use.

Bolle's—and Eck's—terminological version of the tension between the parts as wholes themselves and as participants in a greater whole (religion) received full expression in the discussion following Long's paper. In general, the discussants divided into two camps. Proponents of one position tried to maintain the ultimate integrity of the parts by maintaining their ultimate autonomy (by implying that the parts do not participate in a dialectic with a greater whole). In their view, historians of religions attempt an impossible task. They try to compare two things, such as sacrifice and *yajña,* which are in the end incommensurable, like the Ptolemaic and Galilean cosmologies, and which they know to be incommensurable. Curiously, this ultimate incommensurability does not deter them from attempts to overcome it (that is, to compare). Proponents of the alternate view were perhaps no less concerned about the integrity of the parts, but they did not demand their complete autonomy. In their view, "incommensurable" is a needless and misleading term. We know that "sacrifice" and "*yajña*" are not identical, and this very knowledge demonstrates that they are not wholly incommensurable. The problem is simply that we have not yet reached the point of being able to express their commensurability clearly.

Meslin and the "commensurablists" point to the necessity of dialectical mediation. Green, of course, notes that historians of religions have been discussing how mediation might be achieved for quite some time. As for methods of mediation, however, only Bianchi gave any real indication of how such a dialectic might proceed (inductive analogy and historical typology).

Bianchi and the "incommensurablists," on the other hand, implicitly raise another parts/whole issue, despite the impression the latter may leave. Persons who defend the integrity of the parts rarely succeed in asserting their complete autonomy. Actually, they generally deny one whole's claim to validity (in this case, the claim of religion) in favor of another, "competing" whole. The result is a plurality of proposed wholes, each of which seeks to cast its own light upon the particular. An attempt to adjudicate the claims of varying wholes that transcends mere assertion and denial would itself result in a further dialectic, this time a "dialectic of wholes."

In practice, historians of religions have been most open to the claims of one specific alternate whole, culture. An openness to culture appears among "incommensurablists" as well as among historians (in contrast to phenomenologists). Strictly interpreted, the incommensurablists' position admits of a cultural, or rather, of a linguistic(-theoretical) whole ("paradigm"), but it denies any validity to the cross-paradigmatic whole, religion. Unlike them, Bianchi admits of both religion and culture as wholes, and he attempts to maintain a dialectical tension between the two. Rudolph, too, makes religion a part of the whole of culture, *Religionswissenschaft* a branch of *Kulturwissenschaft*. But he allows religion a relative autonomy which invites (relatively) independent comparative and systematic exploration.

When Meslin invokes the human sciences, he endows the "dialectic of wholes" with greater breadth. By implication he introduces into the discussion wholes such as human society and the subconscious and unconscious workings of the human personality. In general, historians of religions have not related religion so closely to these wholes as at least some of them have related it to culture, partly because, unlike religion and culture, the other wholes encompass religious features as manifestations not of surface but of deeper, hidden structures (see, for example, Sullivan). Historians of religions have frequently met what they have perceived as claims to exclusivity by students of these other wholes with the charge of reductionism and a counterassertion of exclusivity ("religion is *sui generis*"). As defensive measures, both charge and countercharge are understandable, but difficulties of maintaining them aside, they have had harmful side-effects. Lincoln, Green, and Meslin point out, each in his own way, a need for historians of religions to move beyond a position that simply dismisses interpretations of religious particulars in terms of other, nonreligious wholes by characterizing them as reductionistic.

In the form inherited from Schleiermacher, the objective dialectic has a subjective reflex which, according to the psychologistic option, is the real goal of the interpreter's art ("to understand an author better than he understood himself"). We may think of the dialectic of wholes as having a subjective reflex, too. It is, however, a reflex that applies not to religious persons (the precise analogue of a text's author) but to interpreters in their broader community as students of particular wholes: to be exact, to conversations between historians of religions and practitioners of other disciplines. Smart, of course, discusses these conversations in detail, although decidedly not in terms of a subjectively occurring dialectic of wholes. In the conference discussions, particular interdisciplinary conversations received special attention.

On the "import" side, conference participants were particularly interested in what historians of religions could learn from philosophers and theologians. Citing Pettazzoni's difficulties in the shadows of the Vatican, Bianchi voiced the discipline's tradition of defining itself by asserting its autonomy from philosophy and theology. Others, however, felt that at least in North America battles with philosophers and theologians were relics of days gone by. In important respects, Rudolph supports and argues vigorously for the traditional stance, but he also notes that historians of religions could make use of analytical philosophy to achieve a greater degree of conceptual clarity.

Conference participants showed as much if not more interest, however, in the "export" side of the communicative interchange: what historians of religions could teach others. Sullivan suggested that audiences might play a large role in the development of religio-historical methods. Green, Lincoln, and Martin noted that, whatever the discipline's potential, historians of religions had failed to address their academic audiences convincingly. Rudolph takes the academic audience into account, but with his remarks on the significance of the history of religions for Europe and North America, he directs attention to another audience as well, the public at large.

The Interpretive Situation. So far we have only mentioned aspects of the "objective" parts/whole dialectic, together with a particular, social form of its subjective reflex. The second major form in which the parts/whole dialectic has been inherited, the dialectic describing the situation of interpretation, also found its place at the Chicago conference. Of this dialectic we may distinguish two different forms. The first makes interpretation a part of the interpreter's entire existential situation (as with Heidegger and Gadamer). The second grounds the possibility of interpretation in the notion that the interpreter is a part of the whole to be interpreted, that is, in the notion that the interpreter is a human being interpreting human "creations" (see Vico).

The first form received its narrowest expression at the hands of Bianchi and Rudolph. In their views, definition and interpretation occur as a dialectic, but one bounded strictly by the limits of scholarly criteria. Others claimed, in effect, that scholarly method could not totally divorce the interpreter as scholar from non-scholarly dimensions of human life, both individual and social. Lincoln pointed out the hidden and, in his view, harmful role played by religious convictions, even those that have been putatively bracketed. Sullivan suggested that several aspects of the "society" in which historians of religions practice might account, at least in part, for the course of methodological development.

The second form of the "situational" dialectic, that which makes the interpreter part of the object interpreted, receives fullest expression, of course, in Long's essay. Long advocates that historians of religions abandon bracketing the investigator from the object of study and see both the self in the others one studies and the other in the self deserving of study. Because Long recognizes both interpreter and interpreted as fully constituted human subjects, he prefers to label his approach not "science" but "discourse."

Such a designation is reminiscent of another common expression, "interreligious dialogue." In the discussion of Long's essay—and elsewhere, too—questions arose as to whether interreligious dialogue might not be a subjectively incarnate form of the history of religions. Long distinguished himself from a proponent of such an approach over the issue of signification. Historians of religions must remain aware that the questions they ask are their questions, formulated in their language. They must also remain aware that the other as self does not merely respond to the questions raised. His or her meaning still needs to be deciphered.

Perhaps we could say that interreligious dialogue presents a subjective reflex to a dialectic of wholes that are of a different order than the whole defining the history of religions. Interreligious dialogue presents a discussion among persons who adhere to particular religious visions about their religious visions. Maintaining that interreligious dialogue is a subjective reflex of the history of religions confuses a surface subjectivity (the historian as religious subject) with the necessary and unavoidable hidden subjectivity given with the humanity of the investigator. When this particular surface subjectivity is no longer present—when the subject no longer adheres strongly enough to a religious position to speak for it or when the subjects under study are no longer living (prehistoric religions, religions of antiquity, and others)—the dialogical enterprise collapses but not the history of religions. For historians of religions, interreligious dialogue is a form of interreligious contact and as a result an object of study. Still, there are historians of religions who are religious themselves, who feel called to participate in interreligious dialogue, and who hesitate to separate their participation in dialogue from their scholarly activity.

The Future in Dialectical Focus

If the conference at Chicago represents fairly at least the breadth of methodological issues about which historians of religions are currently thinking, these issues include many aspects of the dialectic of parts and wholes: the delimitation of the whole, the integrity of the parts, the means to mediate parts and whole dialectically, the participation of the whole "religion" in a "dialectic of wholes," a subjective and social reflex to that dialectic, the objective dialectic as itself part of the interpreter's entire existential situation, and interpreters themselves as parts of the whole to be interpreted. This rich diversity of parts/whole issues in current discussions contrasts sharply with the place of the dialectic, or more precisely, with the dichotomy in much current, explicit methodological reflection by historians of religions.

As mentioned earlier, methodological reflection in the history of religions has been preoccupied for the last quarter of a century and more with a single dichotomy, history versus phenomenology. These two approaches seem too rigid methodologically, their differences too sharply defined, to allow for genuine methodological vitality. In discussing them, Bianchi evokes shades of Windelband's distinction between "idiographic" and "nomothetic" disciplines. The distinction is not completely beside the point here. Windelband posited two completely different modes of thought, individualizing and generalizing, each with its own objects of study and each incapable of contributing to the other. Having thus removed the possibility of genuine growth in the human studies, he condemned them to pursue a single aspect of a rigid dichotomy, history. Historians of religions, too, have adopted a view that divides thought into two rigid and radically different modes. Unlike Windelband, they may permit both modes to be applied to the same object (religion), but they have been unable to link or harmonize the two in practice, despite their constant claim that some form of linkage or harmonization is necessary.

Perhaps the notion of a dialectic of parts and wholes can help point a way out. Compared with a rigid conception of history versus phenomenology, the parts/whole dialectic has several advantages. As we have just seen, it is more encompassing. It is able to embrace a broad range of current issues which the dichotomy of history versus phenomenology ignores. Second, it is dynamic. It is conceived as a dialectic, not as a dichotomy. It recognizes disjunctions which no serious student can deny, but at the same time it highlights the movement to overcome them. Third, it is flexible. The dialectic of parts and wholes is not a methodological program but a transprogrammatic issue. By referring to parts and wholes, historians of religions may think through various methodological options, but they are not bound to any particular method. Thus, the dialectic should allow for methodological innovation. In the constant, never completed striving for the holistic vision upon which it insists, it should actually stimulate innovation. Finally, it is unifying. The dialectic makes possible a unified notion of the history of religions as a discipline, not methodologically but teleologically. In this view, a discipline is a corporate scholarly enterprise which attempts to understand a whole through the methodical and integrative examination of its parts. What distinguishes one dialectic from others is the specific whole which its practitioners attempt to understand: psychology, the working of the human "psyche"; sociology, human society; linguistics, language; the history of religions, the human religious experience. Each in turn casts peculiar light from its distinctive whole onto various particularities to render them intelligible. Without such light, particularities remain unapproachable (*individuum ineffabile est*).

Given these advantages, historians of religions might do well to focus their attention not so much on what have been the surface features of methodological discussion as on the underlying, perhaps unrecognized issues. That is, they might do well to stop talking about the methodological alternatives of history and phenomenology and start talking in terms of issues that are fundamental to these alternatives because they are fundamental to the entire discipline, such as the issue of parts and wholes. Taking the parts/whole dialectic seriously would have, it would seem, several practical implications. An afterword is probably not the place to explore them in depth. We will only indicate in general terms what these implications might be. No doubt from the point of view of details, our sketch will appear superficial. But details are not our concern here. We will try to convey a preliminary, overall grasp of the possible place of the dialectic in the future of the history of religions. Our hope is that our overview will stimulate and help orient further examination and reflection. The procedure is not dissimilar to the quick reading, oriented toward the whole, with which Schleiermacher initially approached an unfamiliar work.

If the history of religions is conceived as a dialectic, it would seem that work in the history of religions should manifest its dialectic character. One might wonder, then, to what extent writings focused solely on either the whole or the parts actually belonged to this discipline. Might they not participate instead in another discipline (dialectic), despite their author's intentions or claims? Work in the history of religions would seem required to advance, consciously and clearly, the cause of the dialectic which the discipline pursues.

From the dialectical point of view, therefore, it would seeem questionable for historians of religions to undertake simply to describe "religion as a whole." Of course, such description cannot be avoided altogether, just as particular investigations cannot and should not be avoided. But both must be set in dialectical context. The "pseudo-wholes" inherited from the past have been of little dialectical use because, not sufficiently attentive to the integrity of the parts, they seem to render a dialectical movement impossible. Once again the question arises, How can dialectical movement be preserved? Thus, as Green noted at the conference, historians of religions continue to face the issue of generalization. In itself, this is no symptom of disease. As long as the discipline seeks to maintain a continuing dialectic of parts and wholes, discussing how to do so is probably a sign of some rudimentary degree of vitality. The problem with recent discussion has not been that it is taking place; the problem is that it has failed to yield much fruit.

Postponing for the moment the question of dialectical mediation, we note that historians of religions face at least a couple of other questions that center specifically on the whole. Several comments at the conference indicate that the attempt to define "religion" continues, as no doubt it will. But historians of religions should not ignore another basic question at which Rudolph, for one, hints: How is the posited whole, "religion," viable? What justification can historians of religions give for isolating "religions" as a distinct whole worthy of scholarly attention? In other words, whether religion is, is just as fundamental a question as what religion is.

The discipline's dialectical character would seem to have implications no less important for those historians of religions who have opted out of traditional methodological discussions and have turned to particular historical studies. If the parts/whole dialectic is taken seriously, not every particularistic investigation of religious phenomena would be an exercise in the history of religions, despite its possible reliance on "state of the art" methodological tools. Historians of religions would engage in particular investigations explicitly with an eye to the whole which they wanted to understand. They would pursue topics that contributed significantly to understanding the whole of religion, not merely topics that struck their fancies and happened to discuss material commonly considered "religious." The questions they posed and the implications they drew would also contribute directly to a dialectic of the particular phenomena with their discipline's particular whole.

It might be helpful to recall the variety of responses to Windelband's dichotomy between idiographic and nomothetic disciplines. In the years following Windelband's initial proposal, several scholars pointed out the dangers of sharply distinguishing generalizing and individualizing modes of thought and limiting them strictly to the natural and cultural sciences, respectively. Neo-Kantians who rejected Windelband's move, such as Cassirer, tried to bridge the two with the notion of the ideal-type, a general, rational construct never found in reality as such but helpful in highlighting individual features of experience one wishes to understand. Dilthey, the historicistic *Lebensphilosoph,* began not at the generalizing but at the individualizing end with his notion of the typical individual who transcended the bounds of particularity to embody and express the characteristics of his age as a whole. Following the lead of Max Scheler, Joachim Wach sought to mediate the two with a notion of the classical that assumed relative normativity among individual members of classes or types of phenomena. Later, Gadamer, true to his ontological orientation, conceived of the classical in terms of an ability to perdure. In the analytical tradition, Wittgenstein introduced the notion of "family resemblance," according to which classes are defined in terms of a number of general characteristics, none of which can be found in every particular instance without exception. Among the various ways to mediate the particular and the general, we have our preferences, but this is not the place to promote them. Any of these alternatives would be preferable to religio-historical investigations which sought to be either strictly "historical" or strictly "phenomenological."

It has also become clear that historians of religions cannot be so myopic as to limit the dialectic of parts and wholes to a narrow, objective range. Today, such studies as we envision need to take into account further, related applications: the "dialectic of wholes," in both objective and subjective senses, and the dialectical character of investigation itself. On its objective side, the dialectic of wholes appeared at the Chicago conference with reference, of course, to charges of reductionism. Since the charge of reductionism has been one of the walls behind which historians of religions have traditionally bastioned themselves, its appearance at the conference was quite natural. But different formulations highlight in many respects the same issue, and some of them may prove more fruitful in the long run. Examples are the distinction between hermeneutics of retrieval and hermeneutics of suspicion and the widespread endeavor to bridge the chasm established in the nineteenth century between understanding (*Verstehen*) and explanation (*Erklärung*). Obviously, historians of religions cannot simply engage in hermeneutics of suspicion, or formulate explanations, or "reduce," whatever that might actually mean. All three enterprises seem to imply studying religious phenomena as elements of nonreligious wholes. But on the other hand, studies designed to contribute to understanding the whole of religion—hermeneutics of retrieval (in a loose, nonparticularist sense) or "nonreductionist studies"— cannot simply ignore other wholes whose "suspicious," "explanative," or "reductive" approaches illuminate aspects of the parts selected. Wach's vision of an integral science of religion and Eliade's notion of a total hermeneutics may provide inspiration, but the means with which to integrate the various approaches—the means by which investigators can allow the whole they study to participate at the same time in a dialectic of wholes—remain to be discovered.

As significant as the ability to integrate various approaches, and not unrelated to it, is the ability of historians of religions to persuade not only each other but others in academia and the larger public. As we have seen, several participants at the Chicago conference found this to be one area in which historians of religions have not been very successful. Aristotle delineated three sources of successful persuasion, the speaker, the material, and the audience. The details of his rhetoric cannot be applied directly to the history of religions, but these three general categories may be helpful in beginning to see how historians of religions might be more persuasive.

Personally, historians of religions must be clear about their identity as practitioners of the discipline. If our terms are adopted, they must be clear in their own minds how they intend their specific projects to contribute to an understanding of the whole of religion, and they must communicate their intentions unequivocally to others. Such clarity demands at least a rudimentary notion of the whole they study (a working definition) and its relations to other wholes. Materially, the arguments historians of religions employ and the conclusions they advance should be marshaled as persuasively as possible. They must be "factually" accurate, logically correct, analytically precise, and penetrate deeply into the reality of both the particular (be insightful) and the whole (be significant). In addition, the place of the audience, as Sullivan pointed out, should not be overlooked.[3] Historians of religions will never be convincing if they speak to concerns their audiences have long since lost—or have never had. To some extent, their work must be topical. In fact, topicality may help explain why scholars such as Mircea Eliade remain influential even when their methods and their results are called into question. Of course, concern for topicality should never condemn historians of religions to following the latest academic or public fads. They will generate their projects first and foremost from the central problems and concerns of their discipline. But if historians of religions cannot at the same time address the concerns of the present day, their discipline's future will be gloomy indeed.

In general, recent thinkers have advanced the dialectical character of interpretation (interpreter and interpreted as parts and wholes) as ontological description, not epistemological prescription. For example, Gadamer renounces every intention of trying to prescribe how students of humanity should go about their tasks. But those who believe that his description is correct and relevant, quite apart from an investigator's intentions, will inevitably approach their task differently from those who believe it is not. In discussions at the conference, for example, Smart's distinction between descriptive, theoretical, and normative statements was challenged. According to the opposing position, objective description in Smart's sense is not possible. "Description" always takes place within a subjective context which inevitably conditions the end result. The insight may be correct, Smart replied, but in the end it is inconsequential. It still remains possible to distinguish bad, good, and better description, and so long as the possibility remains, accurate description may stand as a scholarly ideal. Others, however, found this dialectic quite pertinent to the future of the discipline, as suggestions by Rudolph and, to some extent, Bianchi on the one side, and by Long on the other, show. Of course, the extent to which these differing approaches actually yield different results cannot be judged from a set of methodological essays.

OTHER ISSUES

Any discussion of methodology in the history of religions encompasses, in an open or hidden manner, a variety of fundamental issues. We have isolated and amplified only one, the parts/whole dialectic, not just because we see that dialectic as itself of central importance to the discipline but also because we envision our overview as beginning a typical part of the entire task which historians of religions must undertake if they are to move beyond the rigid dichotomy they have inherited. Historians of religions must "deconstruct"—but in a constructive manner—the heritage of history and phenomenology (or systematic studies) rigidly conceived. They must be willing to abandon external forms, if necessary, and come to a new appreciation for the life of the discipline within, to a new realization of the identity and creative possibilities of the discipline's fundamental issues. What other elements persist in the midst of change? What are their dimensions? How are they grounded in the nature of the discipline itself? How do they relate to one another? What creative possibilities lie latent within them? As suggested earlier, another fundamental issue might be the distinction between diachrony and synchrony, that is, the paths by which historians of religions approach the dimension of time. What might the rest be?

From the proceedings of the Chicago conference we may note briefly several issues that lie outside the preceding discussion. We do not mean to claim that these are fundamental issues. Here we leave considerations of economy and fundamenticity aside. But the following issues do deserve consideration.

As for the object which the discipline studies, one issues revolves about what each of us perceives of ourselves as opposed to what we perceive of others, that is, the issue of internality and externality or subjectivity and manifestations. Diana Eck raised the perennial question this issue poses to historians of religions: Does the history of religions study religious *phenomena* (for example, cumulative traditions) or the subjective human *religiousness* underlying them (such as faith). The latter has at least formal affinities with Schleiermacher's hermeneutics, Dilthey's concern with human self-consciousness ("worldviews"), and, in a religio-historical setting, Otto's notion of experiencing the *mysterium tremendum et fascinosum.*

Another issue pertaining to the object of study is how historians of religions conceive religious persons. Occasionally participants at the Chicago conference referred to the distinction between mind and body. Such a division can underlie discussions of either external phenomena (for example, expression in thought and action [Wach]) or internal religiosity (Waghorne's "religion as a state of mind" and "religion as a state of body"). Historians of religions know well that "mind/body" is culture-bound. They might want to ask whether it is the best way for them to conceive human personality.

A third "objective" issue is raised by human religious plurality. At its crudest, this issue is expressed grammatically: Is *Religionswissenschaft* a "history of religion in the singular" (Eck and W. C. Smith; Wach) or a "history of religions" (Bianchi, Rudolph, Hiltebeitel, and others)? Claims and counterclaims are advanced in these discussions: the latter, the former might say, ignores that which makes religion what it is; the latter might reply that thinking of such a common core only obstructs scholarly work. Clearly the issue requires more than general claims. It requires full-fledged monistic or pluralistic depictions of the whole of religion which are reasonably capable of withstanding critique from the other side.

Other issues pertain not to the object of study but to the ways in which historians of religions study that object. As comments by

Sullivan and Lincoln illustrate, several questions center on the subjectivity of the historian of religions. In addition to the issues mentioned already, we may note the tension between tradition and creativity raised by Martin. On the one side stands the desire to depart from the past and to create a new tradition of one's own (for Martin, a North American tradition). The new experiences of each scholar and of each scholarly generation make creativity necessary and inevitable. On the other side, scholars not only respect the past; their subjectivity is determined by it. Thus, all creativity inevitably stands within and is conditioned by tradition. The plurality that the interplay of creativity and tradition produces confronts us in a rudimentary way with another issue, the issue of the one and the many: the possibilities and limits of a genuine methodological pluralism between iron-fisted monism and free-floating relativism or eclecticism.

A second issue concerns the inevitable distance between historians of religions and most if not all of the persons they study. Interpretive distance is an issue in hermeneutics today. For example, Gadamer seeks to overcome it; Ricoeur tries to attach new, positive value to it. Like subjectivity, distance raises many questions in the history of religions. One seems particularly inevitable: Must a historian of religions be religious or, in lieu of that, religiously sensitive? A wide variety of answers range from absolute assertion to complete denial. From conference discussions it seems that only one move is common to the way historians of religions deal with this complex issue: the appeal to analogies—the study of music, the study of art—which, because they are themselves neither clear nor clearly applicable to the history of religions, seem only to muddle the issue further.

Sullivan raised yet a third issue most succinctly: "In practice, history of religions at its productive best has been materials-oriented and preoccupied with method mostly in retrospect, when it looked back upon what it had done in order to scrutinize more precisely *how* it did it." The division between hermeneutics as method and as description of practice finds its representatives in E. Betti and E. D. Hirsch on the one side and Gadamer on the other. In the history of religions, supporters of method may go so far as to claim that actual investigation is only important insofar as it has methodological implications (for example, Jonathan Z. Smith). Others may reflect in various ways the comments of Sullivan and Lincoln reproduced here and attach priority to practice over method.

Topography and Its Limits

Our endeavor in this Afterword has been "topographical." We have tried to survey some of the issues (*topoi*) raised, whether explicitly or implicitly, in discussions at the history of religions conference held at Chicago in May 1983. In some respects our topography may seem to have gone too far; in others, perhaps, not far enough. Both failings may be inherent in the attempt to discuss any discipline's issues in and of themselves.

Our topography may seem to have exceeded its bounds by beginning to formulate one specific position to the exclusion of others. Explicit reflection in terms of parts and wholes belongs to a particular tradition of thought, whatever claims one may wish to advance for it in actual practice. If that tradition may be broadly denoted interpretive, a contrasting mode of thought might be labeled investigative. This nonholistic, constructionist mode has been particularly popular in the English-speaking world. To oversimplify somewhat, it focuses on the investigation of particulars and seeks to generalize from them inductively (a "dialectic of parts"?), especially in terms of causes and effects. It begins with hypothetical statements and seeks to demonstrate them experimentally (that is, through verification or falsification of predictions), often with the help of mathematics. From "demonstrated" hypotheses it forms an ever growing picture whose recesses and "final" shape are hidden from view and cannot be properly anticipated. In the interpretive mode, one assesses disciplinary well-being in terms of vitality, in terms of the degree of dialectical interaction occurring between parts and wholes or the degree to which subjectivity and objectivity converge. In the investigative mode, well-being is measured in terms of progress: the quantity of adequate demonstrations that have been established and the success with which they have been integrated.

Of course, investigative as well as interpretive approaches have been applied to religious phenomena. Affinities to investigative modes of thought did appear at the Chicago conference. Some comments by Green, for example, lead one to suppose that in certain respects, at least, he might find investigative thought more congenial than interpretive. So, too, might others who conceive of disciplines not in terms of corporate attempts to understand wholes but in terms of joint efforts to solve a number of limited and related problems by applying specific investigative means. Still further, one might conceive of "disciplines" as unfortunate by-products of academic institutionalization which, in the end, distort the unity of knowledge by drawing lines where they ought not to be. As advocated by Smart, such a position seems to reject a "discipline" of whatever kind devoted to religion and to think instead of a general collaboration of all descriptive (investigative) efforts aimed at religious data ("religious studies"). Thus, in surveying issues in an organized fashion, our topography has gone beyond the various views expressed by participants at the Chicago conference.

But in its concern only to organize issues, our topography admittedly leaves open certain questions that need to be addressed if one is to *think* about those issues seriously. One particularly important question concerns the status of the various wholes and their dialectics. Can one simply collocate the two major forms of the parts/whole dialectic that we have distinguished? Can a dialectic of wholes really be achieved, and how? Are "wholes" merely names, or do they possess some sort of ontological reality? To take only one example, it seems clear that the notion of "holism" in some currents of recent thought—the whole as a theoretical paradigm narrowly conceived—denies a cross-paradigmatic continuity to "religion" which our parts/whole dialectic would require.

Even if our topography takes the most preliminary of steps toward formulating an actual position, it leaves open many questions. Likewise, the second Chicago conference on the history of religions may not have solved many problems. Conferences may not be intended to solve problems. But it did give voice to a wide variety of issues. There is much room for further thought, not just introspective self-criticism but creative thought about the world's religions themselves. Some issues remain problematic; some may seem doomed to being ever problematic. Yet the attempt to make sense of the whole of humanity's religious experience will continue, and not simply out of idle curiosity. As Paul Ricoeur writes above:

> What would be the use of [the history of religions] if it did not aim at producing an echo in the midst of our own experience, and if, at the price of some painful tensions and conflicts, it did not enlarge our own self-understanding, by contrasting what we understand with what we do not understand of the religions of others?

Notes

1. As well as the major works of each author mentioned, readers may find the following surveys useful: Wilhelm Dilthey, "The Development of Hermeneutics," in H. P. Richman, trans., *W. Dilthey: Selected Writings* (Cambridge: At the University Press, 1976), pp. 246–263; Hans-Georg Gadamer, *Truth and Method* (New York: Crossroad, 1975), pp. 167–168, 235–245, and 258–267 (on the hermeneutical circle); Richard E. Palmer, *Hermeneutics: Interpretation Theory in Schleiermacher, Dilthey, Heidegger, and Gadamer* (Evanston, Ill.: Northwestern University Press, 1969); and, for Gadamer's notions against the background of the hermeneutical tradition, David E. Linge's "Introduction" to Hans-Georg Gadamer, *Philosophical Hermeneutics* (Berkeley and Los Angeles: University of California Press, 1976), pp. xi–lviii.
2. Several respondents provided written and revised versions of their comments. We have reproduced these at some length below. Using recordings of the conference proceedings, we have summarized more briefly the remarks of those respondents who did not provide written comments. For the benefit of those who may wish to read the Afterword

before reading some of the major essays and to refresh the memories of those who have read the essays, we have provided brief summaries of them as well. The special lectures by Mircea Eliade and Paul Ricoeur dealt with particular topics within the history of religions rather than with the methodological past, present, or future of the discipline per se. Consequently, we have omitted them from our consideration,

3. For further reflections on audiences and modes of discourse appropriate to them, see the editor's Introduction.

Index

3 9153 00007358 7
PALISADES PARK FREE PUBLIC LIBRARY
a39153000007358 7b

DATE			